Demography and Roman Society

Ancient Society and History

Demography and

TIM G. PARKIN

Roman Society

The Johns Hopkins University Press
Baltimore and London

© 1992 The Johns Hopkins University Press
All rights reserved
Printed in the United States of America on acid-free paper

The Johns Hopkins University Press
701 West 40th Street
Baltimore, Maryland 21211–2190
The Johns Hopkins Press Ltd., London

ISBN 0-8018-4377-4

Library of Congress Cataloging-in-Publication Data

Parkin, Tim G.
    Demography and Roman society / Tim G. Parkin.
        p.   cm.—(Ancient society and history)
    Includes bibliographical references and index.
    ISBN 0-8018-4377-4
    1. Demography—Rome—History. 2. Rome—Population—History.
I. Title. II. Series.
HB853.R66P37   1992
304.6'0937'6—dc20   91-45647

IN MEMORIAM

PATRIS MEI

(1920–1989)

I was ever of opinion, that the honest man who married and brought up a large family, did more service than he who continued single, and only talked of population.

(Oliver Goldsmith, *The Vicar of Wakefield*, ch. 1)

Contents

Contents

Preface

The aim of this book is to introduce ancient historians, and all others who have an interest in societies of the past, to the study of the population structure and dynamics of ancient Roman society. The idea for a study of this kind first arose in 1987, when I was a graduate student at Oxford University, studying the position of the elderly within Roman society, under the supervision of the Camden Professor of Ancient History, Fergus Millar. One of the primary questions I had to ask myself was, What proportion of the population of the Roman world did the elderly represent? In hindsight my inquiries had something in common with those of Socrates; I turned from one potential source of information to another, and in time found the answers each provided unsatisfactory. I gradually—and rather reluctantly—came to the conclusion that there were no shortcuts and that I really had to sit down and start to learn about demography. In this endeavor Fergus was fully supportive, and I was entrusted to the care of the family historian and historical demographer, Dr. Richard Smith of All Souls College, Oxford. One year later, after attending many lectures, reading many books, discussing the subject endlessly with many individuals, and repeatedly trying Richard's patience, I began to put pen to paper.

As part of my research into the demography of the Roman world, I needed to digest a vast amount of modern scholarly literature, both within the realm of ancient history and beyond. In the course of the past one hundred years, since the publication in 1886 of Beloch's *Die Bevölkerung der griechisch-römischen Welt,* scholarly attention has focused increasingly on the population of the ancient world. While great progress has been made in recent years in the field of historical demography, in particular for Europe (especially France and England) of the sixteenth to nineteenth centuries, ancient history has been left far behind. Much of the debate in "ancient demography" has tended to focus on population numbers, rather than on population structure and dynamics. Part of the problem lies in the fact that most ancient historians are daunted by figures, and they tend to write about ancient populations without having any concrete idea of the ways a population works. There are some notable exceptions—for the Roman world, one should mention especially the work of Peter Brunt, Bruce Frier, Keith Hopkins, Richard Saller, and Brent Shaw. Their work has centered around particular aspects of Roman society and population. There is a need, however, for a more general overview of the study of ancient demography, in order to survey the evidence that is available, the methodology needed for the use of the material, and the resources available to an ancient social historian in terms of modern demographic methods and models. This book, in attempting to provide such a critical summary of work done and of work still to be done, is composed of three main chapters.

In the first chapter a detailed critique is given of the traditional methods used by ancient historians in the field of demography, working with such evidence as tombstone inscriptions; mummy labels, census returns, and tax receipts from Roman Egypt; the "life table of Ulpian"; skeletons; and ancient "statistics" as recorded in literary sources. In each area there is given a concise account of the testimony available, the problems inherent in its interpretation, and its usefulness (or otherwise). The basic response here to the use of these types of material for demographic purposes is negative: in every case the biases inherent in the "data," and the uncertainties and demographic improbabilities produced as a result, show that the confidence placed in them by many ancient historians is unjustified.

In addition to this material, therefore, modern demographic methods and models are discussed. The second section provides an easily intelligible guide to the use of modern demographic tools, in particular model life tables, in terms of their construction and the use of the information offered by them. This section also seeks to clarify exactly what is demographically plausible in terms of the ancient world, and what is not.

This leads in to the third chapter, where use is made of both modern techniques and ancient evidence to discuss the probable age and sex structure of the Roman population, and to analyze the effects of various factors, such as changing levels of mortality and fertility, on the population. This discussion in effect goes well beyond the bounds of a study of mere population numbers to consider general population structures and variables, with discussion of such aspects as contraception, infanticide and infant mortality, age of marriage, sex ratios, the human life span, and causes of death.

It is the overall aim of this study to provide the ancient historian with a concise introduction both to modern demographic tools and to varied aspects of the population of the ancient world, in particular during the period of the early Roman empire. It is to be hoped that, with such a basis of knowledge, the field of ancient demography may develop further and may lead us to a better understanding of the ancient world and its people.

This final product is the result of many revisions and has benefited from communication and discussion with many people (though some of them may not have realized the degree to which they have helped me). To name but a few, I would like to thank David Coleman, Arthur Pomeroy, Simon Price, Nicholas Purcell, Beryl Rawson, Richard Saller, and Alex Scobie for their advice and comments. I must also thank all my colleagues and friends in both Oxford and Wellington. But my greatest debt of thanks must go to both Richard Smith, who so patiently and enthusiastically initiated a novice into the mysteries of demography, and Fergus Millar, who had the wisdom and foresight to realize the effort would be worthwhile and who, with characteristic insight and forbearance, allowed me to spend a year of my precious three years in Oxford doing something that at the time neither of us was certain would be of any use to anyone. I myself, however, take full credit for any and all shortcomings or errors in this book.

I must also thank the Rhodes Trustees for financial aid during my time in Oxford, and Victoria University of Wellington for a research grant over the last two years and for funding toward the cost of producing the index. The index itself was compiled by Simon Cauchi, to whom many thanks. For permission to use copyright material in amended form in my tables and figures, acknowledgment is due to the President and Fellows of Harvard College (my table 6), to the Academic Press, Inc., and to A. J. Coale (my tables 7–12), and to E. A. Wrigley and R. S. Schofield (my figure 10). It is a pleasure to express my gratitude also to librarians in both Oxford and Wellington, especially those of the Ashmolean Library of Oxford, whose help and friendship made the initial stages of researching and writing this book not only possible but often a pleasure, and also the Interloan Department of the Victoria University of Wellington Library for going to such lengths to obtain for me material from around the world. I am also most grateful to the editorial staff of the Johns Hopkins University Press, in particular, Eric Halpern, Brian MacDonald, and Carol Zimmerman, for turning my manuscript into a book with such care and patience.

I wrote this book because I felt that an introduction to demography for ancient historians was long overdue and very necessary. There is a danger, however, in undertaking an enterprise of this kind, that one may end up by fully satisfying no one. Those who already have a sound grounding in demography may find some of the material here too simplistic for their tastes. Those who have an innate fear of figures and equations may perhaps be so daunted by the title of this book that they will delve no deeper. If, however, I at least succeed in helping a new breed of ancient historian to find his or her footing in a new and, in my view, essential aspect of ancient social history, then the effort will have been worthwhile.

Symbols Used for
Demographic Functions

BR   Crude birth rate, the number of births in a year for every 1,000 members of the population.

C_x In a stationary population, the percentage of persons aged between x and x + n years.

d_x The number of persons dying between ages x and x + n years.

DR   Crude death rate, the number of deaths in a year for every 1,000 members of the population.

e_x Average life expectancy at age x years.

GRR   Gross reproduction rate, in effect, the number of female births that on average each mother in a population has in her reproductive career.

IMR   Infant mortality rate, the number of deaths under age 1 in a year for every 1,000 live births of that year.

l_x Number of survivors at age x from an original cohort; l_0 is conventionally set at 100,000 in the life table.

L_x Number of person-years lived between ages x and x + n years by survivors at age x.

m_x Age-specific or central death rate, number of deaths in a year at age x divided by the midyear population group of that age.

NRR   Net reproduction rate, the GRR adjusted for mortality, that is, the product of the GRR and $p_{\hat{m}}$, thus allowing for females who will not survive to reproduction age.

$p_{\hat{m}}$ The probability of a female surviving to the mean age of maternity.

p_x Probability of surviving from age x to age x + n years.

q_x Probability of dying between ages x and x + n years.

r   Rate of growth, the difference between the BR and DR, that is, natural increase or decrease in population numbers. Usually expressed here as a percentage per year.

SR   Sex ratio, the number of males for every 100 females in a population. SR_x is the sex ratio at age x years.

T_x Total number of person-years lived after age x years.

Demography and Roman Society

Introduction

Pliny the Elder, in discussing the problem of the height to which clouds extend above the earth, quotes several authorities who give widely diverging figures; one of his sources said that clouds were found some 5 miles above the earth, while apparently most writers stated that the distance extended to 111 miles. Pliny then attempts to justify his putting forward such figures, when no answer one way or the other seems readily apparent:

> These figures are really unascertained and impossible to disentangle, but it is proper to put them forward because they have been put forward already, although they are matters in which the method of geometrical inference, which never misleads, is the only method that it is possible not to reject, were anybody desirous of pursuing such questions more deeply, and with the intention of establishing not precise measurement (for to aspire to that would mark an almost insane absorption in study) but merely a conjectural calculation.[1]

The student of ancient history, who quite naturally asks questions regarding the population of the ancient world,[2] is faced with a similarly complicated and confusing array of apparently contradictory figures. The means of deriving such figures, which depend greatly on our interpretation of the ancient sources, are both intricate and often subjective. Pliny offers the

1

method of "geometrical inference" as a scientific way of analyzing his data, although he leaves the task to someone else who may feel the inclination to investigate the problem. The techniques of modern demography may offer to us the means to get some perspective on ancient population "statistics," though here too—like Pliny—we should not expect exact measurement, but rather conjectural as well as, it is to be hoped, realistic calculations.

Historical demography over the past century, and indeed over the past decade, has seen considerable advances in both methodology and results. In the history of early modern Europe, the use of such material as local parish registers of births, marriages, and deaths has enabled researchers to trace the population history of various isolated villages in order to produce an overall general pattern of population trends over several previous centuries. The methods of aggregative back projection and family reconstitution have produced detailed analyses of the annual changes in population over a long period, and such findings have added much to our understanding of the social history of the era, as well as to our knowledge of the processes of population dynamics in history in general.[3]

In ancient history demography has also begun to have an increasingly recognized part to play.[4] Yet the results have often been unsatisfactory and unconvincing, largely because the necessary initial data needed for demographic calculations (such as birth and death registrations and reliable census material) are almost wholly lacking, but also because most ancient historians suffer from a lack of awareness of demographic technique, which can result in an uncritical adoption and manipulation of the ancient evidence.

In this study I will consider some aspects of how ancient historians have used the evidence and suggest other features that also need to be considered in the field of "ancient demography." Although we may never be able to achieve the accuracy or detail possible in studying other later periods of history, it is still reasonable and worthwhile to apply demographic methods and theories to ancient history in the hope of producing, as with

Pliny and his clouds, a range of probable variables within which the general population of Roman society fits. Clearly one cannot apply with precision any single, simple figures for such factors as average life expectancy or levels of fertility when dealing with an entire population of many millions over a period of several centuries. Differences may well have occurred depending upon time, geographical location, and, to a certain extent, social class. Yet such differences should not be exaggerated, as they have been in the interpretation of data from funerary inscriptions in particular, to produce a field of study known as "differential demography," as will be seen shortly. Certainly, in the short term, significant fluctuations will have occurred in both mortality and fertility levels in regard to both time and place (due to such factors as plague and warfare), but our goal should be an overall picture of the patterns of mortality and fertility in the period and in the Roman world as a whole. Similarly migration must play an important part in any detailed analysis of the age structure of any specific population. However, in a general study of this sort over the Roman empire as a whole, emigration and immigration within the empire (such as military colonization) may be seen to cancel each other out (with some important exceptions, notably the city of Rome), while migration into and out of the empire, though it should not be underestimated,[5] may be regarded as of secondary importance for our purposes as compared with the impact of levels of mortality and fertility. By taking into account general, estimated trends in mortality and fertility, a picture will emerge that, when set out in life table form, provides information on such questions as life expectancy and age structure, both of which are of vital importance in an inquiry into aspects of population in the Roman world.

One

Ancient Evidence

ost "demographic" studies by ancient historians over the past century have attempted to provide answers to two quite different questions. First, how many people (or, more usually and more limited, citizens) were there? Second, which will most concern us here, for how long did these people live?

Establishing the size of a population in history is the practice of historical demography at its crudest level. It is not that the answers themselves are not of interest—certainly they may be—but rather that a population is never static in size and so any single figure is both misleading and an oversimplification, and that the methods used to arrive at such population figures, in the sphere of the ancient world at any rate, are broadly subjective and unable to be validated by modern demographic techniques. Various and widely diverging estimates have been made of the size of populations in antiquity of Rome, Italy, individual provinces, and the empire as a whole, as well as of, for example, Athens in the fifth and fourth centuries B.C.[1] The sources for such population estimates are never open to easy interpretation. They range from reports of census figures, for which—even if accurate—doubt remains as to precisely who was counted, to highly subjective estimates made from such variables as data on food imports and distribution (how much did people eat?), city size and population density (how many people per hectare or per house?), and figures for army size (what exact age group was liable for military service, and what proportion of this age group served or was conscripted?).

Such questions can never be answered satisfactorily, and some very diverse figures have been the result of a century or more of attempts.[2] In a detailed review of the evidence, Maier reached the skeptical conclusion that we cannot acquire sufficiently accurate information on populations in antiquity to make estimates of their size valid.[3] Certainly caution is justified and too often lacking, and again we must not forget that populations fluctuate in size over time—in the case of Rome in particular, where people doubtlessly moved in and out of the capital city continuously and in considerable numbers, with probably quite significant seasonal differences.

However, some general ideas of population extent, in Rome, Italy, and the empire at large at least, are of some use as indicators of orders of magnitude. I therefore append the following tentative estimates, which seem to represent the broad consensus of modern scholarly opinion (though by no means a unanimous one) and which have remained largely unchanged since the appearance of Beloch's masterly work in 1886. All these figures may be held to relate to the early empire. For the city of Rome itself, a figure of between 750,000 and 1 million seems right.[4] For Italy I would accept a figure of between 5 and 8 million inhabitants,[5] and for the empire as a whole between 50 and 60 million (implying a population density of around 15 inhabitants per square kilometer).[6]

The Epigraphic Evidence

To return now to the other question commonly asked, namely how long on average people lived in the ancient world, attention has centered around the very large body of funerary epitaphs available, in particular for the period of the Roman empire. Thousands of inscriptions have been collected on which the age

5

at death of the individual is given. From these a simple calculation can be made:

Average expectation of life

$$= \frac{\text{Sum of total years lived}}{\text{Total number of individuals recorded}}$$

Such was the method of, for example, Beloch, using 1,831 Roman epitaphs; Harkness, with 28,665 inscriptions; and Macdonnell, with 20,758 epitaphs. Since these studies even more inscriptions have been collected and analyzed, and the results have been further differentiated into geographical location, period in history, and even social class,[7] though often the sample size for such isolated areas or groups becomes so small as to be totally insignificant.

Yet even where the overall sample is vast,[8] the inherent problems in the evidence remain and have been frequently spelled out over the past twenty years. Detailed discussion with examples may be found elsewhere.[9] In what follows I want only to highlight what I see as the primary biases discernible in the epigraphic evidence that make the inscriptions of little use in estimations of average life expectancy in the Roman world. Some of these factors are more significant than others. In total, they produce a damning criticism.

Age Distribution　The simple equation just cited may often produce what appears to be a realistic figure for average life expectancy, but when ages at death are sorted into age groups (say, 0–1 years, 1–9, 10–19, etc.), serious problems become evident. That infant mortality (i.e., deaths in the first year of life) is grossly underrepresented in the tombstone records has long been recognized;[10] clearly infant deaths, even when burial took place, went largely unrecorded, or at least any such records have not survived in large numbers. The figures obtained for infant deaths as recorded on tombstones would suggest a rate of mortality considerably lower than that experienced even in present-day developed countries.

At the other end of the age scale, epitaphs commemorating

elderly deceased persons present an image of amazing longevity in amazing numbers, particularly in the case of Roman Africa, where the proportion of centenarians is obviously grossly inflated.[11] That such figures present the absurd image of an elderly population both larger and older than any in the Western world today has not deterred some scholars from believing that Africans really did enjoy such longevity in such great numbers,[12] due apparently to climatic advantages and a healthy life style in the countryside. Apart from the fact that most of the deceased recorded came from urban areas anyway, no life-style—ancient or modern—is so healthy as to produce such a high proportion of people of such advanced ages. Rather what we are seeing here are biases both in the statements of age and in the custom of commemoration of different age groups in different places, features that will be discussed subsequently.

Thus we have evident misrepresentation of the numbers of the very young and of the very old on the tombstones. What of the middle years? In recognition of the problems involved in using age records for these two extreme age groups, some scholars have advocated the use only of evidence for the age groups in between.[13] The results obtained from this method, therefore, take no account of the infant and early childhood mortality rates, but might appear to give some indication of chances of survival after a certain age. This is dependent, however, on the hypothesis that the tombstone inscriptions give an accurate record of mortality in these middle age groups of, say, 10 to 60 years of age. But that they do *not* do this has been clearly shown by Keith Hopkins. In short, *every* age group gives mortality rates that are "mostly demographically impossible and always highly improbable," due to different commemorative practices at different ages.[14] The pattern of mortality that emerges from the tombstone data over the various age classes is untenable in reality. Throughout biases are discernible that render the results of analysis both unreliable and potentially misleading. One bias may be alleviated to some degree by another, opposite one, but the extent of the bias cannot be measured, and the overall result, however realistic it may appear, has little true connection with the underlying mortality pattern. We simply cannot pick and choose among the evidence to find results that fit our preconceived notions.

Geographical Distribution   The case of Africa and its centenarians, which has generated a great deal of interest,[15] highlights the extremes of the variations in life expectancy figures to be obtained from tombstone data from different parts of the empire. Clauss has made this point very clear by setting out the results obtained from analyzing the tombstone records of various localities in the empire.[16] To take extreme examples, Castellum Celtianum in Africa, from a sample of 1,258 individual ages, enjoyed an apparent average life expectancy of 60.2 years; on the other hand Virunum in Noricum, with a sample of only 65 ages, produces a figure of only 18.1 years. Closer inspection shows that in Castellum Celtianum the sample consists of 494 (39.3%) ages of 70 years or more and only 6 (0.5%) under 10 years of age; Virunum, on the other hand, has 19 (29.2%) ages under 10 years and only 1 (1.5%) over 70 years of age. Such distorting variations occur throughout the samples for different localities. This can mean one of two things: either these variations reflect reality, that is, people really did live much longer lives in much greater numbers and suffer from negligible mortality rates in their early years in certain parts of the empire in sharp contrast to others; or these variations reflect differences not in age-specific mortality rates so much as in "the epigraphic habit" in different places—that is, in customs of commemorating different age groups. That the latter alternative is the right one is suggested by the case of Africa alone. It should be noted that tombstone inscriptions on which the age at death is given are only a subgroup of the entire collection of funeral epitaphs. Customs of commemoration differed not only in the age groups commemorated but also in whether age at death is given at all, as Beloch had already noted in 1886. Kajanto has an interesting discussion of this factor, though his figures have become muddled and inconsistent. Briefly, for Rome out of a random sample of 840 epitaphs from *CIL* 6, a total of 537 (63.9%) lacked age records, whereas for Castellum Celtianum only 1 of the sample of 1,258 (mentioned previously) lacked an age.[17] In Rome it appears to have been customary to record the age of those deceased young but not the age of the elderly so often, whereas in Africa elderly ages predominate. The bias produced from such differences clearly distorts the results significantly. Furthermore, the practice of setting up commemorative epitaphs while one was still alive (*se vivo*) adds extra distortion to the data.

Much has been made of the apparent differences in life expectancy in differing areas of the empire on the basis of this evidence. Russell, for example, produced 14 life tables for various provinces based on the tombstone data; one study, that of Blumenkranz, even goes so far as to talk about the demography of a select racial group within the city of Rome.[18] Yet even within such differentiation further problems lie, quite apart from that of sample size. One of Russell's tables, that for Roman Egypt, was constructed on the basis of the work of Hombert and Préaux, who collected 813 tombstone inscriptions and mummy labels.[19] Using the simple equation again of total years lived divided by total number of individuals, Hombert and Préaux came up with a figure of 32.39 years.[20] They were aware of some deficiencies in their data: underrepresentation of the young and of females,[21] and overrepresentation of the elderly, including four centenarians, as well as a bias toward the upper classes and a tendency to age-round. They therefore lowered their figures for average life expectancy to 23.78 years, without explaining how they arrived at such a figure but apparently on analogy with the earlier study by Willcox and his comparison of Roman mortality estimates from epitaphs with early twentieth-century figures for Chinese farmers—a rather dubious comparison, one might have thought![22]

Nonetheless Hombert and Préaux's figures found wide acceptance with ancient historians, as well as with Russell who, as mentioned, adopted their figures in their entirety for one of his life tables. Their figures also gained support from a later study that collected a sample of 168 tombstone inscriptions and mummy labels from a single small locality, Kom Abou Billou in Lower Egypt, and calculated average life expectancy at birth as being 32.88 years.[23] This sample, it is argued by its editor, holds certain advantages over that of Hombert and Préaux's, since (1) it comes from a single locality, (2) it may be dated to a period of only one century (though this is uncertain, with the possible chronological span dating from the second to the early fourth centuries), (3) it comprises a better cross-section of the population, on the grounds that the mummy labels represent the poorer classes,[24] and (4) it gives a better male-to-female ratio than is usual from such samples.[25] At any rate, the picture from Roman Egypt, limited though the evidence was, seemed to prove consistent. Advocates of "differential demography" and of the use of funerary inscriptions in the estimation of life expectancy could claim apparent success here.[26]

But on closer analysis, in fact, the material from Roman Egypt shows the same internal inconsistencies and biases as does the material from the empire as a whole. Boyaval, in a long and often needlessly repetitive series of articles from 1975 to 1981, has highlighted, in the manner of Clauss in 1973, the serious problems and flaws in the material. As he stresses, Hombert and Préaux's sample has no unity of provenance at all and needs to be studied in relation to the precise area of origin rather than being taken as evidence for the whole of Egypt. In bringing the material up to date, he found that the great majority of the inscriptions and labels came from five specific sites in Egypt,[27] one of them being Hooper's Kom Abou Billou. On analyzing each of these sites in turn, it becomes evident that the overall picture obtained by Hombert and Préaux for Roman Egypt in fact conceals enormous differences between individual localities. Average life expectancy at birth for the five sites ranges from 26 to 40 years, depending largely on the variations in commemorative practices. As with the marked differences between Castellum Celtianum and Virunum, other locations in Egypt provide as low an average figure for life expectancy at birth as 14 years and as high as 45 years.[28]

As Boyaval, like Clauss before him, stresses, the difference between geographical areas is an indication, if not of chance, of local variations in "sensibilité" and funerary practices, not of mortality. This cultural variety in commemorative practices has been highlighted by Éry, who provides a very neat example:[29] while the inscriptions from Rome (a sample of 9,980 ages) produce an average life expectancy at birth of below 23 years, if one studies only the *Greek* inscriptions from Rome, one comes up with a figure of 51 years! This serves to indicate clearly the different customs in funerary commemoration of two different groups of people; no one would, I imagine, suggest that Roman Greeks in reality enjoyed such superior life chances over their Latin neighbors.

The conclusion to be drawn is that marked geographical differences are due to cultural practices in commemoration and not to demographic realities. But having stated that, one might ask whether in fact mortality rates might have varied significantly over the empire as a whole. Kajanto thought not: "the length of life was, by and large, equal throughout the Roman empire."[30] This is probably close to the truth. Standards of hygiene and medical care, which still serve to separate the modern Western world to such an extent from the underdeveloped countries in terms of mortality levels today, probably remained uniformly poor over the empire as a whole. Climate may have made some differences;[31] more significant, population density can greatly affect mortality rates, and it is certain that in high-density areas (particularly in the city of Rome, but also in smaller, closely packed urban centers, where epidemic diseases could spread quickly) life expectancy at birth would have been somewhat lower, with noticeably higher infant and early childhood mortality rates, than in the less congested countryside (see chapter 3). But the differences are unlikely to have ever been as great as the inscriptional evidence would suggest. The extreme variations in apparent life expectancy figures as derived from tombstone data, ranging from less than 20 to more than 60 years, are clearly not reflections of reality but rather are indications of how practices of commemoration varied in different places with regard to the recording of age in particular. As such

11

they are also indicators of the dangers in using funerary inscriptions as a basis for demographic calculations. One might also ask how the study of inscriptions from a single town or city can get round the problem of migration into and out of the locality, a factor that might also seriously distort the data.

Thus far we have dealt with the two main biases in the tombstone data, namely age-distribution and geographical variations, factors closely linked to each other.[32] Much more briefly now, I outline other less marked but nonetheless serious faults in the evidence.

Urban/Rural Distribution   Because the vast majority of the epitaphs recording age at death comes from urban as opposed to rural areas—despite some important exceptions, particularly for the western empire—the overall sample is significantly urban-based. It is probable that in rural areas mortality would have been somewhat less severe than in the larger cities due to such factors as relatively better sanitary conditions and availability of food, though it is difficult to quantify these differences. To what extent this bias toward urban centers would affect the life expectancy figures derived from funerary inscriptions is likewise impossible to measure, but must at least be recognized.

Class Distribution   It has long been recognized, though at times it is exaggerated, that not all classes of Roman society are represented on the extant tombstone inscriptions, since only the "respectable" levels of society could have afforded proper tombstones.[33] Certainly crude tombstones have been found and these may commemorate individuals from the lower levels of society, but the vast majority of inscriptions in our sample is derived from the wealthier classes. This fact, rather than deterring investigators, has given rise to a branch of study known as "differential demography," its leading exponent being Étienne. By this method distinctions are drawn as to certain classes, such as the free and freed as opposed to slaves,[34] in the calculation of average life expectancy. Apart from the fact that, as with differences in geography, the dividing up of the sample in this way leads to very small data groups, differential demography fails to take any account of differences in commemorative practices, and sees its results purely as indicators of differing mortality levels within different social groups and not of different social customs.[35] As with the differences in real mortality between urban and rural areas, it is quite plausible to suggest that there was some difference in age-specific mortality rates between the very rich and the very poor in the ancient world. The wealthy were less likely to suffer from malnutrition,[36] and medical aid was presumably available to the wealthy in preference to the poor. That such medical aid may have been of limited effectiveness by modern standards, however, must be remembered, and in the path of epidemic diseases death will have shown little regard for wealth. Clauss is probably right in seeing this class bias in the data as only a minor contributing factor to the overall faults in the tombstone evidence, as compared with distortions caused by age-distribution inequalities and by regional variations in commemoration.[37]

Chronological Distribution   The tombstone inscriptions used in the estimation of mortality rates cover an extensive chronological period. Aside from the problem of the relative size of the sample over different periods of history, there is also the question of whether changes in mortality levels may have occurred over time and therefore whether one is justified in treating as one body a set of inscriptions belonging to a period of some five or six centuries. On the other side of the coin, apparent differences in mortality as evidenced from tombstone data may be due more to changes in commemorative practice—for example, greater representation of certain age groups than before, or changes in the practice of stating age—than to changes in mortality rates.[38] Clauss is again useful here, since he draws a comparison between inscriptions of the first through second centuries and the third century; likewise Éry discusses the differences between early and late inscriptions.[39] Such changes as do occur

13

(they are rarely significant) should again be attributed to changing social customs rather than to any observable change in mortality levels.

Accuracy of Age Statements   The phenomenon of age-rounding is a particularly noticeable feature of the tombstone inscriptions.[40] Clauss found ample evidence in the sample he studied, with some variation due to locality, which again serves to highlight regional variations in commemorative practices. Yet simple age-rounding alone would only give rise to inaccuracies of at most 3 or 4 years, which in the context of demographic analysis could be alleviated by dealing with age groups of 10 years' duration, especially if divided up into groups of 15–24, 25–34 years, and so on, rather than 10–19, 20–29 years, thus to an extent obviating the bias toward ages given as multiples of 10 years.

However, the possibility of significant exaggeration of age, or even of ignorance about age, cannot be overlooked. Problems in calculating exact age have already been mentioned, as well as a lack of interest in precise and accurate statements. Although the bureaucratic system of Roman Egypt enabled officials to calculate and verify statements of age, such precision and accuracy would have only been regarded as necessary or worthwhile in cases where exemption from certain taxes or duties was in question due to the claimant's alleged age. On tombstones, on the other hand, statements of age carried no such bureaucratic implications; no recourse to official records would have been considered warranted, even if such records were widely available outside of Egypt, which may be doubted. In other words, the age recorded on a tombstone reflects how old the deceased and his or her commemorators *thought* the individual was, or even how old that individual *wanted* to be thought to have been at death.

One pertinent example from Algeria will suffice. One Titus Flavius Pudens Maximianus, a *proavus,* is recorded as dying at the age of 83 years and 11 months; yet just below this epitaph an epigram states that "sic fortis centum numerabat tempora vitae."[41] The apparent contradiction here—obvious to us (and to perplexed editors)—probably meant little to the people at the time. This Flavius Pudens is just one of the many elderly people commemorated on tombstones from Africa whom we have already met. It has been seen that this exaggeration in statements of age can create a very significant distortion in the results derived as regards average life expectancy, since a large proportion of very high ages will give the impression of lower mortality levels. Furthermore, this is a bias for which no compensatory calculations can be made with any degree of certainty. We do not know how great the degree of exaggeration was (except perhaps in the case of Flavius Pudens), but we may speculate as to its causes, since it is a phenomenon not unknown in the twentieth century.[42] The suggestion that Roman Africa apparently had so many centenarians because of "l'air pur" has already been ruled out. That it was due to a combination of ignorance and intentional exaggeration seems a much more plausible suggestion, to which one might add the observation that commemoration of elderly deceased with a statement of their age was more common there than elsewhere in comparison with commemoration of the younger age groups. Hence any attempt to calculate average age at death from these tombstones will produce a mean grossly inflated by overstatements of age, just as the mean is overinflated by a lack of recorded infant and early childhood deaths.

Sex Ratio in Inscriptional Evidence   Another very striking feature when considering the thousands of epitaphs collected is the preponderance of males over females.[43] If we assume for the moment that in reality the sex ratio over all age groups was approximately equal, this means that in our sample three males were *commemorated* for every two females. Or is this in fact evidence, as Szilágyi and others would have us believe, that males really did outnumber females by this ratio? It is true that there is some other evidence (to be discussed) that suggests that males really did outnumber females in certain periods of antiquity. But whatever the truth of that, the tombstone inscriptions cannot be used as definite evidence for it. For when the

15

differences in sex are analyzed by age groups instead of as a single unit, the sex ratio varies sharply, from 104 (i.e., 104 males per 100 females) in the 15–29 year age group, to 173 in the 60+ group.[44] Similarly great variations occur in the sex ratio due to the geographical location and even to some extent the chrono-logical period of the evidence.[45]

In some instances females do actually seem to outnumber males, particularly in the 15–35 age bracket, and this has been used as evidence of a mortality increase among females of this age due to childbearing.[46] Whether female mortality rates at these ages were significantly greater than for males of the same ages will be discussed; however, it is unlikely that the epigraphic testimony provides accurate evidence. As Hopkins points out, the difference in the sex ratio at this age is largely due to the proportion of women of this group being commemorated rather than an increased proportion dying; women of this age group seem to have enjoyed heightened status as being both wives and daughters, so that they would have been more likely to have been commemorated by their kin than would females of younger ages. It is also true that wives could only be commemo-rated by their husbands if they predeceased them, and since wives were as a rule some 10 years younger than their husbands, wives who died young stood a better chance of being commemo-rated than did those who lived beyond their reproductive years and whose husbands died before them.[47]

As Hopkins makes clear, therefore, the apparent variations in female mortality over the course of various age classes as appear in the epigraphic data may be due not only to real mortality levels but also (and perhaps more significantly) to habits of commemoration or, more to the point, the availability of a com-memorator. Likewise, Boyaval has argued against the view of Hombert and Préaux that the data from Roman Egypt reflect high female mortality in the reproductive years.[48] Although Boy-aval rightly points out that the sex ratio fluctuates greatly over various localities in Egypt, it is still worth noting that for all the sites males outnumber females in all age groups, a fact he never faces up to. The reason for this, however, is probably again commemorative customs: quite simply, males were more likely to be commemorated than females. Whatever the realities of the sex ratio and female mortality in antiquity, to be discussed in the third chapter of this book, it is evident that the tombstone inscriptions tell us more about commemorative practices due to gender than to mortality levels, and this further undermines their usefulness and validity in attempting demographic observations.

Randomness of Sample The various aspects considered thus far concern habits of commemoration and the way that these factors make the information derived from tombstone inscriptions of highly dubious value. The final consideration I will deal with here is a more statistical one. Advocates of the use of epigraphic material in demographic studies have pointed to the enormous size of the sample as "proof" of its validity. But it is not just size that matters. For a sample such as epigraphic data to be truly reflective of actual mortality rates, not only must we make certain assumptions about the population in question (such as that rates of mortality remained constant over a long period and that migration in and out of the population made no significant difference—very great assumptions indeed), but we must also be sure that the sample is a random one reflecting all levels of society, both sexes, all age groups. As already noted, the sample does not come even close to meeting these criteria. No matter how large the sample, the biases and distortions would remain.

Furthermore, although the overall sample is indeed vast, when one begins to divide it up by region or time period, the evidence becomes sparse. How many inscriptions does one need for a sample to be considered statistically significant? Szilágyi says 75 ages per location. Clauss goes further, stating that we need 75 for each sex and for limited chronological periods of, say, 200 years; a sample of 75 would be satisfactory, he says, but for "certain" results one would need a sample of some 300 to 400 ages at death.[49]

Such a minimum requirement is of course well beyond what

we have at the moment and are ever likely to get, though it still represents only a *very* small proportion of the entire population of the Roman empire. Yet even if we did have evidence in such abundance, all it could tell us would be the trends in commemorative practice, not in mortality rates. In other words, a statistically significant sample of epigraphic data from one site over a short chronological period could do no more than tell us of the population as recorded, not of the population that existed at the time, for all the commemorative biases would still be there; it is just that in a large sample they would be all the more evident.

In sum, then, what the studies involving the tombstone evidence provide us with is a vast array of figures, some of which look reasonable on first sight, others of which are clearly unrealistic in terms of actual demography. Attempts have been made by various scholars to modify and adjust these simple results in order to achieve a greater measure of apparent realism. Such attempts include the elimination of the younger and older age categories, as previously discussed; the use of only selected samples of geographical locations or of particular social groups; the use of median life expectancy values; and the sophisticated manipulation of the figures by mathematical processes.[50] Yet the relationship of such results to reality is still just as difficult to assess.

The basic problem remains that we can never be sure which sample or which result reflects reality. Figures can be made to look plausible even when they are derived from implausible evidence, as with Russell's 14 life tables. The closest we can come with the epigraphic evidence is to say that a large sample of randomly distributed data may accurately portray the population *as commemorated,* with whatever biases were prevalent in the burial and commemorative processes in that cemetery at that time. In other words, at best we may be able to use such data to discover the probable age at death of the population buried at that cemetery, but such a population may not represent the population as it existed at that time, but only (say) middle-aged males of the upper classes of the early third century A.D. Such results, which must still remain conjectural even with such limited parameters, are of little value in an overall demographic consideration of the population of the Roman empire as a whole.

Nonetheless, even in the face of such evidently serious and irremediable shortcomings in the use of the epigraphic evidence for demographic purposes, some scholars continue to expend considerable energy over this kind of work.[51] More generally and with increasing frequency, scholars state that they are aware of the problems but then go on to "tentatively" use the funerary inscriptions to illustrate average life expectancy figures for antiquity. It is not enough to be simply aware of the problems and then go ahead regardless. The material is so plagued with misleading biases and impossible demographic trends that the use of tombstone inscriptions, however selective, is unjustified and potentially fallacious.[52]

The Egyptian Evidence

The use of tombstone inscriptions and mummy labels from Egypt for calculating mortality levels has already been discussed. Clearly this evidence suffers from the same faults as that from the rest of the empire. However, Egypt does provide us with other, unique material in the form of official documents preserved on papyri and ostraka. I have argued elsewhere that the propensity toward age-rounding is noticeably absent from such official documents and that this is due to the singularly effective bureaucratic administrative machine in evidence in Egypt in the first three centuries of our era.[53] The area in which this bureaucracy operated, namely in the collection of taxes and the imposition of public services, has left various records of potential value to the historical demographer, such as notices of births and deaths. Unfortunately, both these forms of documents are very limited in number and provide nothing like a comprehensive collection.

A better sample is provided by the extant census documents. The census was held every 14 years under the principate; I have discussed elsewhere the methods employed in the collection and recording of census data in Roman Egypt.[54] The study by Hombert and Préaux in 1952 remains central to all studies of the census in Roman Egypt. They collected and analyzed some 200 census returns and calculated from the 532 ages cited a figure for average life expectancy at birth, using the simple equation cited earlier, of 26.60 years.[55] They add the warning that because the youngest members of the family tended to be recorded at the bottom of the return, the part of the document most commonly lost through erosion of the papyrus, their figures should perhaps be lowered somewhat.

There are obvious, immediate problems here, of course. Just as with tombstone inscriptions, a stationary population (one that is not growing or declining, or changing through the effects of migration) must be assumed if all ages cited are to be taken as representative of a single point in time; the limited number of data, though individually datable to a precise year (unlike most tombstone inscriptions), does not allow a consideration of the changes in population size or structure over the course of successive generations. Added to this is the further problem that, unlike the data derived from funerary epitaphs, the census returns give not age at death but age at the time of the census. On the other hand, the ages given in the census documents seem to suffer less from the rounding of ages, and therefore, by implication, the tendency to exaggerate ages may also have been minimal. There is always the problem in censuses, even today, that individual declarants may be ignorant of or lie about their ages, the latter case being particularly evident when the census is for fiscal rather than demographic purposes. That such inaccuracies did occur in the ancient world is clear from the figures, apparently derived from the census of A.D. 73/74, recorded by Pliny and Phlegon,[56] in which an incredible number of centenarians is reported, up to the age of 150 years.

But in the case of the Egyptian data, no such exaggeration is evident. Only one person, a male, is said to be over the age of 80 years at the time of the declaration. The age distribution, by sex, of Hombert and Préaux's sample is given in table 1 (see Appendix B). In theory, since all inhabitants of Egypt, both male and female, had to be declared in the census, and since evasion, though it no doubt occurred, was policed and punished, the sample source may be considered a random one and not age-, class-, or sex-specific. The source may be a statistically sound one, but it does not mean our sample is. The census returns we have represent an extremely small proportion of the total universe of Roman Egyptian census returns.[57] But this does not prevent the sample being a usable one, provided that it really is random. Although the sample is not evenly distributed geographically or chronologically, no definite distorting biases can be traced in it, and Hopkins believes that it is indeed representative "of a much wider Egyptian population."[58] Certainly these figures may be regarded as far more representative than the figures from the tombstone inscriptions.

But the evidence is far from perfect. Hopkins noted that young ages are underrepresented (one possible reason already mentioned is the loss of names at the end of documents) and, more seriously, the rate of mortality appears too high at some points to be realistic.[59] Another measure of something strange is the sex ratio by ages. Although the overall sex ratio is nearly equal,[60] the ratios by age groups are very irregular (particularly for females in the 10–39 years group; see table 1) and are unrealistic. It must be remembered, however, that the sample size is small and such fluctuations are not surprising; furthermore, it is a common demographic phenomenon for young females to be missed in censuses. Whatever the causes of these inconsistencies, while they do undermine the demographic value of the sample as it stands to a certain extent, the figures derived from the Egyptian census returns are of far more value than those derived from tombstone inscriptions. An increase in the sample size would be welcome, but we also need to be able to understand the factors influencing the survival of the data that may be producing biases, if indeed the source of the inconsistencies is not in the actual census procedure at the time but in the extant material.[61]

From another, small sample, we have in a single papyrus a record of 122 individuals listed in a register of taxes.[62] Of these

21

122, 85 have their ages extant. The main tax in question, the poll tax, was only paid by males between the ages of 14 and 62 years, so the overall range of this sample is limited to this group. Of the 85 individuals known by age, only 8 are over the age of 49 years, and only 2 of these are over 54. The picture here is of a very young population. But the sample remains too small to be truly meaningful,[63] and size is the main problem here; for information even just on the demographic realities of males aged 14 to 62 years is of value if it is from a reliable source.

Such a source, it has been suggested, *is* available. A much greater body of evidence, similar in character to that of the tax list just mentioned, has been collected and analyzed in what is the most ambitious use of Egyptian data for demographic purposes to date.[64] The authors have edited and studied Theban tax receipts surviving on ostraka of the first to third centuries A.D. This initial body of evidence is enormous and furthermore is confined to a small geographical area. Each complete receipt records the payer's name, the amount paid, and the year in which the payment was made—*but not the payer's age on payment.* Because every male aged between 14 and 62 years had to pay the poll tax (and probably the other taxes as well, as the editors here assume), a very large sample such as this stands a good chance of being nonselective in character. That the sample is "nonarchival"[65] and therefore random is less certain; the fact that for some individuals as many as 64 receipts survive raises the possibility that private archives are included in the sample. But the editors are right, I think, in stressing that their sample is by no means confined to the upper classes (as is usually the case with the epigraphic material), and if anything the bias in the Theban ostraka may be toward the lower classes. This possibility, together with the overall size of the sample, makes it appear a very good source for demographic observations of the Egyptian population.

The method of analysis is laborious and painstaking. The authors sifted through the thousands of ostraka at their disposal to find individuals for whom receipts survive over the course of at least 2 years. A list of 191 men is the result,[66] so already our sample has become greatly reduced. The method now is simple enough. Subtract the date of the first receipt from that of the last for each individual and we have the minimum number of years over which the man paid tax (the minimum possible being 2 years, the maximum being 62 − 14 = 48 years). Then, by adding this tax-paying span to 14 years, the earliest age at which he could have paid tax, we have the *minimum* age at which he could have died, referred to here as the "pseudo-age at death."

But what relation does this pseudo-age have to the actual age at death? For an answer to this question the material was handed over to a statistician, W. K. Hastings, who, via a complicated analysis, assures us that the results derived by this method are likely to be valid—pseudo-age at death is directly related to actual age at death.[67] The results, to which we will come shortly, have therefore found general acceptance, though unfortunately little noticed outside the field of papyrology. Only one review has tried to raise any doubts as to the validity of the results, on the grounds that the pseudo-age at death may reflect a significant proportion of persons stopping payment of taxes not through actual death but because they have fled from payment (*anachōrēsis*), and that therefore the mortality rates as calculated may be slightly too high.[68] This argument holds some validity, but is a minor issue in comparison with a much more significant fault in the use of the data.

This fault is that the receipts used do not cite the age of the individual at the time of payment. Consequently, the pseudo-age, that is, the minimum possible age at death of the individual, fails to relate directly to the real age at death in two ways: the first extant receipt for an individual may relate to an age at payment far in excess of 14 years, since it may not be the payer's real first payment; and the last extant receipt may predate the payer's death by many years, simply because subsequent receipts have been lost. Although the initial sample was indeed a large one, it is still insignificant in comparison with the original universe of Theban tax receipts, and the extant sample has been further limited to only 191 (or, in the final analysis, 150) individuals. I will attempt to show the extent of these faults in the data by reference to the list of individuals given.[69]

In the case of number 15, 4 money receipts survive, dated to A.D. 15, 35, 36, and 40. If the first receipt was not extant, the receipt for A.D. 35 would be assumed to be his first payment at the age of 14 years and thus his pseudo-age at death would be, not 39, but 19 years of age. To take one of the more extreme examples, number 75, only 2 receipts survive, one for A.D. 109, the other A.D. 152—a span of 43 years dependent on a single ostrakon; or again number 14, with 3 receipts, of A.D. 36, 38, and 67, where the final receipt adds an extra 29 years, increasing the apparent tax-paying span from 2 to 31 years. Nor are these isolated references. From a quick perusal of the index of persons I calculate that 60 of the 191 persons listed, almost one in three, have had their pseudo-age increased by at least 10 years through the survival of a *single* ostrakon. The overall sample, reduced to 191 individuals, is too small to allow for such miscalculations as may result, random or otherwise. The pseudo-age at death, as computed, may grossly underestimate the actual age at death in a significant number of cases, both because the first extant receipt may relate to a payment well in excess of the 15th year, and because the last extant receipt may predate the payer's death by many years. That receipts have been lost in a random fashion is argued by Hastings in section five of the book.[70] But that the sample we have is not entirely random is surely suggested by the fact that, whereas for the majority of the 191 persons listed only 2 or 3 receipts survive, for 13 of them (6.81%) more than 10 survive, and in 3 cases 20 or more are extant.[71] This surely suggests that some archival material is involved. In the case of number 90, where 64 receipts are extant, the tax-paying span is 32 years, from A.D. 118 to 150, whereas in other cases where the span exceeds 30 years as few as 2 or 3 receipts survive.[72] Number 94 is a particularly striking example; receipts survive for A.D. 119, 140, and 166—a total span of 47 years (almost the maximum possible) with only 3 receipts, with gaps of over 20 years between each one.

Other limitations in the data[73] include the fact that even if a man survived past the age of 62 years no receipts would exist because payment of the tax stopped at that age—that is, the maximum possible tax-paying career is 48 years, and no allowance is made for those who may live beyond that age. The editors here would argue that, because the numbers by the age of 62 years were so small anyway, this makes no noteworthy difference, but again this rests on their assumption that the pseudo-age at death is directly related to the actual age. That the data deal only with males is rightly stressed, nor can any allowance be made for the effects of migration.[74] The chief fault remains, however, that the method used calculates only the minimum possible age at death, whereas in fact the actual age at death would in reality have often been well in excess of this minimum. The use of receipts between A.D. 77 and 168 only, the period for which most receipts are extant, does little to alleviate this problem, and further decreases the sample size.

A look, finally, at the results as given by Samuel, Hastings, Bowman, and Bagnall confirms these misgivings about the validity of the data and their treatment of them. Their table 6.2 shows the number of survivors from ages 15 to 62 for the various taxes that the receipts cover. Of the sample for all taxes, 150 survive to a pseudo-age of 15 years (i.e., have a tax-paying span of at least 2 years) and the number declines from here. From these figures a survival rate (or, rather, a pseudo–survival rate) is calculated, in the order of 0.887 to 0.937, that is, the probability of surviving from one year to the next. The editors assume that this is a constant, that the chances of surviving from *any* year to the next, whatever the age of the individual after the age of 14 years, is always the same. That this is *not* the case should be obvious and has long been recognized as a demographic principle.[75] Basically, the survival rate remains anything but constant over various ages; the assumption that the survival rate is constant is not only an oversimplification, it is wrong.

This wrong assumption leads the authors to the implausible conclusion that "beginning from any particular age, on the average, each member of the population will live for 14.4 years; expressed differently, it means that a man of 15 can expect to live to reach 29.4 years of age." The authors state elsewhere that this does not apply to expectation of life at infancy or early childhood,[76] but even the idea that the average expectation of life is the same at any adult age is clearly wrong. Hastings at least qualifies these results by stating that the survival rate *may* decrease with increasing age,[77] but in the results as given this assumed constant survival rate remains and further undermines the conclusions reached. Average life expectancy is calculated from the survival rate and hence is dependent on its being constant. The resulting figures from the various taxes, for average life expectancy at age 15 (i.e., the average number of years lived after the age of 15 years), range from 8.3 to 15.4 years. As mentioned, the editors in their conclusion base their arguments on the figures for money taxes only for the period A.D. 77 to 168, and use only the first 30 years of data (i.e., for pseudo-age at death up to 45 years) to give an average expectation of life at age 15 (or any other age above that) of 14.4 years, with 95 percent confidence limits ranging between 11.5 and 19.1 years.

This seems to have raised no eyebrows,[78] despite its evident absurdity. An average expectation of life at age 15 of 14.4 years implies an average life expectancy at birth of less than ten years, something that is absolutely impossible if a population is to survive beyond a single generation. In the worst possible population regime imaginable, where life expectancy at birth is less than 20 years, life expectancy at age 15 is still more than 30 years (see my chapter 2).

For all these reasons, the figures derived from the Theban tax ostraka, as calculated, grossly underestimate life expectancy values. The authors state that "of all the people who reach age 15, only one-half will reach the age of 25, and one-quarter will reach the age of 35,"[79] that is, the population is apparently being halved every ten years. This too suggests impossibly high mortality. Given that in a very high mortality regime only about half the population at birth will reach the age of 5 or 10 years (see chapters 2 and 3), the authors are in fact suggesting the extinction of the Egyptian population, since it would be biologically impossible for the population to reproduce itself under such extreme mortality conditions. They conclude their study by saying that their results point to a higher death rate than had previously been supposed for Roman Egypt (by Hombert and Préaux), but they fail to realize how much worse their scenario is, and how unrealistic their results are as a consequence of shortcomings in the data source and in their method. The use of a statistician was a valiant break from tradition; perhaps the use of a demographer would have proved more advantageous, at least in alerting the authors to the implausibility of their results. I can see no way, unfortunately, that the Theban tax receipts can be used to produce real and meaningful estimates of mortality rates in Roman Egypt. The only potentially usable data from Roman Egypt remain those generated by the census, as small as this sample is.

The Ulpianic Evidence

Thus far the material used as purported evidence for life expectancy in the Roman world has been in the form of raw data on ages at a specific time, data that have needed to be ordered and manipulated in order to even begin to calculate demographic values. Average life expectancy itself is a difficult concept to grasp,[80] and it may be asked whether in antiquity such a concept was understood and used—or indeed whether, in its precise sense, it would have been considered to be of any practical value in the ancient world.

One legal source, it has been stated on many occasions, does give actual figures for life expectancy: the so-called Ulpianic life table, preserved in an edited excerpt from the second book of Aemilius Macer's treatise *ad legem vicesimam hereditatium* in the *Digest*.[81] The text needs to be quoted here in full, and I append a literal translation:

Computationi in alimentis faciendae hanc formam esse Ulpianus scribit, ut a prima aetate usque ad annum vicesimum quantitas alimentorum triginta annorum computetur eiusque quantitatis Falcidia praestetur, ab annis vero viginti usque ad annum vicesimum quintum annorum viginti octo, ab annis viginti quinque usque ad annos triginta annorum viginti quinque, ab annis triginta usque ad annos triginta quinque annorum viginti duo, ab annis triginta quinque usque ad annos quadraginta annorum viginti. ab annis quadraginta usque ad annos quinquaginta tot annorum computatio fit, quot aetati eius ad annum sexagesimum deerit remisso uno anno: ab anno vero quinquagesimo usque ad annum quinquagesimum quintum annorum novem, ab annis quinquaginta quinque usque ad annum sexagesimum annorum septem, ab annis sexaginta, cuiuscumque aetatis sit, annorum quinque. eoque nos iure uti Ulpianus ait et circa computationem usus fructus faciendam. solitum est tamen a prima aetate usque ad annum trigesimum computationem annorum triginta fieri, ab annis vero triginta tot annorum computationem inire, quot ad annum sexagesimum deesse videntur. numquam ergo amplius quam triginta annorum computatio initur. sic denique et si rei publicae usus fructus legetur, sive simpliciter sive ad ludos, triginta annorum computatio fit.

For computation to be made in the matter of maintenance, Ulpian describes [*lit.* "writes"] the following formula: from birth [*lit.* "the first age"] to the 20th year, the amount of 30 years' maintenance will be calculated and the Falcidian portion of this will be due; from 20 years to the 25th year, [the amount] of 28 years [will be due]; from 25 years up to 30 years, 25 years; from 30 years up to 35 years, 22 years; from 35 years up to 40 years, 20 years. From 40 years up to 50 years, the computation will be made by the number of years as are lacking at this age from the 60th year, with one year's remission; then, from the 50th year up to the 55th year, [the amount] of 9 years; from 55 years up to the 60th year, 7 years; and from 60 years, whatever the age, [the amount] of 5 years. Ulpian says that we use this same rule for the computation of a usufruct. However it has been [is?] the practice for the computation from birth to the 30th year to be of 30 years, but from 30 years the computation is of as many years as are lacking from the 60th year. Therefore the computation never goes beyond 30 years. Thus, in the same way, if a legacy of a usufruct is made to the state, whether without restriction or for the provision of games, the computation will be of 30 years.

This excerpt from Macer was included by the compilers of the *Digest* in the chapter on the *lex Falcidia* of 40 B.C., which had provided that legacies should not exceed three-quarters of the entire testator's estate; the "Falcidian portion" mentioned here, the one-quarter minimum, went to the principal heir, while any legacies given over this three-quarter maximum had to be scaled down proportionately.[82] Now if instead of an immediate legacy of property the testator willed the usufruct of property or an annuity to be paid by the principal heir to the legatees for life, then the amount bequeathed had also to be calculated to ensure that the total sum of all such legacies did not exceed three-quarters of the entire estate. In this light, then, the Ulpianic table as recorded by Macer is one method that might be used to compute the capital value of such a legacy over the course of a lifetime, given the age of the legatee.

This is a simplification of a complex law, but it is complicated enough. However, it is only the beginning of our problems in the interpretation of this passage. For the excerpt comes from a work by Macer not on the *lex Falcidia* but on the *lex Iulia de vicesima hereditatium* of around A.D. 6, which imposed a 5 percent tax on most testamentary inheritances. It has long been argued[83] that Macer (floruit circa A.D. 230) originally wrote here not of the Falcidian portion due but of the *vicesima* amount, that is, the 5 percent tax. Since, however, this inheritance tax had been abolished subsequent to Macer's writing and previous to the Justinianic date of the compilation of the *Digest,* the reading was changed by the compilers from *vicesima* to *Falcidia*. This now seems certain,[84] and the restoration of *vicesima* better suits the meaning of *praestetur* in the text, as a tax that is "owed."[85] However, it does make the interpretation of the passage as a whole and of the figures presented in it even more difficult. For if the figures then relate to the calculation of tax on a legacy, how was such a tax to be paid? The text itself offers no solution.[86]

With these difficulties in mind (difficulties that already should make us wary of the demographic use to be made of the figures given), we will set aside the legal intricacies for a moment to look at the actual figures presented. As can be seen from the text, Macer in fact gives two sets of figures, the *forma* that Ulpian describes,[87] and then what Macer describes as the "customary" (*solitum est*) method of computation. Whether this latter system is an earlier version of the Ulpianic table or a later revision is not made clear.[88] At any rate, the figures as recorded are set out in table 2, and are presented in graphical form in figure 1 (see appendix B).

Before we proceed, more textual problems need to be dealt with, this time concerning the customary *forma*. It can be seen that the figures as recorded in Macer's text decline from age 30 to reach zero at age 60 and following. The Greek text,[89] however, states here that the customary table, like the Ulpianic table, gives 5 years from age 60, and on this basis Mommsen, in a footnote to his Latin text, suggested inserting the phrase "ab annis autem sexaginta annorum quinque" at the end of the passage dealing with the customary table, in order to make it match the Ulpianic table from this age. But this would then mean that the customary table would give figures declining to 1 year by age 59 and then rising to and remaining at 5 years from age 60, something that is clearly not right. To make up for this and to retain the impression from the Greek version, Ferrini advocated inserting before Mommsen's phrase the words "numquam vero minus quam decem," so that the customary table would then follow the pattern of descending figures to 11 at age 49, then remain at 10 from ages 50–59, and then remain at 5 from age 60 years on.[90]

This line of argument, though to an extent it tidies up the figures, seems to me untenable. It involves too considerable a reworking of the original text, and there is no sign of any phrase such as "never less than ten years" in the Greek text from which Mommsen first assumed that an insertion was necessary. It seems to me far more likely that the *Basilika* has adopted the phrase "from the age of 60, 5 years" by direct analogy and to bring it into line with the Ulpianic table described immediately before it, and that such a phrase never existed in the Latin original. Thus in the customary table the computation at age 60 stood at zero, something that argues against its purported value as an accurate estimation of life expectancy, as some would have it.

I would suggest at this point that this zero value reflects an apparent Roman premise that after the age of 60 years certain liabilities ceased to be exacted or expected. Examples of such rules of age are fully discussed by me elsewhere[91] and include such factors as testamentary inheritance between childless couples (following the Augustan social legislation), the process of adrogation, and the granting of *vacatio* from public life, including jury service and attendance at the senate. At this point it is enough to realize that a figure of zero at the age of 60 years is not an estimate of average expectation of life at this age, but may be derived from a quite different reasoning.

The Ulpianic table, on the other hand, sets a constant figure of 5 years from the age of 60 onward—again demographically implausible, since life expectancy declines with age, as has already been discussed. So again any assumption that this figure is meant to reflect estimates of life expectancy runs up against difficulties. What it may reflect, if indeed the Ulpianic table postdates the customary one, is a tightening up of the system to make those over the age of 60 years also subject to the tax. Conversely, if the Ulpianic table is the earlier form of computation, then the zero figure in the customary table may have been granted as a concession to old age, just as the age of exemption from *munera personalia* in the empire was lowered from 70 to 65 and later to 60 years of age.[92] At any rate, this must remain speculation, especially in view of the problems with the text of the *Digest* at this point and with the relative chronology of the two *formae;* but at least the suggestion makes more sense of the figures for the age of 60 years and beyond than does any argument relating the figures to average expectation of life.

To return now to the figures given in the passage as a whole, what do they represent? Even in spite of the uncertainties regarding the legal context of the Macer passage and to what use the figures were put at the time, an immediate and quite natural (and very tempting) answer to this question is that they represent estimations of life expectancy from a given age. Overall, the figures decline after the age of 20 or 30 years, in a similar way as do real values for life expectancy. So is this a valid contention? Are these figures indeed the first extant example of life tables, whatever their imperfections at certain ages?

31

Many modern scholars have referred to the Ulpianic (never the customary) table in passing and, while some give brief mention of some of the problems involved with the text, they generally use the figures in the text to support their own assumptions regarding Roman life expectancy.[93] Some of these authors pick out figures for certain ages from the Ulpianic table, glossing over the overall pattern of the figures, a misleading and unjustified practice—how can one accept some but not all of the figures? The uncritical use of the Ulpianic table as a source of demographic information has led to statements like the following, appearing in a work that is otherwise an excellent study of old age in modern society but which rather founders in an attempt to give a historical perspective: "Based upon an analysis of burial records the Roman scientist Ulpianus produced a life table for both males and females. These data . . . probably represent the earliest known actuarial calculations."[94] Riddled with inaccuracies as this statement is, it seems to sum up quite well an impression that is often taken for granted by some scholars.

The negative argument, the statement that these figures as given in the *Digest* bear no real demographic meaning, has for the past half-century rested on the article by Greenwood; it is a rather unsteady base, since Professor Greenwood claimed no knowledge of Roman law or history, and his article represents little more than an informal note on the subject. I think he would have been very surprised to witness the dependence placed on his short discussion by some modern classical scholars who dismiss, almost without comment, the Ulpianic table as irrelevant to demographic considerations of the ancient world.[95] Greenwood does, however, raise some valid points.[96]

Greenwood's central argument against the figures being interpreted as life expectancy estimates is the figure 30 which is given for the ages up to 20 years (in the Ulpianic table, up to 30 years of age in the customary table). The idea that life expectancy remains constant over these years is, of course, wrong, especially in the face of what must have been a very high rate of infant mortality.[97] When something like one in four infants were dying in their first year of life, the idea that expectation of life could be put at 30 years both for a newborn infant and, say, a 5- or 19-year-old, is stretching the bounds of plausibility rather far.

This 30-year figure is much more plausibly to be regarded as a simple legal maximum for the computation, applied not only to an individual but also to the giving of a usufruct to a public body.[98] As Macer states in our text, "numquam ergo amplius quam triginta annorum computatio initur. sic denique et si rei publicae usus fructus legetur . . . triginta annorum computatio fit." The origin of the figure itself is difficult to trace; it is clearly too large to be a multiplicand in estimating an annuity's present market worth if the tax was to have been paid in a lump sum,[99] and it has long been recognized that the figures do not derive from simple calculations of interest rates.[100] It is, however, quite plausible that the figure of 30 years may be derived from an arbitrary notion of the extent of life expectancy at an early age (without it having any bearing on actual or precise demographic reality), or, as one scholar has quite logically suggested,[101] it may be related to the notion of a generation, the average assumed time taken for a man to be born and to have reproduced himself.

From this maximum of 30 years, however it was derived, the figures for computation in the two *formae* were seemingly scaled down or interpolated as the legatee's age increased, reaching its minimum point at the age of 60 years.[102] But this is not quite accurate. Although the customary table does indeed make such a simple and demographically unrealistic interpolation between the ages of 30 and 60 years, the Ulpianic table clearly does not simply interpolate—the progression from the age of 20 years (see figure 1 in appendix B) shows a decrease in the figures for computation in various, irregular steps, with a steady decline only between the ages of 40 and 50 years. Why such a complex procedure? The customary table is more simple but, as commented on already (see n. 88), it does not necessarily follow from this that the Ulpianic table is a later form of computation designed to improve on the simplicity of the customary method. Rather it may be the case that the customary table was adopted as a later, simpler, and more easily memorable alternative to the complicated calculations involved in using the Ulpianic table.

Further intricacies in the Ulpianic as opposed to the customary *forma* may be seen between the ages of 40 and 50 years. Whereas the customary table, as for every other age between 30 and 60 years, merely subtracts the age from 60 to arrive at a figure (i.e., 60 − x), between the ages of 40 and 50 years the Ulpianic table subtracts a further year from the subtraction (i.e., 60 − x − 1). Again, why such a difference? It probably has more to do with legal considerations, the difference operating in favor of the heir rather than of the legatee, than with demographic adjustments. Any argument stating that the change of a year was due to a third-century lawyer perceiving a change in life expectancy values in his society is treading on very shaky ground.

Thus many uncertainties and many questions remain; given our lack of certain knowledge about the legal purpose behind the use of the tables, about their relative chronology, and about the text of the passage itself, I do not believe that convincing answers can be provided. That the Ulpianic table does represent real life expectancy values has been argued most recently and at most length by Bruce Frier, who uses the figures as a basis for a life table for the Roman empire.[103] We will look at his life table in some detail later. At present we need to consider whether his use of the Ulpianic figures to produce a detailed and exact life table is justified. For even if it could be proved, as Frier attempts to do, that the compiler of the Ulpianic "life table" had at his disposal and used contemporary, statistical evidence of mortality rates to calculate life expectancy values, how accurate would such figures be in demographic terms?

At the outset Frier states that the Ulpianic figures represent calculations not of *average* life expectancy (i.e., the average age at which individuals of a cohort or group of a given age may be expected to die), but of *median* life expectancy (i.e., the age by which half the cohort may be expected to be dead).[104] Frier's basis for such a distinction to be drawn is that average life expectancy is "too sophisticated a notion for antiquity"; I agree that it may have been, at least to calculate, but I am not so sure that median life expectancy would have been any more obvious or unsophisticated. The difference, at any rate, is largely minimal. Median life expectancy is generally slightly lower than average life expectancy at any given age, except in infancy in a high-mortality regime, since high infant mortality will account for the deaths of a significant proportion of the original cohort at birth, and therefore median life expectancy at birth will be substantially lower than average life expectancy at birth.[105]

This all presupposes, however, that the Romans had both the means and the need or desire to calculate life expectancy figures with such a degree of precision. The sort of data needed to calculate such values today is as a basis age-specific mortality rates (i.e., the number of people of a certain age who die over a certain period, and the proportion of the total population such an age group represents). There is no evidence that such information, even if it was available through the limited bureaucracy of the empire (which I doubt, except perhaps for Roman Egypt), was ever used in this way.

Did the Ancient Romans Have Statistical Information on the Death Rate? Roby stated that the Ulpianic table "appears to be simply the probable length of life of persons of the ages named"; Stein, following Roby closely, stated that "it is thought [*by whom? not Roby*] that he ["Ulpian"] may have studied the records kept by funeral clubs, which are believed to have kept precise data concerning the ages of their members at death." [106]

This idea found its way into the account by Victor in 1987. It probably stems from a much earlier scholar, not a classicist, but an actuary, one Frederick Hendriks, who wrote in *The Assurance Magazine* in 1852 that the Ulpianic table

> seems to bear intrinsic evidence of some careful collection or observation of facts. These may have been obtained from enquiries on the results of life annuity engagements, or from returns of the number of deaths occurring within a given time at various ages; the former method would seem to have been the most likely to be available, but the other was quite within the bounds of possibility as the foundation of an approximate calculation, for there is ample record of a

kind of registration, or *ephemeris,* of deaths having been observed by the ancients.

Hendriks goes on to compare mortality rates for Stockholm from 1755 to 1763, and then concludes: "Ulpian's estimates must have been based on observation of actual results, though, it may be, limited to a small number, or inartificially combined." There is much uncertainty here; indeed, in the same magazine 5 years later, Hendriks's fellow actuary, W. B. Hodge, dismissed the idea that Ulpian's figures were based on accurate observation.[107] Hendriks's belief in a registration of deaths is as ephemeral as the name suggests. The *ephemeris* was a sort of daybook, a *commentarius*[108] completed by various officials recording daily transactions; it was not a register of deaths as such. Hendriks's assertion may be derived from the statement in the *Chronicle* of St. Jerome under the year A.D. 77 (p. 188, lines 21–24, in the edition by Helm [Berlin, 1956]) that "lues ingens Romae facta ita ut per multos dies in efemeridem [*sic*] decem milia ferme mortuorum hominum referrentur"("a great plague occurred at Rome, so great that for many days nearly ten thousand dead people were recorded in the register"). Even if this statement is historically accurate, it is not proof of regular registration or recording of deaths, not even for the city of Rome on its own. A sharp increase in mortality may have been noted in the official records in this instance, but that does not imply that a daily record of deaths was kept. Yet even if such a record did exist, there is no evidence or implication that it was ever consulted for demographic purposes.

The evidence for the use of precise data on deaths, in Rome or elsewhere in the empire, is lacking. Even if such a register did exist, it is highly questionable that it was ever used for "sophisticated" demographic calculations, by lawyers or by anyone else. Furthermore, even supposing that such material was in existence and was used, there would have been obvious shortcomings in the data (particularly regarding representativeness), too great for us to consider the Ulpianic figures to be reliable and accurate indicators of general Roman mortality levels. If, as

Stein maintains, the burial clubs might be posited as a source for such information, then even more biases are detectable. Although members of burial clubs may have covered a broad social spectrum, with people of slender means and even slaves in some cases able to gain membership, the evidence suggests that such clubs were predominantly male and of urban base.[109] To this we might add the question, If the Ulpianic figures are to be used as the basis for demographic calculations, to whom do the figures relate—males only, the wealthy, those outside Rome? Unanswerable questions, since we do not even know the type of source the compiler of the Ulpianic table used; my impression is that he used his common sense.

But others have argued that statistical data *were* available to the Romans if they ever wanted to make use of them. Hombert and Préaux, as indeed did Levison, laid stress on the census data and notices of birth and death as sources of demographic information.[110] But notices of birth and death seem to have been an irregular feature of ancient life, even in Roman Egypt.[111] What emerges as far as concerns notices of death is that they were not regularly expected or given, and certainly never collected on an official scale as a potential source of demographic data. As for the census, it is only for Roman Egypt that we have evidence of it being carried out on a regular and systematic basis, and even here the census was primarily designed for the efficient imposition of taxes and for ensuring that all fulfilled their public liabilities, never for demographic purposes. Furthermore, as stated previously, census data give age at time of census, not age at time of death, though from such information *median* life expectancy could be calculated, but not average expectation of life. Yet from all our material from Roman Egypt there is no indication that such groupings by age as would be required to make such calculations were ever considered; as for the rest of the empire, scarcely any indication exists that censuses were even carried out regularly and systematically.[112]

Frier himself, while arguing that Ulpian's figures *are* based on empirical research, makes no attempt to suggest what the source for such research was.[113] One source for figures on mortality that might be adduced (but surprisingly never seems to have been) emanates from a rather mysterious figure known as Libitina. Various ancient authors refer to the existence of a list of deceased having been kept in the temple of this goddess,[114] which might suggest that the registration of deaths, at Rome at least, was both widespread and obligatory. Dionysius of Halicarnassus (*Rom. Ant.* 4.15.5) follows Calpurnius Piso in describing how Servius Tullius, in his wish to know the number of inhabitants in the city, and all who were born, arrived at the age for serving in the army, and died, ordered relatives to pay money into the treasury of Juno Lucina when a birth occurred, to Iuventas for those who reached "manhood," and to Libitina when someone died (cf. Livy 1.42.4–43.11). Two points emerge: it is presented as an archaic practice, apparently obsolete by Dionysius's day (i.e., the time of Augustus); and a fee was required for such registration, a practice supported by other references (e.g., Horace, *Sat.* 2.618–19: "Libitinae quaestus acerbae"; Phaedrus 4.21.26: "Libitina lucri"; cf. *CIL* 5.5128 = *ILS* 6726 [Bergomum, N. Italy], where a wealthy citizen is recorded as paying the *lucar Libitinae* for the entire town in perpetuity as patron). So, despite first impressions, this is not evidence for universal registration of death in the Roman empire—the fee alone would have put a lot of people off. Rather the idea behind references to Libitina seems to be to death, or perhaps the undertaker's task, and not to registration of the fact.

What seems far more reasonable and more likely to assume, rather than that the compiler of the Ulpianic (and customary) table worked from an empirical base, is that the figures—if they are to be related to the notion of life expectancy[115]—are based on good guesswork. The hypothesis that these figures are loosely related to Roman conceptions of the number of years a person might be expected to live from a given age seems quite reasonable. Indeed Marcellus, a jurist of the second half of the second century A.D., in discussing the valuation of *legata annua* in connection with the *lex Falcidia,* states that an assessment must be made by the *iudex* as to their capital value:[116] "aestimare debeat, quanti venire id legatum potest, in incerto posito, quamdiu victurus sit Titius" ("he will have to make an assessment of what the legacy could amount to, granted that no one knows how long Titius will live"). Some notion of expectation of life was clearly a factor here, albeit an imprecise one. In the case of alimentary and usufructuary legacies, with which we are concerned with the Ulpianic table, and the calculation of the tax nominally due, though the circumstances are somewhat different legally, a similar method may quite logically have been seen to be needed to apply. To facilitate the computation, the customary and Ulpianic tables set out two different sets of figures. How the differences arose and which is the earlier method are, as remarked earlier, questions we are unable to answer on the basis of the limited information available. But what we can presume, I think, is that the figures are primarily legal in significance, yet that they hold some measure of a concept of expectation of life (to call it average or median is to assume too much precision) in trying to answer the question, How long is your "average" (probably aristocratic male)[117] Roman, Titius, likely to live and therefore what is the estimated capital value of the legacy? Hence the descending scale of figures as the age of the legatee increases.

There is no evidence for, nor need to see, an empirical basis for the figures as given; they must be regarded at most as relatively intelligent guesses based not on statistical research but on observation and common sense. Frier, in a rather circular train of thought, argues for an empirical basis for the Ulpianic figures,[118] and he explains demographic implausibilities in the figures (such as the sharp decline between ages 40 and 50 years) as being due to the biases in the original data used by the compilers of the table (such biases as exaggeration of age by the elderly). This is, however, as Frier himself admits, very tentative a theory, and in my view unnecessary. Indeed, Frier himself earlier in his paper talks about the table being based upon "a limited use of statistics coupled with some shrewd guesswork."[119]

In short there is no external or internal evidence for the use or indeed the existence of the sort of statistics Frier imagines. The figures in the two tables are primarily based on a legal maximum of 30 years being reduced over the course of a range of ages, in line—perhaps—with a vague notion of life expectancy, a notion that in the Ulpianic *forma* is not demographically accurate and can never, I believe, be burdened with modern demographic significance or presumptions. To highlight this, in figure 3 (see appendix B) I have sketched the apparent age to which half a group at any age would, by both the customary and the Ulpianic tables, have been expected to die. Just how implausible the figures are in their transition from one age to the next is clear, though the overall general trend is about right. This is in line with a hypothesis that the figures are based on legal considerations, common sense, and observation, rather than on statistical or detailed demographic research.

Frier sees the Ulpianic table as "probably the best surviving evidence for Roman mortality functions" and he believes "it justified to accord Ulpian's life table a considerable measure of respect as a demographic source for the Roman empire." [120] Although in appearance the Ulpianic figures may seem more useful than the evidence from, for example, the tombstones of the period, they are less useful than the (admittedly numerically small) census data, and certainly cannot be used as the basis for the construction of a detailed and accurate life table. The combined effect of the uncertain legal purpose of the tables and their figures (Frier, to be sure, has taken our understanding further, but certain answers are still no closer), the demographic implausibility of the figures as given and the arbitrary relationship of the figures to actual demographic realities mean that insurmountable difficulties remain. Even if we could be certain of the legal and social context and of the purpose of the tables (and Frier's speculative theory on the latter may be sound), and even if it could be established that the Ulpianic figures were meant to reflect life expectancy trends, I still do not believe that the figures as given could be held to be based on anything but intelligent guesswork and, therefore, that the Ulpianic table could be used to deduce accurate mortality rates for the Roman empire.

The rejection of Frier's basis for his life table should logically mean also the rejection of his life table. It does not, however, for the simple reason that in attempting to "smooth out" the apparent deficiencies in the Ulpianic figures Frier has relied on model life tables, so that his eventual figures for Roman life expectancy hold little close relationship to the Ulpianic figures (as may be seen in my figure 1). We will therefore return to a consideration of Frier's life table for the Roman empire in the second chapter of this study. Firstly, however, we need to consider another alleged source of information on Roman mortality rates, and it is a very different source than those discussed up to this point. From written records on stone, on papyri, or in legal texts, we turn now to the very stuff of mortality: human skeletons.

The Skeletal Evidence

Skeletal remains as a source of demographic information on the Roman empire bring us into a whole new field of study, palaeo-demography, one that in the past has been little utilized in the field of ancient history, in contrast to the use made of the data from tombstone inscriptions of the period. How usable and useful are the data from skeletons? Frier, who rightly rejects evidence from most funerary inscriptions, is very optimistic in regard to skeletons. He sees the way forward in ancient demography as lying in bones: "only new evidence (such as a more complete collection and analysis of skeletal remains) will prove final and decisive." [121] In a subsequent paper, Frier uses one set of skeletal data to lend support to his life table, and he concludes by stressing the greater validity of results derived from skeletal as opposed to tombstone data: "Demographic analysis of skeletal remains is as yet extremely uncommon for the ancient world, despite the fact that the results are on the whole considerably more reliable." [122] And Frier was certainly not the first to come to such a conclusion: Éry noted that "it is widely known that the mortality of bygone ages can be learnt by studying primarily the skeletal remains," though he too adds that there is a comparative lack of such material available for the Roman period. Later in his paper, having also rejected the tombstone inscriptions as a source of demographic data, Éry concludes: "The acquiring of factual knowledge concerning mortality conditions in the Roman era is to be expected therefore only from the demographic elaboration of the skeletal remains excavated from the cemeteries." [123]

Is such optimism justified? Perhaps by comparison with most of the other ancient evidence available and considered thus far, the skeletal evidence is the best potential source we have. But is it good enough for detailed demographic analysis? It may come as some surprise, after the comments of Éry and Frier, to find, in a list compiled by a historical demographer of the relative usefulness of 19 sources for historical demographic information, skeletons and tombstone inscriptions being considered together. It may come as even more of a surprise to find them coming nineteenth in the list! [124] Is such *pessimism* justified? I wish here to consider the nature of the evidence and the problems inherent in its use.

The data to be derived from skeletal age [125] are indeed similar in character to data from tombstone inscriptions: both relate to the age at death of a given cemetery population over an ill-defined and usually extensive period of time. Thus data from skeletal evidence inevitably suffer from many of the same potential errors: How *representative* of the population as a whole are the remains that we have, in terms of age, sex, and social class? Furthermore, as with tombstone evidence, the data derived from skeletal remains must be assumed to relate to a stationary population. [126] If the population under study was in fact naturally growing, in other words where the birth rate exceeded the death rate, then any analysis of the mortality data derived from skeletons will overestimate mortality and thus underestimate life expectancy; the converse would be true if the population was in decline.

This problem affects the usefulness of evidence both from skeletal remains and from tombstone inscriptions. Other problems discussed in relation to funerary epitaphs are also relevant here, particularly the question of burial custom. Just as it was seen that apparent differences in mortality in different parts of the empire were in fact due to different customs of commemoration, so it is true that different practices for the selective burial of people of different age, sex, or social class will affect the reliability of the data derived from their skeletons. For example, infants, whose deaths are greatly underrepresented on epitaphs, appear also to have been comparatively rarely given proper burial,[127] or at least burial in adult cemetery sites. As a result infant mortality may be greatly underestimated. Similarly the difference between rural and urban areas may be difficult to assess. Sample size is a problem here too as with funerary inscriptions; to date the number of cemetery sites of the Roman period excavated and properly recorded for demographic purposes remains very small, and the number of skeletons to which even approximate ages can be assigned is far below the 43,000 inscriptions Szilágyi collected.

Nonetheless one of the major problems with funerary inscriptions, the question of the reliability of age statements in epigraphy, might be considered to be avoided with skeletal evidence. With skeletons we do not need to depend on the inaccuracies or vagaries inherent in the recording of ages on epitaphs; instead we have the actual evidence of age before us. Certainly this much is true: a skeleton cannot lie about its age. But on the other hand, the accurate estimation of the age—and indeed of the sex—of a skeleton, especially one that has been buried for hundreds of years, is far from a straightforward matter, and the possible margins of error may be very significant. It is worth outlining here the principles behind the aging and sexing of skeletons, since the use of the skeletal evidence for demographic purposes relies on the data derived.[128]

The Sexing of Skeletons Differences exist between the male and the female human skeleton even at the fetal stage, but only adult skeletons can be sexed with any degree of confidence; the sexing of a child skeleton is little more than subjective guesswork. In adults, the pelvis serves as the principal means of differentiation between the sexes, due to the female reproductive capacity. In female adults as a rule the pelvis is broader, though in males it may be heavier and more robust. The sciatic notch of the pelvis, at the junction between the ilium and the ischium, is wider in females, whereas the auricular area of the pelvis is flatter in males. The preauricular sulcus, a groove between the auricular area and the sciatic notch, is usual in female adults, but seldom found in males. When it is found in males, it is always shallower by comparison, though a high level of expertise is required to detect the difference. Finally, the pubis is longer in females, and the subpubic angle is wider.

All these differences are detectable by experts, but wide variations in the pelvic features may be encountered, not only over time and space but also between individuals of a single population group. Furthermore, in archaeological excavation, the pelvis may not always be recovered, and other remains (particularly the skull) must be used, though the ability to differentiate between the sexes in such cases will inevitably be less certain. The male skull generally has larger features with greater cranial capacity, and is heavier than that of the female. Differences between the sexes may also be detected through inspection of the mandible and teeth. Furthermore, the size of the skeleton as a whole may be considered, but the degree of certainty in sexing on such a criterion diminishes. Females, it must be remembered, generally grow and mature at an earlier age than males, so even in questions of sex, age confounds the matter and must be taken into account. Relative sizes of the long bones, the vertebral column, sacrum, sternum, and the heads of the femur and humerus may all be taken into account, but inevitably serious doubts and uncertainties arise, especially due to the increasing variability of such measurements in different places and over different periods of time.

In short, where the skeletons are complete and a definite standard for comparison is possible, the sexing of adults is feasible and reasonably accurate, yet still often depends on observation of the grave goods found with the skeleton rather than on the skeleton itself. The best method for sexing employs a variety of approaches, relying principally on the pelvis and skull, in which the results obtained from the different methods may be compared, to avoid as far as possible any subjectivity in the process.[129] If a demographic analysis is to be carried out where differentiation is drawn between the sexes (possible only in adult age groups when skeletal evidence is employed), then the results of sex determination need to be objective and certain, with few cases undecided. Such precision and certainty are rarely achievable in Roman cemetery sites, and an unequal sex ratio is often the result, for a variety of reasons. Some obvious causes are the incorrect determination of the sex of a significant number of skeletons, the incomplete excavation of the site, and the erosion of female as opposed to male skeletons. Another possible cause may be that the cemetery site excavated itself contains an unequal sex ratio, due to historical reality. The population itself, if the sample excavated is indeed representative of the population as a whole, may not have had an equal balance of the sexes,[130] or indeed—and this is probably more plausible—the cemetery site itself may have been predominantly used for a certain sex, and thus will not be representative of the real population of the area. Instances where the latter explanation is clearly the case will be considered subsequently.

The Aging of Skeletons   Here our problems are even more acute. The human skeleton experiences changes with age just as the living body does, but the different changes occur at different times and at different rates in the different bones and structures in different persons. It is generally possible to classify a complete skeleton as being that of an infant, child, adolescent, or adult, but obviously for demographic purposes greater precision is needed. A further problem is that the living skeleton is affected not only by the influences of age but also by conditions of environment, nutrition, working conditions, and disease, all of which may give a false impression of the actual chronological age (as opposed to the "biological" age) of the individual at death. Again, variations in the various features used to determine age may occur over time and space, and indeed between individuals of the same population group. Here, as with the determination of the sex of a skeleton, a variety of tests needs to be applied. Again, we depend on good preservation and excavation, and on skilled and objective analysis (also often involving expensive equipment), if results are to be sufficiently precise and accurate to be of any value in demographic analysis.

The various criteria employed and their interpretation in regard to the aging of skeletons are both very complex and liable to subjectivity and error in the attempt to achieve precision— but precision is certainly necessary, as is accuracy: "It makes little sense to attempt a detailed demographic statement about a population if the methods of estimating age incorporate errors of 20 years or more." [131] Yet such errors are always possible and, in the case of archaeological material from Roman cemetery sites, quite probable.

Different methods need to be used for the aging of a skeleton depending on the approximate age at death, that is, whether the skeleton is that of a child, an adolescent, or an adult. In children calculation of age is carried out primarily by the inspection of the condition of the teeth, since the relative stage of the calcification and eruption of the deciduous ("milk") and permanent teeth is an indication of age, although the margin of error may be substantial. Ideally the sex of the skeleton would need to be known first, but (as noted) in the case of young skeletons that is practically impossible. Furthermore, the teeth need to be well preserved and in a complete state if such inspection is to be fruitful. Failing this, the length of the skeleton may give some indication of age, though obviously this is uncertain and is highly liable to error, especially when the sex is unknown.

With a skeleton from the age of around 15 years, other criteria need to be employed. Teeth are still important, particularly the stage of formation, eruption, and full development of the third molar, though even here there may be a great degree of variability between individuals. The skull can be used by considering the degree of closure of the cartilaginous joint between the sphenoid and the occipital bone, such closure usually occurring between the ages of 17 and 22 years. A third indicator is the length of the long bones, [132] although this can be used only for general estimates, and wide variations do occur. More exact is the stage of the fusion of the epiphysis and diaphysis of the long bones at their extremities, since union generally occurs around the age of puberty.[133] Obviously, this will differ between the sexes, so the sexing of the skeleton is a definite prerequisite, but is not often possible and is rarely certain in such cases. This feature also differs in different population groups and, even when the bones are well preserved and complete, margins of error from 2 to 8 years must be allowed for.

The second traditional method employed for the calculation of the age of adult skeletons has been the degree of closure of the cranial suture, that is, the lines or joints between the 22 bones of the skull, lines that disappear gradually and at differing rates, beginning from within, as the individual ages.[134] The sagittal suture is often chosen as the easiest to observe and measure over the longest period, but even here there is wide variability and the method is now considered generally unreliable.[135] While these methods may continue to be employed, other criteria need to be used in conjunction with them in an attempt to derive some measure of precision and accuracy. One such indicator is the metamorphosis of the symphyseal face of the pubis from the age of about 18 years (the importance of the pelvis for both the sexing and the aging of the skeleton cannot be stressed too much). Although definite stages in this process of change can be delineated, there is still debate as to their exact relationship to age, and yet again wide variations occur, particularly between the sexes. Even when the pelvic section of the skeleton is well preserved and the skill and equipment needed are available for the analysis of the pubis, the margin of error may still exceed 10 years.[136]

Other indicators of the age of the individual at death to be found in the skeleton as a whole, such as the degree of degeneration measured by ossification and the appearance of bony extensions, the resorption of cancellous bone, and the degree of expansion of the medullary cavities of the humerus and femur, are both inexact and variable. More precision may be obtained by analyzing the degree of cortical remodeling in the long bones: with the increasing age of the individual, osteoclast cells cut longitudinal channels through the layers of the cortex and these holes are gradually filled by concentric layers of bone produced by osteoblast cells, leaving a small opening in the middle. These structures, called ostea, increase in number with age, and by counting them over a given area under a microscope as well as by measuring the size of the channels, an estimation of age at death can be made. Yet even with this exacting process, which is obviously destructive and highly specialized, a significant margin of error, in excess of 5 years, must be allowed for.[137] Further tests of the chemical constitution of the bones, such as the phosphate, calcium, and collagen contents, all of which decrease with age,[138] are also, besides being destructive, highly variable and are affected by decomposition of the skeleton following death and burial, a factor that clearly is liable to occur in skeletons of Roman date, and the extent of which may vary according to soil and burial conditions.[139]

In short, the methods of estimating the age of a skeleton, while continually increasing in sophistication and in the degree of expertise required in carrying out such tests, are still vulnerable to variability between individuals and also to the degree of subjectivity in analysis. Indicators of age may also be distorted by environmental, social, and economic factors that might lead to the overestimation of individuals' ages at death. It has been argued, on the other hand, that most adult skeletons are systematically *underaged*:[140] an underestimate of 10 years in the age of every adult skeleton in a sample may produce an error in the calculation of life expectancy at age 15 of anything between 17 and 67 percent. Such systematic underaging is extreme, but nonetheless the combined effect of the uncertainties in the various techniques of aging a skeleton and the relative subjectivity and expertise of the analyzer may produce significant and immeasurable distortions in the resulting data. Add to this the fact that skeletons may be extensively eroded or damaged, not only by soil erosion but also by excavation, and thus will prove more difficult to analyze, and it must be doubted whether the data derived from a sample, especially when small, can be used for detailed and reliable demographic analysis.[141]

The difficulties inherent in the aging of skeletons are highlighted when one looks at the results of tests in two separate cases, as listed in table 3 (see appendix B). In the first test case,[142] four different indicators of age were employed (symphyseal face of the pubis, degree of closure of cranial sutures, and age changes in the epiphysis of both the femur and the humerus) to estimate the ages of five *complete* skeletons of individuals *recently deceased* for whom the ages at death were already known. Allowance was made for a margin of error of 2.5 years in their estimates. The results as given in table 3a show that for the first three test cases the results are encouraging: 3.2 years out at most. But in the last two cases the estimation is out by 20 or more years either way. This serves to illustrate the complexities and variability inherent in the process. When skeletons are much less well preserved, the margins of error must inevitably increase.

The second test case that highlights the inaccuracies and subjectivity inherent in the methods of determining the age and sex of skeletons, in this case ones that have been interred for a long period, is provided by excavations at the late Roman cemetery at Pécs in southwest Hungary (Pannonian Sopianae). Of 134 skeletons that were aged and sexed independently by two anthropologists,[143] I have noted in table 3b 18 extreme examples of difference between their results. The divergences are striking: in five cases different sex is determined; in some cases the differences in determined age amount to as much as 50 years. Overall such distortion would greatly affect any demographic interpretation made from these data.

In questions of both the sex and age of skeletons, therefore, our final data may be defective, even when the most detailed and sophisticated methods of analysis are employed. In this regard the apparent advantage of skeletal evidence over tombstone inscriptions in regard to demographic data is less significant than many have thought. But even if we could achieve absolute accuracy in regard to the sex and age of the skeletal sample we have for a population, how can we be sure that the sample we have is representative of the population as a whole and over a long period of time? For not only may there have been distorting factors due to the customs of burial at the time, leading to the exclusion from or underrepresentation in a particular site of a particular sex or age group, but also the actions of time and the method of burial may have affected the preservation of certain types of skeletons. Infant, elderly, and female skeletons are less sturdy and are therefore less likely to remain intact. Their fragments are less likely to be retained in excavation and are more difficult to analyze with precision even when not discarded. Furthermore the best-preserved skeletons may be not only the toughest but also those of individuals who were given the best burials, due perhaps to social class, a factor that might further distort the validity of the results. For demographic analysis we need both a representative sample and accurate estimations of age; with skeletal remains we cannot be certain of either.

Some Skeletal Data   It may be worthwhile now to turn to some actual excavation reports of cemeteries to consider the nature of the evidence available. For Roman cemetery sites, as mentioned already, such demographic evidence is sparse; other historical periods have produced greater finds, as for example the Anglo-Saxon cemeteries, where the data resulting are more abundant, though problems in methodology still remain. I cannot attempt here a complete survey of excavations of cemeteries of the Roman period, but it will be of use to consider some site reports to see what sort of evidence is produced. It must always be remembered that for such purposes we must rely on the statements of age and sex given in these reports. For this reason we are hampered both by not knowing what methods were employed and how accurate and precise the figures as given are, and by the fact that figures from different sites cannot be compared directly since the data come from different methods and different archaeologists, so that no overall objectivity is possible. These sorts of problems regarding the variability in the reports should become clearer as we proceed. For ease of reference, I have focused primarily on Romano-British sites.

First, however, let us consider Frier's Pannonian evidence. In his 1983 paper he uses as support for his life table the data from a single cemetery, that of Keszthely-Dobogo in Roman Pannonia.[144] Generally the Keszthely-Dobogo life table does appear to follow the trends of Frier's table, but it is only an isolated example and the reader is left with the impression that the skeletal evidence in general presents a unified picture of Roman mortality in accord with this evidence from a single cemetery. But this is far from the case: the evidence from Keszthely-Dobogo has been selected for the very reason that the trend is in accord with Frier's estimates, and no clear indication is given that biases may be present in the data,[145] that the figures may not reflect general reality, or that other skeletal data produce very different results. Frier regards the 120 skeletons in this sample as statistically significant, but whether they are representative is quite another question. Certainly other sites may be found where the sample is greater in size but where the results produce quite a different picture of the population of the time.

For example, the Roman cemetery at Lankhills in Winchester provides a usable sample of 284 skeletons from the fourth and early fifth centuries.[146] It is noted here that the determination of age and sex was preliminary and that "a more leisurely examination of each skeleton may reduce the uncertainty concerning the age and sex of some individuals." Skeletal preservation ranges from "almost perfect" to "almost entirely decomposed," though such criteria are in themselves highly subjective. Of the 284 individuals to whom ages are assigned, 37 (13.03%) are said to be under the age of 2 years, 46 (16.20%) between the ages of 2 and 15 years, and 16 (5.63%) from 16 to 20 years. In other words, only 34.86 percent of the sample is held to be under the age of 20 years. Of the remaining 185 skeletons, 64 are classified as dying in their early 20s, and 117 over the age of 25 years. The authors suggest that this is an indication of very high mortality in the early adult years,[147] but such apparent high mortality in early adulthood would be very surprising, and the figures are probably more a reflection of biases in burial practice or excavation and analysis. It is also noted in the text that the preliminary examination of the skeletons to determine age may have systematically underestimated the age of adults by comparison with a subsequent examination. As far as sexing goes, of the sample 181 determinations were made, revealing 111 male and 70 female skeletons, a sex ratio of 158.57. It is stated that adult male skeletons appear to have been better preserved than the female ones, which may account for some of the sex bias. Other biases are also detectable: in the 17–20 age group there is only 1 male skeleton for 12 females, whereas in the 30+ age group there are 31 males as opposed to 7 females. Significant differences in age and sex structure may also be noted in different sections of the cemetery as excavated.[148] Hence, although the sample is comparatively large, important doubts remain as to the representativeness of the sample and about the reliability of the estimates of age and sex.

The Romano-British cemetery at Trentholme Drive in York[149] also serves to highlight the dangers in using skeletal material for demographic studies. Out of a usable sample—again quite large—of 290 individuals, 231 (79.66%) were classified as probably male, 52 (17.93%) as probably female, and in only 7 cases (2.41%) was the matter considered too uncertain to decide. If we are to regard this as 231 males to 52 females, then the sex ratio derived from these figures is 444.23, that is, well over 4 males for every 1 female. If this is indeed representative of the population as a whole (and is not due to biases in burial, excavation, and analysis), then it may reflect the status of York as a garrison town, a factor that will also have affected the age structure of the population. In the excavation report the breakdown by age is in 5-year groups for those under the age of 30 years, a method that gives no indication of the uncertainties of the age-determination process (these figures are given in table 4 [see appendix B]). If we are to regard these numbers as an accurate portrayal of the ages of the skeletons, then the first very noticeable feature is the very low mortality rate at young ages (only 8.28% under age 15 years). It is suggested in the text that this may be due to the combination of the decay of young skeletons and the usual interment of such skeletons elsewhere. The high proportion of skeletons in the groups between 25 and 50 years is also very striking: 73.10 percent in all, with only 1.72 percent over the age of 50 years. This too may be due to a combination of factors: York as a garrison town, again; the use of this cemetery predominantly for middle-aged males; or a tendency in the age-estimation process toward this age group. By computing life table values from these figures, on the assumption of a stationary population, I calculate a figure for average life expectancy at birth[150] of some 31 years, which seems reasonable when we remember the underrepresentation of infant deaths. But this figure plummets down to a life expectancy at age 15 of only 18 years, little more than 8 years at age 30, and less than 3 years at age 45. If this was indeed a reflection of reality, then it would suggest a population in which mortality in the early adult years was incredibly high, and it would raise doubts as to how such a population could have reproduced itself. It seems much more likely that these results reflect the use to which the cemetery was put, if indeed the sample we have is representative of the population buried at the cemetery and the age estimations are not wildly inaccurate. The question of infant burials aside, the predominance of males of the 25–50 age group does suggest that the cemetery reflects the status of York as a garrison town and that burial at this site was chiefly reserved for this group. Needless to say, the demographic usefulness of the data in this regard is rather negligible.

The cemetery at Cirencester likewise produces very strange and potentially misleading demographic data.[151] The site is divided into two main sections. From the first and main half, 347 inhumations were discovered from which 362 individual skeletons were recovered (there were some double burials). It is noted in the report that in general the skeletons were in a very poor condition, and in 62 cases (17.13%) sex could not be determined. Of the remaining 300 skeletons, 207 (69.00%) are classified as male and 93 (31.00%) as female, a sex ratio of 222.58, and this imbalance may be put down, as with York, to the garrison nature of the town, if not also to uncertainties or mistakes in sex classification. In regard to age, of these 362 skeletons, only 63 (17.40%) are held to be under the age of 18 years—so, again, the young are drastically underrepresented.

These biases become even more evident in the other section of the cemetery site: of the 45 skeletons excavated, 38 are classified as male, only 7 as female (a sex ratio of 542.86), and of these 45 only 1 is described as being under the age of 18 years. As a consequence, these data can hardly be regarded as representative of real mortality levels, even if the determination of age and sex is accurate.

We need not dwell here on other similar sites. In a review of the evidence for five late Romano-British cemetery sites (third to fifth centuries)[152] that provide an overall sample of 238 skeletons, all from within a relatively small geographical area, children are again seriously underrepresented. Of the total of 238, only 39 (16.39%) are described as being under the age of 30 years, and 23 of these are from a single site. Also, and importantly, a significant proportion of the sample (62, 26.05%) apparently survived to at least the age of 45 years. But, just as importantly, 58 (24.37%) skeletons are described as simply "unaged adults"—the inclusion or exclusion of this group could markedly alter the results. The sex ratio for the five sites varies from 67.65 to 190.91.

Other problems in both skeletal samples and their demographic analysis may be made clear by considering early Anglo-Saxon cemeteries. For example, a recent study of a fifth or sixth century cemetery in Hampshire,[153] which was only partially excavated, recorded a sample of 98 individuals, for which the sex ratio of the 72 skeletons for which the sex was determined unusually showed a surplus of females: 40 females to 32 males (a sex ratio of 80), a feature the authors attribute to male migration or high male death rates due to warfare. They stress also that their age estimations are very rough, with a margin of error for adult skeletons of up to 20 years, and with one-sixth of all the skeletons being classified simply as adults.[154] Despite these drawbacks, the authors feel confident enough in their data to argue for a healthy population at this site with fairly high longevity, since their mean age at death is calculated at about 37 years. This ignores, however, the very low level of infant and (to a lesser degree) juvenile representation: only 6 (6.1%) skeletons under 2 years of age, and in total only 27 (27.6%) under the age of 18 years. The low child mortality rate is regarded by the authors as authentic, as is the high proportion (33.6%) of individuals surviving beyond the age of 40 years, but this fails to take account of the uneven distribution of the ages overall (cf. their table 14). The original warnings given by the authors on the uncertain nature of their classification by age and sex seem to have been forgotten in their subsequent demographic discussion.

Reports from outside Britain, relatively few as these are, also may be seen to suffer from similar handicaps. For example, a Graeco-Roman cemetery at Gabbari (Alexandria) in use from the end of the fourth century B.C. till the end of the seventh century A.D.—an enormous length of time and itself a potential source of distortion—produces a usable sample of 55 skeletons, as described in table 5 (see appendix B).[155] On first sight the age spread of this sample seems reasonable: infant mortality is very high (over 30%) by comparison with most other samples, but is not so high as to be unrealistic,[156] and deaths under age 20 account for nearly two-thirds of the sample. But on closer inspection, when the data are laid out (as in table 5), it is evident that the sample is very uneven over differing age classes and is too small (especially in view of the vast chronological scope of the sample) to justify confident statements about mortality levels. One also wonders at the precision of the age classifications, and notes too the irregularities in the classification of sex of the adult skeletons. All those over age 50, for example, are described as males. Perhaps if the sample were larger and the estimations of age and sex were more reliable, this cemetery population might prove useful, but then again one must be wary of picking and choosing among the bodies of evidence available merely to find examples that support one's preconceptions. The high proportion of young skeletons in this sample, if it is not due to errors of analysis, may reflect external reality—or it may simply be due to the use to which this cemetery was put. At any rate, from such a small and uneven sample spread over so long a period of time, no worthwhile demographic conclusions can confidently be drawn.

To take another case, that of a cemetery site in late Roman Carthage, the British report of the human remains from this site comprises only 10 inhumations, from the fifth to the seventh centuries.[157] Of these 10, 6 are said to belong to individuals between the ages of 10 and 16 years, 1 from 18 to 20 years, and only 1 over the age of 20 years; the remaining 2 are classified as infants under the age of 6 months at death. Sex determination here is, not surprisingly, fraught with uncertainties. These results, where most of the skeletons are roughly the same age at death, tell us quite a lot about the probable use made of the cemetery, but absolutely nothing about the demography of the population outside the cemetery.

Even cremated remains of human skeletons have been used to reach demographic conclusions, as for example in two English reports in the last decade[158] where age classification can only be made in *very* general terms (i.e., as child, adolescent, or adult, at most), and where sexing is equally hazardous.[159] Their usefulness as a source of demographic data is highly dubious.

That the problems we have already considered are still prevalent in the use of skeletal remains for demographic analysis may be illustrated, finally, in the results of two recent excavations, both of Anglo-Saxon burial sites but both showing the present state of our knowledge and technique. The first of these is that of an Anglo-Saxon cemetery in Yorkshire with a skeletal sample of only 59 (and a demographic report of only three pages).[160] Determination of sex was carried out using both biological and cultural criteria, the *latter* being preferred in contradictory cases. Of the sample 19 are described as female adults, 14 as male adults, 8 as adults of indeterminate sex, 8 as juveniles, and the remaining 10 are unclassified as to either age or sex. No attempt is made to classify age beyond the juvenile or adult distinction.

More detail is given in the second recent report to be considered here, that of an Anglo-Saxon cemetery in Kent, where the sample is larger (172) but where the skeletons are described as badly eroded.[161] The criteria used in the determination of sex are very illuminating. Grave goods are cited as the primary source before analysis of the skeleton itself. In 21 cases the two methods produce conflicting results, and in 11 cases the sexing by bone evidence is regarded as definite but still differs from the determination made by inspection of grave goods. Furthermore, preliminary skeletal reports on age and sex sometimes differed from the final report quite markedly, pointing again to levels of subjectivity and possible error. These problems are explained in the report as follows: "Reasons for confusion include: pelvic features in the female resembling the male form, double graves where one body has decayed, and a consistent proportion of individuals whose skeleton is genuinely intermediate in form between the sexes (around 5% to 10% even in well preserved series . . .). The very young and the very old are not easily distinguished either." This is an honest reflection of the uncertainties that still hamper us in our attempts to use the skeletal material for demographic purposes. Of the Buckland sample, sex is determined in 120 cases: 54 males and 66 females (a sex ratio of 81.82). Juvenile deaths are again underrepresented (only 6 skeletons under the age of 6 years), while 22 percent of the sample is classified as having died between the ages of 20 and 30 years. Of the total sample of 161 skeletons, only 96 (59.63%) have been assigned estimates of age. Overall the data are unsatisfactory, as the author of the report is well aware: "With a cemetery of incomplete data such as at Dover, where a number of graves were destroyed, and where a definite age is assessable for only a proportion of the skeletons, no meaningful life expectancy figure can be produced." Perhaps, therefore, the most recent trend, despite all the sophistication being brought to the area, is to realize the difficulties in attempting broad demographic statements based on data from incomplete and inexact evidence.

All of the skeletal material, when considered together, presents anything but a coherent picture of mortality and life expectancy rates. Like the inscriptional evidence, it points to wide fluctuations, due more to the customs of burial and variability of surviving evidence than to actual differences in demographic realities. The apparent advantage that the skeletal material has over tombstone inscriptions, namely that exaggeration or inaccuracy in the statements of age found on epitaphs is not a problem when dealing with skeletons, is undermined by the fact that the estimation of age (and indeed the determination of sex) in skeletons is a very haphazard and inexact process, and is prone to inexpert and subjective conclusions. Add to this the fact that skeletons from the Roman period are rarely preserved in a complete state—and indeed even when they are they are widely uneven in distribution—and their value as sources of vital statistics is put in serious doubt. Skeletons do provide us with valuable information, especially on pathological questions,[162] but the optimism of some scholars on the information to be derived from skeletons for detailed demographic analysis of the Roman empire is wholly unjustified.[163]

Ancient Statistics

What should emerge from the earlier sections of this study is my conviction that the various sources that have too often been supposed to be useful in producing data for demographic studies of the ancient world are in fact so plagued with biases and produce such potentially misleading or improbable information that they cannot be considered as usable. The evidence from the tombstone inscriptions reveals more about habits of commemoration than about mortality or population trends. The Ulpianic table, though it may well have been influenced by some vague contemporary notion of life expectancy, does not provide sufficient precision or accuracy to generate confident and meaningful statements on the demography of the time. The skeletal evidence, with the sample size as it stands and the lack of precision inherent in modern methods of determining the age and sex of skeletons, likewise provides data that are inadequate and also liable to biases. The census data from Roman Egypt, on the other hand, seem to me to be of greater potential value, especially if enough census returns from a wide chronological and geographical space could be employed so that any slight biases, and factors such as migration, could be taken into account; even in this eventuality, of course, the results could only be held to be valid for this particular province. But as things stand at present, the relative paucity of the returns and the rather irregular nature of the data produced from them mean that such data are of very restricted applicability and are inadequate for a detailed survey of the demographic reality of the Roman empire.

The fact of the matter is that there is a general lack of vital statistics from the ancient world.[164] The sort of material that historical demographers work with as the basis for their studies— notices of birth (or baptism), of death (or burial), and of marriages—exists only in very small and insignificant numbers (if at all) for our period. It is true that some ancient authors at times and quite casually give us snippets of demographic information of a sort, which it is very tempting to seize upon and exploit. But to what extent can we trust such information? It is worth pointing out that it is notoriously difficult to detect contemporary fluctuations in population size or structure merely by observation, however intelligent such observation may be. This is as true today as it would have been in antiquity.[165] Today we can refer to demographic documents generated from censuses to detect and measure such changes. It cannot be assumed, however, that ancient authors referred to—or even had at their disposal—similar sources of detailed information.[166]

It may be as well to consider one or two ancient observations on population in order to highlight the problems involved, for in what follows in chapter 3 much reference will need to be made to the literary sources. We will look here at some rather detailed observations which, as it happens, are made by Christian authors. Tertullian dismisses the idea propounded as part of the doctrine of metempsychosis that the number of people living at any one time never changes.[167] He points to the fact of large migrations due to overpopulation and argues that the population of the earth is ever on the increase.[168] Along with such natural increase, he sees the effect of natural forces as a remedy against overpopulation.[169] These comments are of interest and quite reasonable, remarking on long-term effects over the course of history which in hindsight and with intelligence may be seen to have operated; one can find similar discussions in Plato and Aristotle, for example.[170] But in the middle of this discussion, Tertullian comments on the contemporary scene—specifically, the flourishing and growth of the earth's population as he observed it in Roman Africa at the time, a description culminating in the famous exclamation "ubique domus, ubique populus, ubique respublica, ubique vita." This is what Tertullian observed, and it led him to believe (or perhaps reinforced his preconceived belief) that the population of Africa and of the world at large was growing at a quite considerable rate. No figures are given—we are dealing here with observation and impression, not detailed mathematical or statistical analysis.

Tertullian's assumption here may be in tune with the reality of the day, but it is not (nor was it intended to be) a demographic statement and should not be used on its own as evidence for the growth of the population of the empire at this date. As it happens it is *not* used for such a purpose. In fact it is generally overlooked because the consensus of scholarly opinion within the last 30 or 40 years has been that the overall population of the empire was in decline from the late second century A.D. One literary reference that is often cited in this context is that of Saint Cyprian, bishop of Carthage, who writes in A.D. 252 of the chronic shortage of workers on the land and of soldiers in the army, and of the drying up of the resources of the land.[171] This observation supports the current scholarly view of the decline in population at this time[172] and indeed may reflect contemporary reality to a greater degree than does the statement by Tertullian: the crisis of the third century entailed both economic and demographic emergencies, the latter being most noticeable in the shortage of manpower and leading to the state enforcement of labor.[173] But depopulation of the empire is a generalization over space and time and should not be thought of as a continuous, one-way process. Furthermore, although severe shortages of manpower may well have been observable over a long period of time, such shortages may have been due to a variety of causes: not just natural population decline through increased mortality or decreased fertility, but also by mass migration away from a particular area (e.g., from rural to urban, or vice versa), as well as by an increase in demand for production and a subsequent increase in demand for manpower to facilitate such increased production. It has been suggested that the new stress in this period on the enforcement of free labor may have its roots in a change of mentality in the late empire where the status of the free laborer becomes assimilated to that of the slave.[174] This may be true but the decline in manpower may also be evidenced in the large tracts of land increasingly being left uncultivated. Many factors may have brought this state of being about,[175] and no single explanation, nor any single term such as "depopulation," will help us to understand a complex reality.

The *cause* of manpower shortages and of depopulation is another question again. One can point (just as Tertullian did for a different purpose) to such natural phenomena as plagues, food shortages, and epidemics in the third century, as well as to the devastation of the land by "barbarian hordes." At a basic level it is possible that the peasant family was failing to reproduce itself, something Tertullian and Cyprian would probably have been just as unaware of then as we are unable to measure it today. One can point to the economic decline experienced at the time (again a broad generalization), but the relationship between the economic and demographic realities, presuming that there was such a relationship, is difficult to judge. Did one cause the other, or were both symptoms of the same cause? Such theoretical questions have taxed the minds of scholars for centuries: Plato and Aristotle both but in different ways argued for an optimum population size that would safeguard the economic and political structures of the state. It was also a question that concerned Thomas Malthus (1766–1834), whose various editions of the *Essay on the Principle of Population* developed a theory that saw preindustrial populations as growing only until they reached the maximum number possible as dictated by economic factors, basically the carrying capacity of the environment. Once a population had reached this peak, preventive checks (in Malthus's terms, late marriage with sexual abstinence beforehand) and positive checks (disease, war, and famine leading to higher mortality levels) would restore the balance. Similarly in the theory of a homeostatic regime rapid population growth is checked by the general environment through regulation of the birth and death rates.[176] These oscillating processes occur repeatedly over the course of history as long-term trends. The industrial revolution, which had hardly begun to make its presence felt as Malthus worked on his theory, brought new complications to the model. It is beyond the scope of this book to consider this theoretical question in any depth, but it is certainly something that needs to be taken into account in any study of the economic history of the ancient world, yet all too often is not.

The question that concerns us here is more elementary. In hindsight we can point to some evidence, not necessarily conclusive, for a long-term decline in the population of the Roman empire from the late second century A.D. Cyprian seems to confirm it, Tertullian does not. But on what criteria can we reject one and accept the other, other than subjectively to pick and choose pieces to suit our arguments? Cyprian wrote at the time of a plague, and his vision was perhaps clouded by his philosophical and religious conviction that the whole world was "in a state of senile decay, changing and passing away." [177] Tertullian wrote with a flourish of optimism and to suit his own philosophical argument. Both wrote from what they could (or chose to) observe, and both were dealing in short-term phenomena, which they might have assumed to have been indications of more extensive trends in population. Cyprian's observations were determined by the negative images surrounding him, Tertullian's by clearly more positive images. To use such observations as the bases for arguments about long-term population increase or decrease is as invalid and misleading, I would suggest, as believing that the population of any modern city is growing (whether by immigration or by natural increase) because one notices that the shops are busier than they were last year; the city's population may well be flourishing, but it needs more than observation and impression to measure and be sure of this.

The sort of population movements or changes in antiquity that might have been detectable by simple observation, even in the long term, would have to have been on a drastic and dramatic scale. In the light of the comments by Tertullian and Cyprian, it is perhaps worth quoting here a letter which Eusebius records as written by Dionysius, bishop of Alexandria, to a bishop elsewhere in Egypt, one Hierax, around A.D. 261/62, at the time of plague and sedition in the Egyptian capital:

> Yet men wonder and are at a loss as to the reason for these continuous pestilences, these chronic illnesses, all these kinds of deadly diseases, this varied and vast destruction of mankind; [they cannot understand] why this greatest city of ours no longer bears in it as great a number of inhabitants as before, beginning from infant children right up to the most advanced in age, as it once supported of those whom it called *hōmogerontes* [hearty old men]. But at that time those aged between 40 and 70 years were so much more numerous that now their number cannot be filled out when all those from 14 to 80 years of age are enrolled and counted together for the public corn dole, and those who appear youngest have become, as it were, the contemporaries of those who in the past were the oldest. And thus, on seeing the human race on the earth constantly diminishing and wasting away, they do not tremble, though their complete obliteration is increasing and advancing.[178]

If the figures quoted here are at all accurate then we are looking at a severe decline in population numbers,[179] so that, by Dionysius's account, in A.D. 261 the total number of people aged between 14 and 80 years is smaller than the number of those aged between 40 and 70 years at an earlier date. The severity of such an alleged population decline may be illustrated by supposing that, at its height, the population of Alexandria stood at half a million. A reasonable estimate of the proportion of this number aged between 40 and 70 years, male and female, assuming for the moment a stationary population with life expectancy at birth of around 25 years, would be 25 percent, that is, 125,000 individuals aged between 40 and 70 years.[180] Now if 125,000 was the total number of people aged between 14 and 80 years in A.D. 261, then this would suggest a total population (if the 14 to 80 age group represented about two-thirds of the population) of only 190,000, a fall from the earlier figure of 310,00 or 62 percent. This is indeed a catastrophic decline in numbers, though not impossible as a short-term phenomenon.

What makes this reference so interesting in this context is not so much the alleged reality of the demography of Alexandria in A.D. 261, but both the awareness of the different relative sizes of age classes within a population (however inexact), and also the way a decline in population numbers has been measured. A catastrophe of this order, if it were really to occur as described, would be clearly visible to the intelligent observer, as it was apparently to Dionysius.[181] Whatever the real dimensions of this decline, Dionysius discusses its magnitude by reference to the numbers eligible for the corn dole, one way in fact in which population numbers and large shifts in size would have been detectable at the time. But again increased mortality or decreased fertility may not have been the only possible causes of such a decline in numbers of people applying for the dole. Such factors as migration, or simply an unwillingness to apply for whatever reason, would also lower the numbers and present the image of a decline in population size. It is unlikely that Dionysius's description of the situation in Alexandria is an accurate reflection of *long-term* demographic reality: the sort of decline he implies, over what is apparently a relatively short space of time, would have been too severe for the population of Alexandria to have survived through successive generations. Perhaps a significant degree of exaggeration (to suit the argument of the letter) must be assumed, whatever other interest the passage may hold in terms of demographic perception. The effects of the combined devastation brought on by plague and war may have caused in the short term a dramatic increase in mortality rates, but if these effects were really experienced over the longer term in terms of mortality and fertility levels, then Dionysius had very good cause to be concerned!

The basic point to be drawn from the examples discussed is that we cannot believe precisely everything an ancient author tells us about population sizes and trends, at least not without considering the author's source of information (was he merely making an observation or was his statement based on census material?) and his purpose in giving this information. But what of such details—for example, when the population size of a city is given? No one today would seriously regard as accurate Pliny's figure for the population of Seleucia of 600,000, yet Pliny clearly believed his source;[182] to us the figure seems an obvious exaggeration. We have less trouble, however, in believing that the population of Roman Egypt was around 8 million because this figure sounds fairly reasonable and is apparently based on official records, although the matter is far from as simple as that. The main piece of evidence is a statement in Josephus[183] where Herod Agrippa in A.D. 66 notes that Egypt has a population of 7.5 million, not including the inhabitants of Alexandria, as may be evidenced from the poll tax receipts. Diodorus Siculus[184] states a century earlier that in times of old the total population of Egypt was about 7 million and that now (mid first century B.C.) it is 3 million—this latter figure is regarded by almost all scholars as a textual error and is amended to read 7 million also. Diodorus also states that the free residents of Alexandria total 300,000, as recorded by those who kept the census returns.[185] One final gem of information to be gleaned from the literature: Philo records that there were 1 million Jews in Egypt.[186] Again it is a case of picking and choosing among the literary references to find one that "sounds about right," a method that is obviously too subjective and arbitrary to be satisfactory in terms of historical demography.

Another example of the misuse of literary references to provide, in this case, absurd statistics was pointed out by David Hume more than 200 years ago and remains instructive. Appian states that Caesar subjected 400 *ethnē* in Gaul. Diodorus Siculus states that the largest *ethnos* in Gaul had 200,000 men, the smallest 50,000. If we take the average, 125,000, multiply by four to allow for women and children, and then multiply by Appian's 400, we reach a total population for Roman Gaul of 200 million![187] As Hume states, "such calculations, therefore, by their extravagance, lose all manner of authority." The absurdness of the example is patent. Yet all too often modern scholars assemble such disparate tidbits of information in order to arrive at some ingenious but highly dubious conclusions.

Even when we have citations of ancient census totals the problems remain. Roman census figures from the republic and early empire are illustrative of this.[188] Even allowing for scribal error in the past,[189] we cannot be sure exactly what the figures represent. In 86 B.C. the figure for Roman citizens is given as 463,000, in 70/69 it is 910,000. To correct such an implausible *natural* growth, Beloch suggested that the earlier figure should be amended to read 963,000, but then the previous figure (of 394,336 for 115/14 B.C.) must be regarded as too low—one can only make so many amendments.[190] From 910,000 in 70/69 we leap to 4,063,000 in 28 B.C., and so on through Augustus's reign as recorded in the *Res Gestae*. The final figure, of 4,937,000 for A.D. 14, contrasts with the figure for the same year in the *Fasti Ostienses* of 4,100,900. Which figure is to be preferred and on what grounds? Furthermore, it remains unclear whether the figures relate only to adult men or include women and children.

Or do we in fact have here evidence for a growth in the general population of Roman citizens over the last years of the republic and the beginning of the empire? Perhaps we do; certainly the established view since Beloch has been that such a growth did occur, though not necessarily among all strata of society.[191] But the evident increase in the census figures may not be due to natural population increase alone, if at all. It may reflect better methods in the collection of data, or it may be due to people being counted who had not been before, not just women and children but also enfranchised allies and ex-slaves. This apparent growth is also contemporaneous with a noted shortage of army manpower. Is this to be taken as a sign of declining population numbers, or again as a symptom of a general unwillingness to serve? In short, the census data present more questions than answers.

Two

Ancient History
and Modern Demography:
Methods and Models

n the face of such uncertainties and difficulties it is perhaps little wonder that demography has yet to make its presence felt in the study of ancient history. Usually, when demographic techniques or studies are brought to bear on ancient populations, the union is not a fruitful one, due not so much necessarily to their incompatibility as to the often uncritical use of modern comparisons with ancient material. Boak in 1955, for example, professed to use demographic "laws" and more modern case studies to illustrate his thesis that the fall of the Roman empire was directly related to the (alleged) decline in population. But his method had the opposite effect: rather than illuminating his thesis he blinded the reader with drawn out discussions of numbers from China and medieval England without ever making it clear why such particular comparisons were valuable or relevant. To give such a discussion "an aura of scientific demography," as Finley called it in his 1958 critique of Boak, is both misleading and unproductive. The later work by Salmon in 1974 suffers from similar drawbacks. Having ascertained that statistics from ancient sources are both scarce and unreliable, Salmon nonetheless goes on to cite them selectively to suit his arguments. His book is of use, at least for highlighting various aspects of information on ancient population, but it does little to inspire confidence in the value of demography in the realm of ancient history.

Brunt's book, *Italian Manpower, 225 B.C.–A.D. 14*, which first appeared in 1971, is probably the most systematic and critical evaluation of the demographic sources for a particular period of ancient history to date.[1] Although his underlying thesis regarding the decline of the freeborn population of republican Italy with a corresponding surge in the numbers of freedmen may be questioned, Brunt's careful consideration of the census figures in particular and of other related demographic features such as army manpower and internal migration adds much to our knowledge of the period. It is when demographic methods are applied uncritically, however, to a question such as the extent of exposure or infanticide in the ancient world that the audience becomes wary and skeptical (see chapter 3). Oldenziel, in her 1987 review of the contribution made by demography to the study of this particular aspect of ancient life, probably reflects the reaction of many. She notes that in dealing with exposure and infanticide the tendency has been in recent years to turn from the ancient literary evidence to demographic considerations, "as scholars fell under the charms and their promise of exactness. . . . It is dubious whether demographic arguments are any more precise or conclusive than arguments based on literary sources. . . . The statistical data from antiquity are so weak that it is difficult to see why any scholar would trust them any more than literary sources."[2]

This is precisely where the problem lies. What we as ancient historians should look for in demography is not a precise statistic exact to four decimal places as the answer to all our questions, but rather an awareness of the way populations work. "Ancient demography," if such a branch of ancient history is to develop, should not confine itself to the collection and discussion of figures that can be extracted from the ancient sources (the "lure of aggregates"), but should relate these and other data to what we know both of the social and economic conditions of the ancient world and of the general principles of population dynamics. We should not become bogged down either in tedious and unfruitful quibbles about numbers that ancient authors throw out to us in passing, or in protracted comparisons with specific modern populations as if the ancient world as a whole was directly comparable. For even if it was, how would we know? Hopkins makes a typically blunt comment in this regard, which is worth repeating here: "it would be awful if we came to regard comparative history like ancient sources as quarries from which we could make corroborative examples."[3] Yet this is increasingly becoming the tendency.

In the remainder of this book I shall discuss some ways in which modern demographic studies and theories may usefully help us to gain an awareness of the sort of factors relevant to a study of the dynamics of population size and structure in the ancient world, by highlighting the indirect evidence we have and by bringing to bear on the subject some of the tools, such as model life tables, which may be used to elucidate aspects of ancient populations. It needs to be stressed that what we are dealing with here are inference and impressions—not the sort of impressions that Tertullian and Cyprian wrote about in dealing with a specific time and place, but general impressions in hindsight of populations over a vast span of time and place. What we should aim to end up with are not answers to such questions as "How many thirty-year-old men were there in ancient Rome in A.D. 100?" or "How many children did each Roman mother have?" but rather probable answers to such questions as "What was the approximate age structure of a population experiencing certain factors such as high mortality rates?" and "How many children on average would a mother need to have given birth to in order for such a population to have remained stationary or to have grown?" It is true that demography as a mathematical science deals in facts, not impressions.[4] But in the absence of hard factual statistics we can hope to increase our awareness of the demographic realities of the ancient world on a broad scale.

General statements on population trends in the ancient world can rarely ever be "proved" by reliable evidence from the literary sources. They must rest on what may be held to be plausible or probable rather than on what is certain or proved.[5]

It needs to be understood that, while the population of the ancient world may not be directly comparable in terms of mortality and fertility levels to any single present-day or other well-documented historical population, the basic concepts in the study of demography as developed this century are of universal application in the trends they describe. Nancy Howell has argued for a uniformitarian theory of human palaeodemography, by which is meant that one can apply the known demographic patterns of the present to the past, on the assumption that the basic biological responses of humankind to the environment have remained the same over the course of history, that is, "in processes of ovulation, spermatogenesis, length of pregnancy, degree of helplessness of the young and rates of maturation and senility."[6] In other words, although the *rates* of these processes may have changed, with differing levels of mortality, fertility (including nuptiality), and migration in different periods and populations, the responses to these variables have remained similar. Expressed graphically, this means that, for example, the levels of mortality over various ages of the life-course fall into a pattern: the shape of the mortality curve is a constant, the overall rates being dependent on the underlying demographic conditions at the time.[7] This is the principle underlying much of historical demography and it is most evident in the use of model life tables, to which we shall come shortly. To speak of "laws" of demography would be a misnomer; rather what we are dealing with are notions of mortality and fertility, which may be applied hypothetically to any period of history and into which any given population may be expected to fit.

"I think nobody will deny that from a social and economic viewpoint ancient Italy can be compared with an under-developed country."[8] This is rather a sweeping statement but, demographically at least, I think it is true. Our notions of population are perhaps too greatly affected by the society in which we live today. From the nineteenth century the population structure of the developing and developed Western world has seen unprecedented and dramatic changes, sometimes referred to as the "demographic transition," where the combined effect of a significant drop in mortality rates (due largely to improved hygiene and medical standards) and of an extreme decline in fertility rates, sometimes to below replacement levels, together with a rapid rate of population growth, led to a quite different demographic regime than had ever been experienced before.[9] This century we have experienced an enormous increase in the proportion and number of elderly people in our society. In England today, for example, some 15 percent of the population is over the age of 65 years, compared with less than 5 percent a century ago. Average life expectancy at birth in the United Kingdom and the United States today is something approaching 80 years for females and is more than 70 for males, and it continues to rise. But it must be stressed that this does not mean that people are living significantly longer lives today than people did 2,000 years ago, only that *more* are surviving into old age because of a lowered risk of mortality in earlier years, and that the proportion of the elderly is growing because of lower fertility rates. Average life expectancy, as has already been noted, can be a misleading concept, especially in high mortality regimes where so many die in infancy. If, to take a highly hypothetical but illuminating example, in a population group of 100 individuals, 50 people died at or shortly after birth and the other 50 all died at the age of 60 years, then the average life expectancy would be $(50 \times 0) + (50 \times 60) / 100 = 30$ years. So average life expectancy at birth of 30 years clearly does *not* mean here that most people die at the age of 30 years; often quite the contrary might be true where infant mortality levels are high. In such a regime it is often useful to talk also of average life expectancy at age 5 or 10 years, that is, the average number of years lived after reaching this birthday, for this method obviates the bias produced by high infant and early childhood mortality. In modern, so-called posttransitional populations such as those of the United Kingdom and the United States, infant and early childhood mortality is minimal, and indeed the age group of 10 to 15 years is seen as the least at risk. In ancient society, on the other hand, as with other preindustrial populations, quite the opposite was true. While some people did live on to extreme old age, mortality was severer throughout the earlier years, and this dramatically affects the demographic picture.

The three basic factors that determine the size and structure of all populations in purely demographic terms are mortality, fertility, and migration, and it is with these three factors that demographers begin their analysis, as may be seen in any good demographic handbook.[10] It is on mortality and fertility that we shall focus here, because migration, while it may affect a population very significantly in terms of age and sex structure, is of more concern when dealing with a specific rural, urban,[11] or national population, and in our discussion of the population of the Roman empire as a whole may for the moment be considered as of secondary importance.

Fertility levels indicate the number of people entering a population through birth, mortality those leaving through death. Consider a hypothetical population group or cohort of 100,000 people all born in the same year. We can trace their life careers through their various life-courses, to see how many survive to certain ages. For convenience and brevity the life-course may be divided up into 5-year stages, with the first stage, the 0–4 year group (from birth to the end of the 5th year) being further divided into the 1st year and the remaining 4, in order to allow for a record of infant mortality. So we may follow our population cohort to see how many survive to the end of their 1st, 5th, 10th, 15th year, and so on. At the end of each period we record the number who have died since the previous period and the corresponding number who survive. Hence, if in the 1st year of life, 35,822 of the 100,000 die, then the number of deaths in the 1st year, termed d_0, equals 35,822, and survivors at exact age 1, l_1, is $100,000 - 35,822 = 64,178$. Then if, in the 1–4 year age group, $d_1 = 15,210$, l_5 will equal 48,968, and so on.

The number of deaths in any age group, divided by the number of survivors at the beginning of that age group, tells us the probability of dying under these conditions between these ages, and is termed q_x. Hence q_0 is 35,822 divided by 100,000, which equals 0.3582, and q_1 is 0.2370, and so on. The complement of q_x, that is, $1 - q_x$, is the probability of *surviving* to the next age group, and is termed p_x. Thus, $p_0 = 0.6418$ and $p_1 = 0.7630$; that is, the probability of an individual surviving from age 1 to age 5 years under these conditions is 0.7630 or, expressed differently, 76.3 percent of the group who survive to age 1 year may be expected to survive to age 5 years.

Because $q_x = d_x/l_x$, as defined, we can also say that $d_x = l_x \cdot q_x$ and that $l_x = d_x/q_x$; that is, the number of deaths within a certain age group is equal to the number of survivors multiplied by the risk of dying; and the number of survivors is equal to the number of deaths divided by the risk of dying. These three values, d_x, q_x, and l_x, form the basis of the life table. Through knowledge of one of them, all the remaining functions of the life table may be calculated.

Before we turn to these other functions, however, we need to remember that we are dealing with a hypothetical population and that we are making certain assumptions about that population. The basic assumption is that the birth and death rates are constant over an indefinite period and that the population is closed, that is, that there is no effect from migration and that any short-term fluctuations due to such factors as plague, war, and famine are smoothed out in the long term. The population returns to its previous age structure within a few generations.[12]

In such a population as assumed in the last paragraph, the age composition is self-replicating and becomes fixed. In a stable population natural increase or decrease in size occurs when the birth rate exceeds the death rate, or vice versa, the change in size occurring at a constant, cumulative rate. Where the birth rate is equal to the death rate, that is, where the numbers born each year are balanced by the numbers dying, the population is said to be stationary, with a zero rate of growth. The main benefit of such assumptions and of working with a stationary population is that from the basic information on age-specific mortality rates a complete life table can be constructed, and the full size and structure of the population can be analyzed.

In reality, of course, no population is perfectly stationary or, for that matter, stable. Nevertheless, the stable population theory provides a useful and illuminating model of population dynamics which, for our purposes, is sufficient. But it needs always to be borne in mind that the information to be obtained from this method and the use of model life tables reflect probabilities, an idea of the structure of ancient populations. For this reason I am surprised by the comments of Brent Shaw, who criticizes the utility of model life tables as little more than "an interesting heuristic device legitimate in certain [*which?*] contexts for ancient demographic studies."[13] He states that they cannot be regarded as generally applicable because the population of the Roman empire was not stable. This is strictly true but need not prevent the use of the tables. It is worth quoting Shaw here, for there seems to be some doubt as to what he understands by the term "stable":

> It is abundantly clear to most Roman historians [*who?*], however, that the overall population of the Roman empire in the period between the first and the fifth to sixth centuries A.D. was not at all a "stable population." For western parts of the empire, between the second and fourth centuries, at least, it seems fairly certain that the population was growing at a considerable rate, and that certain sectors of it (especially those related to urban centres) were rather mobile.

Although it is certainly true that large urban centers (and it is these with which Shaw is principally dealing), especially Rome, were not stable, due partly to mass in-migration, it is not so clear that the empire as a whole, even if it were "growing at a considerable rate" (though I wonder at the evidence for this), does not approximate to a stable population. Remember that "stable" does *not* mean stationary. As Newell states, "it is important at the outset to realise that the word 'Stable' describes the unchanging *shape* of an age distribution, not the total size of a population. A population which is Stable may, despite its name, actually be growing or declining in size very rapidly." [14] On this basis model life tables may be very useful in discussing ancient population trends. [15]

That we are dealing with probabilities, not certainties, is something that is not, I feel, made sufficiently clear by Frier in his construction and discussion of a life table for the Roman empire. [16] Frier assumes a stationary population and leaves questions of fertility and growth rates largely unconsidered. However, because his life table is probably the one most accessible and of immediate interest to ancient historians, it is worth continuing our analysis of life table functions by reference to Frier's figures. How valid his table is as a model of population trends in the Roman empire will be considered shortly.

In table 6 (see appendix B), beginning from the left, one can see the functions we have already introduced: x, the exact age; q_x, the probability of dying between age x and the next age (commonly referred to as x + n); and l_x, the number of survivors at age x. The initial number or radix of survivors, known as the birth cohort, l_0, is conventionally set at 100,000, and we follow these 100,000 individuals throughout their life-courses until they have all died. At age 80 years, 671 survive, and as these survivors will all eventually die the probability of death from age 80, q_{80}, is 1, and the number of deaths from age 80 onward, d_{80}, is 671. Graphs of the values of q_x, p_x, [17] d_x, and l_x are given in figures 4–7 for illustration of the types of curves to be expected in high mortality regimes (see appendix B). What is most important here is not the precise figures but the generally applicable trends that may be seen in each function.

The next function in table 6, m_x, is added here mainly for the sake of completeness. It represents the age-specific mortality rates or central death rates at age x, and differs from q_x in that m_x is the ratio of deaths in a *single* year to the *mid*year, not the initial, population. From a census in modern demographic studies, one first calculates the age-specific mortality rates, by taking the number of deaths at a certain age in a year and dividing it by the average number of the population at that age at the beginning and the end of the year.[18] These m_x values are then converted to q_x values (the method of which need not concern us here) in order to generate a life table. In a life table like Frier's, however, q_x values are generated from the d_x and l_x values, as described, and in this regard m_x values are superfluous. Values for m_x are always greater than the corresponding q_x values, since the denominator in the former is smaller, and is calculated in Frier's table by the equation $m_x = d_x/L_x$. It would be wrong to take, as Frier does, m_0 as an indication of infant mortality, since (as stated) it tells us not how many died in their 1st year from an original cohort of 100,000, but from the midyear population.[19] So Frier is wrong when he states that, according to his table, the infant mortality rate (IMR) was 466.9 per 1,000;[20] the rate his table in fact gives is 358.2 per 1,000, that is, q_0. But even this is very high. What it actually implies is that in the Roman empire more than one in three people died in their 1st year of life. Furthermore, by adding up the d_x values, we can see that, according to this table, over half (51,302/100,000) from an original cohort was probably dead by the age of 5 years, and that little more than a third survived to the age of 30 years. This is a bleak picture of high mortality—a little too high, perhaps, to be realistic, as we shall discuss.

First we need to consider the remaining four columns of the life table in table 6. The L_x column represents the number of person-years lived between age x and age x + n. What this in effect means is that, for example, at age 20 where there are 40,385 survivors (l_{20}), if all of these individuals lived to the age of 25 years they would have lived together over the 5-year period a total of $40,385 \times 5 = 201,925$ years. But of course some of them will die during the interval and will not live for the full 5 years, so L_{20} will be less than this total. The actual figure for L_{20} is most easily approximated (as it is here by Frier) by averaging l_{20} and l_{25}, that is, the average of the number of survivors at ages 20 and 25 years, and multiplying by five for the 5 years lived, on the assumption that the mortality rate is linear, that is, that people of this age group are dying at a constant rate over the 5 years. Therefore, $L_{20} = (40,385 + 37,047)/2 \times 5 = 193,580$.

This method of deriving L_x is valid for all ages except the initial years of life, since in infancy and early childhood mortality does not occur at a constant rate. Mortality is severest in the time immediately following birth and declines sharply thereafter in an hyperbolic curve. Therefore more complex equations are necessary to derive L_0 and L_1, but these need not concern us here. Indeed in the model life tables to be considered shortly a more complex method has been used to derive all L_x values, but the method here described is sufficient to explain the meaning of the figures.

The next function, T_x, is simply the sum of all the L_x values. That is, T_x represents the *total* number of years lived after age x. Therefore T_{20} is the sum of L_{20}, L_{25}, and so on through to L_{80}. For a stationary population T_0 represents the total population size if 100,000 people, the radix, are born and die every year. As T_0 is the sum of all the L_x values, the L_x column gives us the numbers in each age class. For example, in table 6, with a population of 2,110,730 individuals, 76,716 would be under the age of 1 year, 216,573 between the age of 1 and 5 years, and so on, at any one time. This enables us to calculate the proportion of the total population that each age group represents, termed C_x; that is, $C_x = 100 \cdot L_x/T_0$. Thus, in table 6, assuming a stationary population, 3.63 percent of the population is under the age of 1 year, 0.12 percent is over the age of 80 years, and so on. The C_x function is thus very useful in telling us, from the age-specific mortality rates existing in a population, what the approximate probable age structure of that population is.

The final function of the life table to be considered is the demographic factor which is most well known and most frequently cited, though too often without precise knowledge of its method of calculation or even its exact meaning, namely average life expectancy. It is calculated for any age by dividing the total number of years left to live at any age by the number of survivors at that age; that is, $e_x = T_x/l_x$. Average life expectancy tells us how many years on average each survivor may be expected to live from a given age. Hence, in table 6, average life expectancy at birth, e_0, is 2,110,730/100,000 = 21.107 years;

$e_1 = 2,034,014/64,178 = 31.693$ years, and so on. In other words, at the age of 1 year, the individual members of the group of survivors to age 1 year may on average be expected to live another 31.693 years each. Average life expectancy is actually significantly higher at age 1 than at birth in this life table because of the high rate of infant mortality in this population. As noted, average life expectancy can be a misleading concept for this very reason. It needs to be remembered that it is an average for the entire age cohort, and is not an upper limit by which time everyone will die or be dead. Many will live beyond that age, many will die before it; very few will die at that precise age. So when it is stated that average life expectancy at birth in the Roman empire was 25 years (or whatever), it does *not* mean that most Romans died at that age, as many seem to assume.

Some further information may be derived from the basic life table as illustrated in table 6. In a stationary population, the birth and death rates are by definition equal, and they are defined as the initial birth cohort divided by the population size, that is, l_0/T_0. Now, because $e_0 = T_0/l_0$, one can see that the birth and death rates therefore equal $1/e_0$, the inverse of the average life expectancy at birth. Thus, in Frier's life table, the birth and death rate is 0.04738, or in other words 47.38 births or deaths per 1,000 individuals per year. This is actually a very high rate. By comparison the current birth and death rates in modern Western countries today are generally in the 10 to 15 per 1,000 range. A figure in the high 40s for antiquity is not impossible[21] but it is improbable for the long term, and it leads one to believe that Frier's figure for average life expectancy at birth in a stationary population is a little on the low side. This is one reason why I believe that Frier's life table is not as useful a tool for ancient historians as it may at first appear or promise to be. I have argued already that the Ulpianic table is not a satisfactory basis for deriving a life table for the Roman empire. Nevertheless, Frier's table *is* demographically plausible for the simple reason that his figures are in effect modeled or modified in the light of model life tables, mention of which needs to be introduced here now, though they are not entirely new to some ancient historians.[22]

But the use of model life tables by ancient historians has too often taken place without adequate explanation or justification and thus has aroused, naturally enough, some skepticism.[23]

The basic idea of a model life table is to provide information on populations for which insufficient data are available or where data are of dubious value,[24] in order to test the validity or demographic plausibility of certain assumptions about the population being analyzed. They have been progressively developed since the 1950s, and various sets of model life tables are now in existence. We will deal here with only two, the ones most commonly employed by demographers, both of which have been used by one or two ancient historians. The basic and proven assumption on which such model life tables work is that age *patterns* of mortality are basically the same irrespective of time and place. The precise mortality rates may differ, but the overall pattern is constant: a high level of mortality in infancy (though exactly how high may differ widely), a sharp decline to low mortality levels in later childhood and adolescence, and then gradually increasing mortality levels into old age.

The first sets of model life tables were those published by the United Nations in 1955–56, 24 tables for both sexes with e_0 ranging from 20 to 73.9 years, computed from 158 empirically based life tables. These model life tables are rarely used now.[25] The main criticism of the U.N. tables is twofold. First, their original data were subsequently found to be inexact, biased, and based upon inadequate evidence, especially in the higher mortality models. Second, they make no allowance for any variations outside of mortality levels, that is, the entire age structure of the population is defined simply by the overall level of mortality without reference to age patterns; in this respect the U.N. models are too rigid.

The Coale-Demeny tables, first published in 1966 with a revised edition appearing in 1983, are the most widely used tables today.[26] Not only are 25 tables for each sex given, over a range of values for average life expectancy at birth from 20 to 80 years (for females), but also four different types of age patterns of mortality are considered, so that a total of 100 different models for each sex are generated. The four different types, or "families," are termed "North," "South," "East," and "West," and they differ in the relative mortality levels in infancy, childhood, adulthood, and old age. The tables are based on a collection of 326 real life tables for each sex, bases that have been scrutinized and judged to be demographically accurate. Inevitably, this means that the sources are predominantly from the developed world of the nineteenth and twentieth centuries.[27] Briefly, the four families are distinguished as follows:

East: generated from central European (including northern and central Italy) life tables; high infant mortality and increasingly high mortality over the age of 50 years.

North: generated from life tables from Scandinavia; low infant mortality and old age mortality relative to adult years.

South: generated from Mediterranean life tables (Portugal, Spain, Italy—particularly southern Italy and Sicily); high infant and early childhood mortality, low mortality in the 40 to 60 year age group, high mortality from age 65 years onward.

West: represents a "standard" or "average" pattern of mortality, recommended for use where vital statistics are too inadequate to provide a certain allocation of the population to one of the other three families; based on varied empirical life tables from around the globe.

In using these model life tables as the basis for a general study of ancient populations, the West region tables are probably our best and safest bet, though the South region tables, with their Mediterranean basis and particular mortality pattern, are also worth considering.[28] The East and North tables are less relevant for our purposes.

It must be added, however, that in high mortality regimes such as that of the Roman empire, these types of differences in mortality patterns are less significant than in modern-day, low mortality regimes, especially since in this context we are looking only for general indications of demographic characteristics and not four-decimal-place accuracy. Yet the differences between the four regions are important and represent one of the

primary benefits of the Coale-Demeny[2] tables over their prede-
cessors, the 1956 U.N. tables, since allowance is made for variability in the age patterns of mortality due to more than just age
itself. For the subtle differences between the West and South
regions, compare figure 9 (appendix B), a graph that shows average life expectancy values as given in Coale-Demeny[2] Level 3
female, where $e_0 = 25$ years, for both the South and West families.[29] Basically the same pattern is evident in both regions, but
there are some important points of divergence. In the South
table, infant mortality is lower than in the West, but early childhood mortality is higher. Then, from age 5 to 60 years, South
mortality is lower and thus one finds higher e_x values at these
ages. In old age South mortality becomes slightly higher than
that in the West table.

One very real criticism of the use of the Coale-Demeny[2] tables
for the study of the population of the ancient Roman empire is
that these model life tables are based on real life tables of the
nineteenth and twentieth centuries where average life expectancy at birth never fell below 35 years. How can one apply tables
based on such empirical data to a historical population where e_0
is assumed to have been significantly lower than this? Hollingsworth noted this problem in discussing the value of the first edition of the Coale-Demeny tables, which appeared in 1966: "The
mortality schedules calculated for expectations of life at birth of
20 to 35 [years], which are important for historical demography
in Western Europe because they are what is usually found before
1800, are really only extrapolations of observation."[30] Part of
our justification for this method is that demographic principles
are of universal application, and tables for high mortality can be
calculated from lower mortality tables by regression. But this is
not the whole answer, since age patterns can change over time,
though not so significantly as to render the results from the
model life tables invalid.

The criticism remains, however, a valid one. But there is every
reason to believe that the demographic patterns of age structure
and mortality trends that the Coale-Demeny[2] tables illustrate
are broadly applicable to ancient populations, and are at any rate

the best source of information available. The work of anthropologists in the field of demography has proved productive.[31] Their studies are of some interest to us here since they often deal with populations with mortality levels as high as we envisage for ancient society. Weiss has gone so far as to construct model life tables for anthropological populations, models that appear to fit well with the Coale-Demeny[2] high mortality tables.[32] A test of the validity of such tables concludes that, so long as it is remembered that the results given in such tables are smoothed estimates of population structure and average life expectancies and are not exact reconstructions of historical reality (a fact I have tried to stress thus far), then the tables produced are an invaluable tool in the study of preindustrial populations.[33]

I believe that it is preferable for ancient historians to use the Coale-Demeny[2] tables rather than to confine themselves to Frier's life table, for various reasons, some of which have already been noted. First, Frier's eventual figures owe more in their specific details to the Model West Level 2 table from the first edition of Coale-Demeny than to the Ulpianic figures, which I have already argued are not an adequate basis for a life table anyway. The similarities between Frier's life table figures and the relevant Coale-Demeny table (male and female combined) are quite clear and striking when the two are compared: the rates in the birth to 10-year age groups are identical, since Frier has used these figures where the Ulpianic table is considered inadequate. After that age, Frier's mortality rates are generally slightly lower up to age 35 years, and then become higher over the remaining years. The differences are not significant by any means: the relative e_x values never differ by more than 1 year, and the age distribution of the stationary population, that is, the C_x values, is virtually identical between the two tables, Frier's population being slightly younger. The lack of any close relationship between the Ulpianic figures and those of Frier's table may be seen in figure 1.

It seems to me more useful to take advantage of the more detailed and wider range of information obtainable from the Coale-Demeny[2] models, rather than to confine ourselves to a single life table, however plausible it may appear overall. Moreover, Frier, in acknowledging that the Ulpianic figures make absolutely no allowance for infant and early childhood mortality, uses the Coale-Demeny West Level 2 table for the various q_x values below the age of 15 years, on the assumption that mortality rates for infancy and childhood may be derived from the mortality rates for the adult age groups.[34] Frier remarks that this assumption renders the portion of his life table from birth to age 10 the weakest part of it all, but one might think that his assumption about the comparability of early and late mortality rates a justified one;[35] this assumption also underlies the 1956 U.N. model life tables. But in fact the assumption is a false one. It has been clearly shown by demographers that infant mortality rates may fit into a significantly different pattern than those of adult mortality.[36] Adult mortality rates do *not* necessarily reflect infant/child mortality levels, and vice versa: Frier's assumption is both unfounded and misleading.

It would be a mistake to regard the Coale-Demeny[2] model life tables as exact or definitive descriptions of any actual populations. To state it again, for it needs to be understood, the tables illustrate probabilities for hypothetical stable populations, probabilities that suggest approximate dimensions rather than strict limits. Furthermore, it needs to be stressed that when we refer to Level 3 "female" or "male" these tables need not be related to a single, specific sex.[37] In what follows attention will be focused on the "female" life tables, but only because in these tables e_0 is expressed as a rounded number (20, 22.5, 25 years, etc.). The actual details of the table as discussed here are meant to refer to the general population, not specifically to females alone. The possible difference between the demographic characteristics of each sex in the Roman empire will be considered in chapter 3.

Frier's incorrect assumption that he can derive infant and childhood mortality rates from the adult rates has given rise in his table to a very high infant mortality rate of 358.22 per 1,000, in my opinion too high by comparative standards to be generally applicable (see table 6). Even if Frier's figure for e_0 of 21.11 years is in the right region[38] this need not mean that infant mortality was as high as he suggests in his table. In Coale-Demeny[2] Model South Level 1 female, where e_0 is 20 years, the infant mortality rate is only 307.21 per 1,000, with the mortality rate remaining high over the early childhood years. The problem with such a low e_0 figure as Frier supposes is that in a stationary population (which is what Frier assumes and does not go beyond) it implies a birth and death rate of 47.38 per 1,000, which in the long term, as regards the birth rate, would have been very difficult to achieve in the social and economic context of the ancient world.

If we are to use the Coale-Demeny[2] model life tables as the means for gaining an awareness of the probable population structure of the Roman empire, we need to have an idea of the sort of population in actual terms with which we are dealing. There is every reason to believe that the average life expectancy at birth of the population of the Roman empire as a whole was in the range of 20 to 30 years. If it fell below 20 years over a long period the population would have fallen into rapid decline. The upper limit is set on the comparative evidence of preindustrial populations in general: an e_0 in excess of 30 years would imply a quite different demographic regime, with infant mortality in particular far lower than might be anticipated with medical care and environmental conditions being what they were.[39] An estimate in the 20 to 30 year range is clearly right, I think, as a generalization, allowing for significant variations over time and space.[40] With this in mind, in tables 7 and 8 (appendix B) I have given the relevant figures, from models West and South respectively, describing a stationary population with average life expectancies at birth ranging from 20 to 30 years. In each case the e_x column gives the various values for average life expectancies at different ages, and the C_x column the proportion of the population in this age group—for example, $C_{30} = 7.11$ means that 7.11 percent of this stationary population at any one time may be expected to be between the ages of 30 and 34 years inclusive. Below these two columns are given the crude birth and death rates (which are equal because the population is stationary), the gross reproduction rate required to sustain the stationary population (to be discussed) and the average age of the living population, and the dependency ratio, the latter being a standard measure of the ratio of those under the age of 15 years and over 59 years of age as compared with those in the population between these age limits. For the population of the Roman empire, "dependency" is something of a misnomer, since there was no notion of a retirement age nor is it clear how much of a "burden" the young and the elderly were held to be. The measure itself, however, is a useful one for helping us to understand the age structure of the population. In figure 8 (see appendix B), the various values for average life expectancy from Model West, from 20 to 30 years at birth, are displayed.

It is important that we bear in mind that such figures as these are meant only to illustrate long-term trends. Quite marked fluctuations are bound to have occurred in the short term, due to such natural or artificial phenomena as plague, war, endemic disease, and famine. Nor is this the only area in which we must allow for variables. Up till now we have considered the Coale-Demeny[2] tables only insofar as they give us the sort of information that Frier gave in his life table, that is, in questions of mortality. In fact model life tables can tell us much more, and it is time now to move from the stationary population model to that of the stable population, by introducing notions of fertility and population growth rates. For changes in fertility levels can have a greater effect on the structure of a population than may changes in levels of mortality. When the birth and death rates are not equal, population increase or decrease will occur. Such growth, positive or negative, may numerically appear very small (say 0.5% per year at most), and indeed over the long term in the course of history, before the demographic transition, rates of growth were probably very small and close to zero.[41] Yet such apparently insubstantial rates of growth can have quite significant results in terms of population size over a long period of time.

If we focus on a specific average life expectancy at birth of 25 years,[42] midway between our range of 20 to 30 years, we can use the Coale-Demeny[2] tables to illustrate the effect of differing rates of fertility and the various consequences of growth or decline in a population on its age structure. If the crude birth rate is, say, 42 per 1,000 per year and the death rate is 37 per 1,000, then clearly in a stable population where birth and death are the sole factors in determining natural increase, the population will grow by 5 per 1,000 or 0.5 percent per year. This may not seem numerically significant but in fact, at cumulative growth rates, the population under these conditions will in theory double in size in less than 140 years; a growth rate (r) of 1 percent per year will lead to the population doubling in under 70 years, and of 2 percent in under 35 years.[43]

But for such rates of growth (or, for that matter, rates of decline) to occur, there need to be quite considerable changes in mortality or fertility levels. Mortality we can measure by values for average life expectancy. Fertility may be conveniently measured here by the gross reproduction rate (GRR), a measure that can be interpreted as the average number of daughters that a woman in a hypothetical cohort would give birth to if she survived throughout her reproductive life course (conventionally a mean of 29 years, from—say—age 15 to 44 years) and if she experienced typical female fertility rates in that period. Hence, if we assume for the moment that on average an equal number of boys are born as are girls, a GRR of 1 represents one daughter or a family of two children. In the case of Coale-Demeny[2] Model West Level 3 female, a stationary population with e_0 of 25 years, the GRR required to maintain a stationary population is 2.543, or a family size of just over five children ever-born per woman. For Coale-Demeny[2] Model South Level 3 female, the corresponding GRR required for a stationary population is slightly higher at 2.635, the difference being mainly due to differing infant and early childhood mortality rates. Gross reproduction rates at different values for e_0 in both models may be seen in tables 7 and 8. As an average family size a figure in excess of five may seem to us very high, accustomed as we are to an average family size in our own society of around two children. But it needs to be remembered that we are referring here to *live births,* not necessarily to complete family size. High infant and early childhood mortality rates would mean that a significant proportion of these live births would not have survived into adulthood, as the l_x columns in tables 9 and 10 illustrate: Of 100,000 live births, only 45,734 and 43,123 respectively survive to the age of 20 years (see appendix B).

The degree of influence of differences in e_0 and GRR on growth rates may very usefully be illustrated by figure 10 (see appendix B). The vertical axis represents, on a logarithmic scale, different GRR values, from 1.5 to 3.4. The horizontal axis gives e_0 values from 20 to 30 years. The $p_{\hat{m}}$ scale on the horizontal axis measures the approximate probability of a female surviving from birth to the mean age of maternity; the product of the GRR and $p_{\hat{m}}$ is known as the net reproduction rate (NRR), that is, a value less than the GRR because allowance is being made for females who die before achieving reproductive capacity. In modern developed populations, where mortality levels at young ages are very low, $p_{\hat{m}}$ is nearly one and the NRR is thus practically equal to the GRR, since most females survive to the mean age of maternity. In a high mortality regime such as that of the Roman empire, the NRR is much lower in comparison with the GRR, with many females dying before reaching the average maternity age. Thus $p_{\hat{m}}$ is directly linked to mortality.[44]

Figure 10 shows, for example, that where $e_0 = 25$ years, a GRR of 2.543 will give a zero growth rate, that is, keep the population stationary. If the GRR were to rise to 2.926 (i.e., almost six live births per woman of reproductive age), the growth rate would as a result increase to 0.5 percent per year; one extra birth per woman is needed, in other words, to achieve such growth, a significant difference in fertility levels. Looking at the other axis, if the GRR remains the same, mortality rates would in effect need to change from an average life expectancy at birth of 25 years to an e_0 of nearly 30 years, for the growth rate to increase to 0.5 percent per year, again a very significant change in demographic terms.[45]

Figure 10, then, serves as a useful means of illustrating the way that changes in mortality and fertility levels may affect the rate of growth of a stable population, and of how significant such changes must be in order to bring about what are in appearance relatively small changes in the rate of growth. It may be noted that in a high mortality regime such as the one described here, increases in fertility levels will be made more difficult to achieve because such a significant proportion of females does not survive to a fertile age anyway—$p_{\dot{m}}$ is much lower than 1 and NRR is significantly lower than GRR. In view of this fact, one can reflect on the problems in the concept of the Augustan social legislation facing the legislators in their apparent attempt to increase the fertility of the elite class at Rome.

Taking a stationary population in which $e_0 = 25$ years, we can tabulate the effect on the age structure of the population (i.e., the C_x column in tables 9 and 10) of differing rates of both the GRR and of levels of growth. In table 11 (see appendix B), Coale-Demeny[2] Model West Level 3 female is used to show the effects on the age structure when the GRR varies from 2 to 3.5. Hence, for example, in a stable population where $e_0 = 25$ and GRR $= 2.5$, the proportion of people aged above 60 years is 7.15 percent of the total population; where GRR $= 3$, this proportion decreases to 5.47 percent. It should be clear from table 11 that as the GRR increases (i.e., with increased fertility) the population becomes younger, that is, there is a greater proportion of young as opposed to old people. In table 11, below these population percentage figures, are appended other values: first, the birth and death rates and the growth rate, r (expressed as a percentage). We already know that a GRR of 2.543 is needed to achieve a stationary population in this model, that is, a growth rate of zero. When the GRR falls below this mark, the death rate exceeds the birth rate, and the rate of growth is expressed as the difference between these two values. Note that for a GRR of 3.5 to exist in this population, the birth rate required is well in excess of 50 per 1,000, and is therefore unlikely in practice. The NRR is also given in table 11; it is significantly lower here than the GRR. Finally, the average age of the living population and the average age at death are given, to highlight the fact that as fertility levels increase, the population becomes correspondingly younger and more deaths occur in the younger age groups.

In table 12 the same population, Coale-Demeny[2] Model West

Level 3 female, is used to show the differences in age structure that occur under different levels of growth (see appendix B). The growth rate, r, varies from -1 to $+1$ percent per year. Where $r = 0$, that is, in a stationary population, the age structure of the population is that given in the C_x column of table 9. Where negative growth occurs, that is, when the death rate exceeds the birth rate, the proportion of young to old people becomes smaller. As the growth rate increases, the population becomes younger with increasing fertility, as highlighted at the bottom of table 12 by the increase in the GRR, and the decrease in average living age and the average age at death. The difference in age structure due to changes in the rate of population growth can be fairly significant. For example, in this model population, the percentage of people under the age of 15 years when $r = -0.5$ percent per year is 29.92 percent, but when $r = +0.5$ percent per year this proportion increases to 36.65 percent. In the same circumstances the proportion of those over the age of 60 years decreases from 8.51 to 5.68 percent. But what is even more striking is the increased level of fertility necessary to effect such a change. The birth rate must increase from 34.72 to 45.65 per 1,000, while the death rate is little affected. Similarly the GRR must increase by over 0.7, in other words an extra 1.5 children born per woman on average. Such increases may, in reality, be very difficult to achieve. It should be added, however, that a drastic lowering of fertility, especially through the extensive practice of efficient contraception, induced abortions, or frequent and prolonged breast-feeding (see chapter 3), may lead to quite significant falls in rates of growth in a population, where mortality levels remain largely unchanged. It is much simpler to limit fertility than to raise it when the level is already low, in a society in which the incidence of marriage is high and the age of first marriage low. This will be of great relevance when we come to discuss the apparent failure of the elite at Rome to reproduce itself, and the apparent failure of the Augustan social legislation to raise the fertility level of this class.

What I hope to have indicated in this section, with a general discussion of the construction of a life table and of the use of

model life tables, is that these methods and models are very useful tools in showing us the way that population dynamics work.
That the population of the Roman empire was not stationary or
stable is certainly true—no real population was or will be. But
the stable population theory offers the ancient historian a means
of understanding the basic structure of and possible changes occurring in an ancient population at a general level. It allows us
to make reasonable and probable assumptions about the mortality and fertility levels that existed in such a population, and to
understand the consequences of changes in these levels. The
tables used here give figures to several decimal places; the exact figures themselves are not so important, however, as are
their relative magnitude and their relationship to one another.
Furthermore, it must not be forgotten that averages tend to dis-
guise variations over geographical space (as well as between urban and rural areas), over time, and over class differences. I am
not suggesting that, for example, 6.98 percent of the population
of the Roman empire was over the age of 60 years, but that a
proportion of this magnitude is probable as a generalization
over space and time, and that the proportion of this age group,
the elderly, would have increased if fertility levels fell and the
population was in decline. Such approximate calculations can
be used, for example, to give probable answers to such questions
as the proportion of the Roman elite class who would survive
from birth to reach the minimum age for the consulship or who
would live to see a son reach such an age, the proportion of the
male population eligible for military service, or the numbers
who would live to see their grandchildren born, or to estimate
the probability of a 14-year-old male surviving to the age of 62
years (or whatever) and thereby enjoying tax exemption.[46] In
effect, the cautious and informed use of model life tables can
help us to gain a greater understanding of the population and of
the society of the ancient world, in ways that have hitherto been
unattainable because of the lack of direct and realistic data on
ancient populations.

Three

Demographic Impressions
of the Roman World

My main aim in the remaining sections of this book is to pinpoint some factors I think are relevant to a study of the demographic regime of the ancient world, particularly those factors in Roman society that had demographic consequences in terms of levels of mortality and fertility.[1] I am not attempting to cover in full the aspects I raise; much work has already been done on some subjects, others will require more study in future. Inevitably some familiar problems will reappear. Since for a discussion of this kind recourse must frequently be made to the ancient literature, we must again be wary of biases—of class and sex, for example—and of potentially misleading impressions. Enough has already been said of the dangers of using literary evidence as the sole basis for an argument on the extent or prevalence of a particular demographic phenomenon (such as rates of population growth and decline). But the literary evidence is still of use, at least to tell us something about the state of knowledge regarding population structure and dynamics at the time, if not also to guide us in our discussion of the relative importance of various factors that may have influenced population size and structure, such as contraception and infanticide.

The relationship between mortality and fertility in regard to population growth is a difficult question. The traditional view has long been that mortality levels set the tune and that changes in fertility levels follow as a natural consequence. Hence, where mortality is high, fertility will be high also, and where the mortality level falls, fertility will fall as a consequence. Debate about this view reaches a head in discussion of European demographic history from the eighteenth century and of the demographic transition that followed.[2] It is emerging that fertility may play a more important and independent role in population dynamics than had previously been suspected, and may directly influence mortality levels, rather than vice versa.[3] In the long term over the course of history, however, levels of mortality and fertility probably remained "at closely similar levels."[4] For the Roman empire, our model is of high death rates, with a correspondingly high birth rate if the population size was to be maintained at a fairly stationary level. What this means in reality needs now to be considered, first in terms of mortality.

Mortality

A population in which mortality and fertility levels are consistently high is referred to as a "high pressure" regime. To generalize, we are working with a stable population model where birth and death rates are both around 40 per 1,000 per year, with only short-term fluctuations; average life expectancy at birth is in the region of 25 years, and the gross reproduction rate is about 2.5 to 3 (i.e., on average each woman bore five or six children). In terms of mortality and age structure, this means that about 30 percent of an original birth cohort dies in its 1st year, and 50 percent dies before the age of 10 years. From that age on life is somewhat less hazardous. Of those who reach age 5, over 80 percent will reach age 20 and over 30 percent age 60 years. It is mainly the severe rates of mortality at infancy and childhood that produce such a low expectation of life at birth. Those who survive to age 5 can on average expect to live at least another 40 years (for all these figures, see the tables relating to chapter 2).

It is impossible to give a simple breakdown of the relative importance of different causes of death in the ancient world;[5] tombstones very rarely record (alleged) cause of death, and the medical knowledge of the time being what it was, the extant medical literature offers few clues. What *can* be said is that causes of death now are quite different on the whole than the causes were then. Today degenerative diseases, that is, endogenous mortality, account for most deaths—ischemic heart disease, cerebrovascular disease, and cancer, to name some obvious examples. Historically the predominant form of mortality was due to famine, epidemics, or war (Malthus's positive checks)—exogenous mortality. Exogenous mortality levels are dictated largely by environmental conditions (notably hygiene, sanitation, and nutrition), as well as by standards of medical practice; obviously war has other factors that also contribute. As such conditions and levels of skill have improved, deaths through such causes have been progressively, though not yet completely, eliminated. In the ancient world exogenous mortality was high to a great extent because of the conditions of life, any account of which, particularly for the crowded city of Rome, makes grim reading.[6] Attempts have been made to highlight specific aspects of ancient society that might have led to high mortality (and even to the fall of the empire), one favorite being lead poisoning.[7] But it probably makes more sense to consider the *underlying* causes for high mortality, as with other preindustrial populations, in the general conditions of life, whether for the elite or for the poor. The latter may have suffered to a greater degree, due to undernourishment and a less sanitary environment, but at both ends of the social scale, especially in urban areas, infectious diseases would have taken their toll indiscriminately.[8]

It has been suggested in the previous chapter that the infant mortality rate (IMR) in the early Roman empire was around 300 per 1,000 per year.[9] This compares with a rate in the modern developed world of less than 10 per 1,000, an extreme difference;[10] in poorer countries, on the other hand, the IMR ranges from 50 to over 200 per 1,000. Infant mortality was and is due to a combination of endogenous and exogenous mortality.[11] In the time immediately following birth, when the newborn infant is particularly vulnerable and may suffer from birth trauma, the risk of mortality is the highest, even today, and such severe mortality risk must have been far more prevalent in ancient times.[12]

It is one thing to realize that the infant mortality rate in the Roman empire was high and to suggest an order of magnitude based on comparative evidence; it is quite another to try to measure the rate by reference to literary or inscriptional evidence.[13] As discussed in chapter 1, records of infant burials are drastically underrepresented in the extant funerary inscriptions. One can point to isolated instances from the literary sources where high mortality rates are recorded (though not necessarily infant deaths). Perhaps the most famous and most frequently quoted example in this context is that of Cornelia, mother of the brothers Gracchi, who had 12 children[14] and who was to become a symbol and an ideal of maternal fertility and discipline.[15] Apparently all 12 children were born between 163 B.C. and the death of Tiberius senior around 152 B.C.[16] At any rate, of these 12 all survived their father, but only 3 (the two famous boys and one sister) survived childhood, and—so it is alleged—none survived their mother.[17]

Similar cases of high fertility and high mortality may be pointed to. Agrippina and Germanicus had 9 children, 6 boys and 3 girls, only 6 of whom survived their father. Quintilian laments the loss of his young wife, as well as of his two young sons who died at age 4 and 9 years. Fronto, of 6 children born to his wife, had only 1 daughter left, while Marcus Aurelius and his wife Faustina had at least 12 children, of whom only 1 son, Commodus, survived to adulthood.[18] Interesting as these cases are, they are highly selective and tell us nothing of the general demographic realities of the time. Nor are direct comparisons with more modern populations to be regarded as indicative of the infant mortality rate of the ancient world, except perhaps as indicators of possible orders of magnitude.[19] An IMR of 250–300 per 1,000 is what may be expected from comparative preindustrial history, though much higher rates are possible, especially among populations that practice no or only minimal breast-feeding of infants. A society in which such a high rate of infant mortality existed, together with high childhood mortality, might therefore, it could be suggested, view the death of their small children quite differently and perhaps with less grief or concern than we do today.[20] This is one of many aspects of life in ancient society where the situation was so different from today that judging actions or situations by our own moral or ethical criteria would be unjustified and misleading. There are many indications that, at least in theory, parents were able to deal philosophically with the death of an infant son or daughter, but at the same time there are indications of parents whose grief was very powerful and presumably very real. That infants were not regularly accorded full burial or commemoration, as noted earlier, should not be interpreted simply as parental indifference.

One aspect of infant mortality in the ancient world that has generated a great deal of controversy and interest among scholars in recent years, perhaps because it is so foreign to our own cultural morality, is that of infanticide. An enormous amount has been written on this phenomenon, so much in fact that the subject is fast becoming a literary *topos* in its own right.[21] Whole books could (and no doubt soon will) be written on infanticide in the ancient world, but I doubt that our knowledge on it will be much extended. The evidence for the practice of infanticide from the literary sources is sketchy and heavily moralistic. Often the practice of "exposure" is confused with that of infanticide, by writers both ancient and modern.[22] How often exposure did in fact result in the death of the infant is unknown, as is the prevalence of exposure or the extent of willful infanticide.[23] One can with some confidence apply demographic models to gauge the extent of natural processes, but one cannot use such models to measure the effects of social customs and practices. The "demographic" argument in this context has focused on whether extensive infanticide, by which seems to be meant 10 percent or more of all live births, was theoretically possible. It is clearly right that extensive infanticide was *possible* in demographic terms,[24] yet this is far from proof that infanticide was extensively practiced in antiquity (much of the literary evidence relates to the Greek world of the fourth century B.C), only that it was theoretically possible. A recent discussion of the relevance of these demographic arguments dismisses them as "simplistic and blind-sighted" on the grounds that the significance of infanticide is not so much in how extensive it was as in the fact that it actually occurred at all and was a perceived threat to all newborn infants.[25] True enough, but the demographic question is of relevance to ancient demographic studies all the same.

Another point worth noting is that many of those who were killed in infancy would most likely have died in infancy and early childhood anyway, since the killing of physically defective children was apparently routine. So perhaps more pertinent questions to ask in this context are, what constituted physical defectiveness,[26] and what proportion of live births in antiquity might one expect to have been "defective"? Again answers are not apparent, but at least comparative evidence may be more applicable if the right questions are asked. Patterson discusses other categories of infants who might have been exposed: illegitimate children, children of families whose numbers were already large or who suffered from poverty, and "unwanted" females.[27] Some of these categories, in particular the poor, she regards as generalizations that may not reflect reality, though poverty is a very real reason for parents not being able to bring up all their children.[28] Patterson quite rightly, however, points out that such general categories as these may mean something quite different at the individual family level; there is a vast difference between a general recognition that certain infants are routinely exposed and an individual decision to expose one's own son or daughter. It was the father, the *paterfamilias*, who decided the infant's fate, not the state.[29] Dionysius of Halicarnassus mentions a "law of Romulus" whereby all Romans were obliged to raise all their male children and the firstborn of their daughters.[30] Furthermore, no child under the age of 3 years could be killed unless he or she was "maimed or monstrous from birth"; such infants were allowed to be exposed with the approval of five neighbors. Those who disobeyed this "law" were punished, most notably by the loss of half their property. Yet elsewhere Dionysius states that "all of the proper age were obliged to marry and to rear *all* their children."[31] Quite apart from this inconsistency about the exposure of daughters, it may be doubted whether the Romulan law existed in reality in the archaic history of Rome or whether it was in fact invented in later times as part of the moralistic tradition. A wealth of sources can be and have been collected to show that exposure and infanticide were widespread and were not.[32] Literary tradition and isolated historical incidents may not represent everyday reality, and generalizations tend to overlook differences in time and place, such as different economic circumstances.

In all this, exposure and infanticide become too easily confounded. Exposure can be widespread without willful infanticide being widely practiced if a significant number of exposed children were in fact taken up and reared by others, whether as adopted members of a family or as slaves, prostitutes, or whatever.[33] Again, there is some evidence for such survival, but no way to measure the extent of it. Laws to prevent infanticide only appear in the late fourth century A.D.,[34] but *not* laws to prevent exposure. That some considered exposure as tantamount to infanticide may be comforting but it is not very relevant.[35] Even the extent of exposure may have been exaggerated; it was certainly a practice that was commented upon, but this need not necessarily mean that it was common, only that it was noticed, without any idea of numbers.[36] The traditional assumption, for example, that people in Roman Egypt with names linked to *kopros* ("dung") were foundlings left on dunghills has been well refuted recently by Sarah Pomeroy, with 279 examples: the names may relate to the *tradition* of a foundling in the family ancestry but not necessarily mean that the person himself or herself was exposed at birth.[37] I do not mean to imply that infanticide, or even exposure, was not widely practiced in antiquity, only that the evidence does not allow us to generalize on the practice as a social phenomenon. Too much attention is paid to this aspect without considering infant mortality as a whole. Even if social practice as compared with "natural causes" did have a significant effect on the infant mortality rate, it may also be asked whether this manifested itself only in the abandonment or killing of children, or may also have found expression in so-called benign neglect, the deliberate, or even unconscious, favoring of firstborn or male offspring to the detriment of others, particularly of female children. Aristotle states that females require less food than males, and Xenophon implies that most Greeks put such a notion into practice.[38] Roman authors, perhaps characteristically, seem to have had no interest in the question, but we know that in the Italian alimentary schemes of the second century A.D. girls received a lower payment than boys and for less time.[39] The literary evidence for benign neglect is sparse, but then it is a practice much less striking than exposure and infanticide, particularly to an aristocratic male audience.

This possible difference in practices of exposure, infanticide, and neglect between the two sexes inevitably leads us to a consideration of the sex ratio. By convention the sex ratio is expressed as the number of males for every 100 females in a population. At birth, as a general rule, the ratio is around 105; that is, slightly more males are born than females, but this slight imbalance tends to have balanced out by the end of early childhood.[40] The sex ratio of any age group in a population need not necessarily be 100, due to sex differences in mortality and migration. In the modern world it is well known that female mortality is lower than that of males, that women have a higher average life expectancy at birth than do men.[41] But in India in 1971, for example, female mortality was higher than for males, "probably due to worse malnutrition among young females and the risks of maternity."[42] As a consequence, the sex ratio for the population of India at this time remained above 100 at all ages.

What of the ancient world? Attempts have frequently been made to gauge the sex ratio from inscriptional evidence. This method leads almost invariably to an image of marked male predominance.[43] The ratio varies sharply, however, according to age. Similarly, in the census data from Roman Egypt, although the overall ratio is 103.6, there are significant fluctuations of an uneven nature over the life-course.[44] In the case of the Italian

Demographic Impressions of the Roman World

alimentary schemes, the sex ratio appears very extreme. From the Table of Veleia (*CIL* 11.1147), where 300 children are recorded as beneficiaries, we find 264 boys and only 76 girls, an apparent sex ratio of 733.33. Obviously this is not an accurate reflection of the sex ratio at any age, at least not of a natural population. Rather it represents *social realities*: more males received the *alimenta*, for whatever reason.[45] Sarah Pomeroy has stated that the sex ratio indicated in historical documents "reveals the practice [of female exposure] to serious scholars."[46] To support such an argument and to show that exposure and infanticide were more common for females than for males, stock literary references are frequently cited by various scholars.[47] But again one cannot generalize from isolated incidents or literary references. More substantial evidence seems to come from the inscriptional records of Greek immigrants to Miletus of the late third and early second centuries B.C.[48] The sex ratio for 762 immigrants is 294.8, in other words, almost 3 males for every 1 female, and there is no *obvious* reason why females would not have been recorded here if they existed. However, apart again from the fact that this sample cannot be regarded as indicative of the entire ancient world, it is also worth pointing out that the ratio of children to adults in this sample (215:548) is very strange, and that the sample may therefore represent an unnatural population, where children and females are heavily underrepresented. The data do in fact relate to mercenaries, so perhaps the unusual character of the sex ratio is not so surprising. In short, I would not agree with Pomeroy's statement that this sort of evidence reveals the practice and extent of female exposure. It is *possible* that more females than males died in their 1st year of life because of social practices such as exposure, infanticide, or neglect. But this does not mean that such practices led to marked imbalances in the sex ratio at later ages, or that such a male predominance, even if it did exist, is proved by the inscriptional evidence. What this kind of evidence does highlight is perhaps rather the inferior position of females in a male world.

Dio states that, in 18 B.C., "the free-born population [of

Rome] contained far more males than females."[49] Before one can accept such a bold statement as fact, however, one must ask how Dio arrived at such a conclusion. Presumably it reflects observed conditions among the upper classes (the context is the Augustan marriage legislation). Could one accurately make such an observation? We have already commented in chapter 1 on the problems inherent in the interpretation of contemporary observations: perceived reality may be something quite different from reality itself. On the other hand, the aristocracy at Rome was such a small proportion of the population as a whole that the sort of marked imbalance in the sex ratio that Dio implies for 18 B.C. as an observation may be close to the truth.[50] Among such a small group such an imbalance might have been observable.

But having said this, we must note the context of Dio's statement. It is presented as part of the introduction to Augustus's marriage laws: in 18 B.C. the *lex Iulia de maritandis ordinibus*. Later, with the *lex Papia Poppaea* of A.D. 9, Dio has Augustus address in the forum the *equites,* who are divided into two groups, those who are unmarried and those who are married.[51] The members of the second group, Dio records, "were far fewer in numbers than the former." Both passages, and in particular Augustus's speeches to the two groups of equestrians in A.D. 9, are heavily imbued with propaganda and oratory for effect. Dio's statements of "demographic reality" are in fact, I would suggest, to be interpreted in the same way—bold statements designed to emphasize at a much later date the nature of the Roman society, particularly at the aristocratic level, that Augustus sought to remedy and improve.[52] Such statements are bound to be enhanced for effect with some degree of generalization or exaggeration, and at any rate the observation is secondhand at best: 200 years might tend to distort the details.

That the sex ratio of the Roman aristocracy in 18 B.C., as at other times, was over 100 is perhaps right, due to various social practices that favored the advancement or indeed the survival of males over females. That it was significantly male-dominant I find unlikely or at least unproven. Simple observation on the streets of Rome of even a minority like the aristocracy would tend to give an illusion of male supremacy in numbers. A significant number of bachelors in a society need not reflect a shortage of eligible females; it may have more to do with the expectations of elite males and the apparent advantages of bachelorhood and especially of childlessness.[53] Again there is the problem of contemporary literary sources and of their value in estimating demographic trends. But what is perhaps more relevant in this context is the apparently widespread *belief* that being married and having children were disadvantageous. Such a belief, whether based on reality or not, may have considerably affected the proportions who married and hence it may have had a direct effect on the demographic regime of the period, especially among the aristocracy.

If secure and convincing evidence for the extent of the difference in the sex ratio in Roman society is lacking, the possibility remains nevertheless that such an imbalance did exist in reality. The reasons why males might be preferred as offspring to females, as some sources indicate, are varied, according to some extent to the social class we are dealing with. Leaving aside for the moment the question of the perceived optimum number of children as a whole, one possible reason for a Roman aristocrat hoping for a son rather than a daughter was the alleged financial burden of providing a dowry for the daughter.[54] However, it has recently been shown that in Roman society, as opposed to that of Greece, dowries were not as substantial as is often supposed: "relatively small but not negligible . . . dowries usually did not play a very large part either in aristocrats' strategies for financial success or in their financial ruin."[55] So while a father might have hoped for a son so as to avoid having to provide a dowry in later years for a daughter, one might wonder whether he would have automatically exposed a daughter or would rather have accepted the fact that a girl had been born. Abandoning offspring is, after all, quite a dramatic move, and it was perhaps dictated more by necessity than by the concern over the loss in fifteen or so years' time of a "relatively small but not negligible" amount. Of course we are faced with the problem that not only do we not have evidence for the extent of such abandonment, but we do not know the emotions of those who did expose their offspring. But again the negative aspect of financial expense in having a daughter might in a father's mind have been compensated by the prospect of a useful marriage alliance—if not also by paternal joy at having a daughter!

At the other end of the social scale and perhaps more realistically, a son held the promise of maintenance in the parents' old age, whereas a daughter might be expected to leave the family house at a young age and to have no independent means to support her parents. This makes sense, but, if it was true to any significant extent, the literature is strangely silent on it, perhaps because Roman aristocratic writers and readers had no worries about their financial well-being in old age. Here as elsewhere, one must be wary of equating public, male, aristocratic attitudes with general reality. While tombstone inscriptions for young children may sometimes express the parents' grief at the death because of the loss of potential solace and support in old age,[56] no differentiation emerges as to sex.

The question extends beyond sex ratios to comparative mortality levels between the two sexes. As noted, women in the modern developed world live on average some 6 years longer than males. In the discussion of mortality models in chapter 2, no differentiation was attempted between males and females. The models are meant to represent general trends, not sex-specific ones. The models used here are called "female" but, as stressed, they should not in this instance be regarded as applicable only to females. The parallel "male" tables given in Coale-Demeny[2] uniformly give higher male mortality, at varying degrees of difference between the four regions. This is on the analogy with modern developed countries, but need not be true of ancient populations, as indeed it is still not true of all Third World countries. So, in our discussion of the model life tables, we have focused on the "female" life tables without suggesting that the associated "male" life table is relevant or that the "female" table reflects only female mortality.[57] The reason I have not up to now attempted to give male and female tables is that I do not believe that we can be sure of the difference in mortality levels for the two genders in the ancient world. Even if mortality for females was higher in infancy than for males, this may affect e_0 but not expectation of life in adult years.

That, contrary to the modern-day trend in most developed countries, males on average lived longer than females in antiquity, is quite likely.[58] It is a common feature of preindustrial, high-mortality societies, as with some Third World countries today, where higher female than male mortality in early childhood is also common. We need now to consider reasons why female life expectancy at birth may have been lower than that for males in antiquity, and the answer seems readily at hand, so often is it stated by modern scholars.

Dixon states, without references, that "It is accepted that women had a lower median expectation of life than men, but that their expectations [*sic*] were higher if they survived the dangerous reproductive years."[59] That this view is accepted as fact is overstating the case. Dixon is clearly influenced by the demographic study published by Burn in 1953 and his use of inscriptional evidence to calculate median life expectancies.[60] Burn describes the apparent differences in male and female mortality as evidenced in the tombstone data as "the most striking—one might almost say sensational—discovery emerging from these figures." In short, he calculated that median life expectancy at age 15 for males exceeded that for females by 5 years or more. The reason for this difference is, Burn insists, obvious: there is, he states, "no reason for hesitation over accepting the evidence of a very heavy female mortality at reproductive ages under the empire."[61] This view has been accepted and widely repeated, and has the appearance of being authoritative.[62] But it is not that simple or that evident.

The largely overlooked study by Appleton in 1920 preempted Burn in many ways, in its use of the inscriptional evidence to indicate "la mortalité vraiment effrayante qui sévit sur les femmes de la classe aisée . . . pendant la période de maternité possible." In reviewing earlier discussion of this aspect of female mortality[63] and discussing possible causes, he veered away from the conventional talk of the precocity of marriage and "les dangeurs de l'accouchement" to consider the often fatal results of induced abortion.[64] Appleton's brief discussion is illuminating and ahead of its time; it is unfortunate that many subsequent scholars failed to take note of his arguments.

However, in this context, the inscriptional evidence is misleading. Hopkins has shown that the numerical superiority of females over males on tombstone inscriptions in the 15–29 age group cannot be attributed solely to increased female mortality levels in these years. As noted in chapter 1, women of this age bracket probably enjoyed "heightened social estimation" as being (usually) both wives and daughters, and they were therefore more likely to be commemorated than females of other ages. Likewise, wives could only be commemorated by their husbands if they predeceased them. As females were in general some 10 years younger than their spouses, wives were more likely to receive commemoration if they died relatively young, from whatever cause.[65] It might be added that in the data from the censuses held in Roman Egypt (see table 1), females again outnumber males in the 10–39 age groups, as well as in the 60–69 group. But this cannot be held to be due to increased female mortality, since the census returns record *living* individuals. Again, the more plausible explanation is that females of these age groups enjoyed heightened status and a greater chance of being recorded. Burn's evidence, therefore, rests as much—if not more—on social customs as on real mortality levels.

Certainly in preindustrial societies maternal mortality was higher than it is in developed societies today, due to such factors as poorer standards of hygiene, less efficient medical practices (particularly in regard to abortion), and increased vulnerability to disease during pregnancy.[66] But there is a tendency to exaggerate the effects of maternity on female mortality rates in history. This fact is well demonstrated in a recent paper by Schofield, who examines rates for England from 1550 to 1849. Traditionally historians, as with ancient Rome, had assumed severe mortality levels in this period. But Schofield shows that the rate was on average around the 10 to 15 per 1,000 level for females aged 15 to 49 years,[67] varying depending on the age of the mother and the number of children she had previously given birth to. This rate is still high, to be sure,[68] but it is nowhere near as high as had been previously supposed. I would suggest that similar generalizations and unfounded presumptions on the severity of maternal mortality in antiquity are likewise exaggerated. Individual cases can be found, but they tell us nothing about the real extent. That difficult births did take place is certain, then as now;[69] that babies were born stillborn is likewise inevitable, though the literary references are surprisingly few; that many babies died in the period immediately following birth as part of birth trauma is certain. But that a very significant number of mothers died giving birth or that maternity was a *demographically* significant factor in differentiating between male and female average life expectancy (even if it was perceived as such) is unproved and unlikely on comparative grounds.[70] Similarly, the assumption that women who survived their reproductive years had a higher life expectancy than males of the same age is assuming too much. It is not, I would maintain, maternal mortality that is the primary explanation for the low sex ratios at ages 15 to 39 years, but, as with the general picture of apparent mortality to be derived from funerary inscriptions, this bias is due to questions of commemorative practice. One must add, however, that mortality may have been higher for females than for males, but the inscriptional data cannot be used as evidence for this. At best we must rely on comparative evidence. The extent of such differences, if they existed at all, remains uncertain.

We remain, then, with probable models that are not sex-specific. Moving now to the end of the life-course, what was the maximum possible life-span in antiquity? Demographically this question is only of significant interest if maximum life-span was different in antiquity than it is today, or if a considerable number of people in ancient societies reached such an age, thus distorting the figure for average life expectancy. We have seen in chapter 1 with the alleged centenarians of Roman Africa that a significant number of people recorded as living into extreme old age can distort the e_x value upward, especially for figures of life expectancy at high ages. It is worth looking briefly, then, at notions of maximum life-span, in order to consider their demographic importance.

The first very important point to realize is that, despite the "demographic transition" and the advances in medicine this century, a person does not live significantly longer today than his or her ancestor did in the historical past. The simple fact is that *more* people survive into old age today, not that they live any longer than the elderly in past times.[71] This is not the place to consider in depth the biological phenomenon of human aging; enough to say that it remains imperfectly understood exactly what causes and regulates the aging process, and it is unclear whether medicine will ever be able to significantly extend the human life-span. We may eventually be able to eradicate most forms of exogenous mortality and even to alleviate degenerative diseases to such an extent that people live healthier lives into extreme old age. But the chances are that people will not live considerably beyond a certain limit, the maximum potential life-span. No precise figure can be given for such a limit—something around 115 (± 5?) years seems to be about right.

In dealing with records of longevity in history we have the obvious problem of the reliability of our sources, which is as much a problem for antiquity as it is for more recent history.[72] How do we know whether an apparent Methuselah really did live as long as a literary source or a tombstone inscription claims? Objectivity in such cases can be difficult. Comparative evidence tells us that the number of alleged centenarians in Roman Africa is a gross exaggeration. But that is not to say that *some* people did not survive the century mark and beyond.

Pliny the Elder was at least aware of the problem. In a quite lengthy section on human longevity,[73] he begins by stating that various fabulous ages attributed to legendary figures are "uncertain" due to problems of chronology ("inscitia temporum"). Pliny dismisses such stories as Arganthonius king of the Tartesii living to the age of 150 years, yet a few paragraphs later he states that it is admitted fact ("confessum") that Arganthonius reigned for 80 years, from his 40th year of age.[74] To ignorance of chronology we might add ignorance of precise age. Whole races of people, mostly far distant if not mythical, were routinely credited with fantastic life-spans, just as were various species of animals who were synonymous with long life. Various kings, poets, and seers of archaic times were credited with ages well in excess of a century, sometimes with spurious accuracy.[75] Figures of 300 or 500 years occur for pseudohistorical individuals, while mythical characters, such as Tithonus, Teiresias, and the Sibyls, were attributed with lives of several centuries, if not of eternity. Old age was conventionally associated with wisdom, since the time of Homer's Nestor at least, and so, for example, the Seven Sages of Greece were not surprisingly credited with extended life-spans.[76] Likewise Pythagoras in the sixth century is credited with 80 or 90 years, though Galen gives a figure of 117 years.[77] This confusion concerning ages at death is a common one, and it seems clear that often the age of someone long dead, especially of someone famous, tended to be exaggerated more and more as time went on and as circumstances suited.

Nevertheless, in reaching more "historical" times, there is ample evidence of people surviving into their 90s and beyond, and often there is little reason to doubt the figures quoted. A brief, representative sample is given in the next section; for brevity's sake, most references are omitted.

Examples of Very Old Greeks and Romans Xenophanes of Colophon, philosopher and poet of the sixth and fifth centuries, lived to the age of at least 91 years, 67 of them as an exile; other accounts say he lived to be more than 100. Another poet, Simonides of Ceos, lived around the same time as Xenophanes, and died at about the age of 90. The old comic poet Epicharmus died at the age of either 90 or 97 years. Sophocles was about 90 when he wrote his last extant play, and apparently died in his late 90s. The philosopher Empedocles (fifth century) highlights the varying life-spans attributed to a single individual: Diogenes Laertius (8.52–74) quotes figures of 60, 77, and 109 years. Probably the most striking case of longevity from antiquity is that of Gorgias of Leontini, a sophist of the fifth and early fourth centuries, for whom all sources agree on a life-span of 107 to 109 years and, so tradition has it, his health never deteriorated (one of his secrets for long life was said to be that he never accepted an invitation to dinner!). The comic poet Cratinus lived to be 97, the philosopher Democritus to either 104 or even 109 years, and the lyric poet Timotheus into his 90s. Euctemon, a wealthy Athenian (ca. 460–364 B.C.) lived to the age of 96 years, as Isaeus records, and the orator Isocrates to 98 or 99 years. The historian Xenophon lived to be over 90, the comedian Alexis of Thurii apparently to 106,[78] the poet Philemon to at least 97, the historian Timaeus to 96, the Stoic philosopher Cleanthes to 98 or 99, the philosopher Timon to around 90, and Zeno the Stoic of Citium to 98 (though other authorities give figures as low as 72 years). Hieron II, tyrant of Syracuse, is said to have ruled for 70 years and to have died at the age of 90 or 92. Ctesibius the inventor and historian died at the age of 104 while out for a walk (though one manuscript reading gives 124 years—probably a case of an extra 20 years being thrown in for good measure). In later times the historian Hieronymus of Cardia died at the age of 104 years, Xenophilus the musician at 105 years or more, and Lucian's Cynic Demonax starved himself to death when nearly 100 years old.

Turning now to Roman figures (which for various reasons are rather more difficult to find than their Greek counterparts), the grammarian Orbilius Pupillus is recorded by Suetonius as dying at almost 100 years of age. Valerius Corvus, six times consul in the second half of the fourth century B.C., lived to be 100. Caecilius Metellus in the third century was *pontifex maximus* for 22 years and died at the age of 100 years also (the round figure is suspicious). Massinissa, a famous king of Numidia in the third and second centuries, reigned for 60 years, had a son at the age of 86, and died 4 years later. Marcus Perperna, consul in 92 B.C. and later censor, lived to be 98, while Servilius Vatia, consul in 79 B.C., died aged 90. Cicero's secretary and friend Tiro lived to be 100, and Cicero's first wife Terentia was 103 years old at her death. Piso, consul in 15 B.C., was *praefectus urbis* for 20 years and died at 80 of natural causes. Volusius Saturninus, *consul suffectus* in A.D. 3, died as *praefectus urbis* in A.D. 56 at the age of 93 years,[79] the same age as Seneca the Elder. Gaius Manlius Valens reached his first consulship at the ripe age of 90 years and died in office, while Iulius Ursus Servianus, three times consul, was forced by Hadrian to commit suicide at the age of 90 years. Less prestigious personalities also emerge: Statilia (or Sattia) in the time of Claudius is recorded as dying at the age of 99 years (cf. Pliny, *Nat. Hist.* 7.48.158; Seneca, *Ep.* 77.20; Martial 3.93.20; *CIL* 6.9590 = *ILS* 9434), the actress Lucceia at at least 100 years while still performing, and one Clodia, a mother of 15 children, died at the age of 115 years. Women, it may be noticed, are few in this list, but this is a reflection of a male world, not necessarily of higher female mortality in younger years. A Sabine slave belonging to Hadrian, named Faustus, is said by Phlegon to have lived to be 136, and one Lucius Terentius of Bononia was recorded in the census of A.D. 74 to be 135 years old.

These figures range from the quite possible to the highly suspect, and doubts remain as to their accuracy in many cases, particularly with the individuals listed from the census of A.D. 74 by Pliny and Phlegon. Typical of the extreme is one Zocles, a Samothracian of whom, according to Pliny,[80] Mucianus wrote that he saw in the first century A.D. at the age of 140 years, having just grown a new set of teeth!

But while the borderlines between history, fable, and myth may at times become hazy, it does emerge both that some people in antiquity lived into extreme old age, just as some (and proportionately many more) do today, and that ancient writers were aware of the fact, and sometimes dwelt on it at some length. Notions of maximum life-span do occur in antiquity, though without any wide consensus and usually without reference to purely biological aspects of aging. A certain mathematical and astrological atmosphere pervades many of the references, due largely to Greek influences. Favorites for maximum life-span are numbers that are multiples of seven, of nine, or both (63 years was regarded by some as a limit).[81] One estimate of maximum life-span goes as low as 54 years, at least for some people.[82] Pliny the Younger states that few exceed the age of 67 years, and Solon speaks of a figure of 70 years, though this was later amended to 80 in the light of his own experience, apparently.[83] Hesiod stated that 96 years was a limit, while 100 years was a natural favorite for many.[84] Such a limit is also reflected in the traditional timing of the secular games, 100 or 110 years.[85]

These figures are somewhat on the low side. Often, however, ancient estimates of maximum life-span are strikingly similar to our own figure of around 115 years. Pliny gives a variety of figures derived from "sideralis scientiae sententia," ranging from 112 years as a practically impossible upper limit, to more than 116 years, and 124 in Italy, while a figure of 120 years emerges as a common notion of maximum life-span.[86]

Enough figures and references. What I hope emerges from all this is the recognition of an awareness in antiquity that some people could and did live well beyond the life-span of the average individual. We cannot deduce from all this, however, how many lived to such advanced ages, but clearly they were regarded as exceptional. That the proportion of centenarians in antiquity was in reality far smaller than it is in the modern world today is an obvious assumption. The model life tables described in chapter 2 would suggest that in a stationary population with average life expectancy at birth of 25 years and where the risk of dying increases sharply after the age of 50 years,[87] only 30 to 60 individuals from an original cohort of 100,000 would on average survive to the age of 90 years, at which age average life expectancy would have been less than 2 years. Of this group only a handful would have reached the age of 95 years. This number would increase very slightly only if the population was in decline, that is, if fertility was relatively low.

In other words, only a very select few ancient Greeks and Romans could have genuinely boasted of passing the century mark, and demographically that is not significant, however significant it may have been to those individuals at the time. While many of the "records" of ancient centenarians should be regarded as fabrications, whether on tombstone inscriptions in Africa or in census returns from Italy, there is every reason to believe that Gorgias did indeed live to be 108 years of age. But it is certainly just as true that at that advanced age Gorgias must have been very aware that he was alone of his generation.

This much, then, on mortality. The general impression is of a high mortality regime, with relatively high infant mortality, around 300 per 1,000, but considerably lower mortality rates among the older age groups. As has been discussed already, the factor that probably affected population dynamics more over time, space, and social class was fertility, a factor that could be influenced to a greater degree than could mortality by social customs and attitudes.[88] It is to that factor that we will now turn in the final section of this study.

Fertility

It has already been seen in our discussion of the model life tables that in a stable population with high mortality levels, a high fertility rate is required to maintain the population size. In a stationary population with an average life expectancy at birth of 25 years, a gross reproduction rate of over 2.5 is required; that is, each woman on average needs to bear 2.5 daughters, or about five children. In such a situation a GRR of only 2 (i.e., four children) will mean the population is declining by some 1 percent every year, a drop in the birth rate from 40 to around 30 per 1,000. Such a drop in fertility would therefore lead to a severe decline in the long term. We need now to consider ways in which fertility levels in Roman society may have been affected, in particular by social practices of the time.[89]

Fertility levels are affected by many variables, such as the age at first marriage of both males and females, the "spacing" of children, the use and efficacy of contraceptive and abortive techniques, the extent of breast-feeding, the level of natural sterility in the society, and the social "rules" governing celibacy, nonmarriage, and remarriage. That the aristocratic class at Rome was aware of ways by which fertility might be influenced is clear enough from the legislation enacted at various times, particularly under Augustus, which aimed to some degree to increase fertility levels. But at the same time it needs to be noted that it is very difficult to increase general fertility levels or indeed to improve social mores through legislation. That much is still true today, but even more so in ancient times when high mortality levels at younger ages lowered the numbers of females reaching and living through their reproductive years.[90]

Fertility levels in demographic terms are customarily measured against the very high levels achieved by a religious community, the Hutterites, who live in the High Plains of the northern United States and southern Canada, and who, while not marrying at a particularly young age, practice no form of contraception (what is known as "natural fertility"), breast-feed only for a short time, and thus have achieved the highest known fertility levels for which reliable information is available.[91] Average family size in this community is over 10 (i.e., a GRR of over 5). Certainly individual cases have been recorded from elsewhere where a woman has given birth over 20 times,[92] but here we are talking about the *average* number of births per woman in a population. By comparison the GRR of most modern developed countries is usually around 1, the replacement level, or even below. Where mortality levels are much higher, as in the ancient world, the replacement level is correspondingly high.

So a total marital fertility rate of around five is not impossible, even if a situation of "natural fertility" does not exist. If a mother in the ancient world during her reproductive career gave birth to five children, the chances are that only one would survive to the age of 55 or 60 years.[93] Our information on family size in the ancient world is severely limited. We may know how many children (or often only sons) were born without knowing how many survived to adulthood, but usually the reverse is true: we know only of those who survived, not how many were born originally. A few examples of high fertility (and high mortality) were already given. Generally a family with more than two adult children would have been considered remarkable.[94] Attempts to calculate family size from literary sources are limited by the amount of information available and the uneven nature of the data produced;[95] a large family might be mentioned simply be-

cause it was unusual, daughters often remain anonymous or un-
mentioned, and ancient authors rarely show any demographic
interest in average family size. The use of the Egyptian census
data is more promising, though the sample is small. It has been
calculated, on the assumption of an average expectation of life
at birth of 20 to 22 years, that families *with children* (in other
words childless couples are not considered, thereby inflating the
GRR) on average had between six or seven children per
mother.[96] But this figure is misleadingly high for the very reason
that couples without children are omitted. It tells us only that
some households were very large. Nor can this be considered as
typical of the Roman empire as a whole, since a quite different
marriage pattern appears to have operated in Egypt at this time
(see further discussion). On average the size of households in
Roman Egypt as calculated from the census returns was around
six, including parents and slaves.[97]

What did arouse the interest of many ancient authors in this
regard were the novelties. Superfetation, for example, held some
fascination.[98] Alleged cases of prodigious fertility were remarked upon, particularly instances from Egypt and Africa
where fertility—of the inhabitants as well as of the soil—was
traditionally held to be high and produced many novelties. Five
children at one birth seems to have been the established record,
with an oft-quoted case from Egypt.[99] Apparently one woman
gave birth to 5 children on four separate occasions. Pliny also
mentions a woman who gave birth 30 times in her lifetime; he
goes on to relate stories of women giving birth to elephants and
snakes, so perhaps too much credence in his narrative at this
point is unjustified. Aulus Gellius adds a case from the time of
Augustus where a mother gave birth to 5 children—all 6 died as
a result. In contrast to this, we have already seen the case of a
woman who gave birth to 15 children in total and who lived to
the age of 115 years.[100]

To return to less fantastic figures, twins are quite commonly
referred to.[101] But the high infant mortality rate combined with
superstition to produce the apparent belief that, when one twin
is male and the other female, only rarely will both survive. Mar-

tial composes an epitaph for a woman stating that she gave birth to 10 children, 5 sons and 5 daughters (compare similarly Cornelia, mother of the Gracchi), all of whom survived her to be at her funeral.[102] Such an instance was remarked upon for its rarity (if indeed it was true), and this is part of a natural mentality that regarded it as a matter of great satisfaction and honor, a great blessing, to leave many children behind you when you die, descendants who might be expected to tend your grave, cherish your memory, and grant you a form of immortality.[103]

Such a desire is understandable, especially in view of the fact that it must have been very difficult to achieve. As Pliny the Younger states, most people in his day remained childless, though apparently this was due to preference. But Pliny himself was in a position to know how difficult it was to acquire a large family: he remained childless after three marriages. His third wife, Calpurnia, did become pregnant but subsequently miscarried—Pliny's desire for children is evident.[104] Similarly, Cicero's daughter Tullia had only one child after three marriages and as many miscarriages. One can point to other childless couples among the elite at Rome where clearly childlessness was not through choice. This is particularly true of the emperors, very few of whom produced natural heirs, however much they may have wanted to.[105] A high level of natural sterility is probably to be assumed, albeit impossible to measure.[106] One famous case was that of Spurius Carvilius Ruga who apparently divorced his wife (against his will) because she had produced no children. The traditional maxim was that marriage was undertaken "liberorum procreandorum causa."[107] Those who were unable to "do their duty" and produce children suffered as a result, not just in archaic times but also in the penalties facing *orbi* as a result of the Augustan marriage legislation.[108] Further allowance for natural sterility[109] may be seen in the system of *adrogatio,* according to which a man was only permitted to adopt a son when he was considered no longer capable of begetting children, that is, when he was over 60 years of age, and had been unsuccessful in begetting children before that age.[110] One can perhaps gain some awareness of how common natural sterility was, in both males and females, by considering the superstitious stories related of causes of and remedies for sterility and infertility. Factors included the drinking of wine or the taking of certain drugs—concocted from, in one case, willow seed; and the Druids, Pliny reports, believed that mistletoe imparts fertility (mistletoe Pliny regards as superstition, willow seed on the other hand as accepted fact).[111]

Much scholarly attention has centered on one particular aspect of declining fertility, that of the elite class at Rome in the late republic and early empire, a perceived decline that the Augustan marriage legislation apparently attempted to reverse. It has been argued, most notably and forcefully by Brunt, that the elite class was failing to marry and reproduce itself in this period.[112] As a result of this fall in the fertility rate, Augustus is said to have faced a shortage of manpower ("penuria iuventutis")[113]—again, an observation in retrospect but, if accurate, a sign of an aging population due to a fall in fertility levels.

This is not the place to become embroiled in a protracted account of Augustus's social legislative program: If studies on infant mortality could fill a book, the secondary material on Augustus's marriage legislation could fill a library.[114] The basic purpose underlying the legislation appears to have been to encourage aristocratic Romans to marry and have *legitimate* children. This was attempted by granting various benefits to those married with a certain number of children, and by imposing penalties on the unmarried and childless ("caelibes et orbi"), such as their capacity to inherit; divorce and adultery also came under the scrutiny of the legislators. It must be stressed that the laws appear to have been aimed primarily at the upper classes, though their implications also affected freed slaves, and indeed ultimately all those who lived under the system of Roman law.

One aspect of this social legislation of obvious relevance to us here is the number of children that the law "required." The *ius liberorum* in its purest form (as opposed to many honorary grants of it to the childless) was granted to those in Rome who had three children, four for those in the rest of Italy, and five for those in the provinces and for freedmen in Rome. These rules are clear enough. But is the reference to *living* children or to children ever-born? The difference is very important because of high infant and early childhood mortality. Three children ever-born would for many have been a relatively easy figure to achieve, whereas three living children would have been far more difficult; of three born, on average only one would survive to age 35 or 40, and one would probably be dead before its first birthday. To achieve three living children, therefore, a father would have had to have produced significantly more than this number, depending upon at what age he wished or needed to apply for the *ius liberorum*. The answer to the question, three living or ever-born, is not readily apparent, and confusion is the result. This problem is discussed in the next section.

The ius liberorum: *Living or Ever-born?*   One might expect the question of *ius liberorum:* living or ever-born?[115] to be at least raised by someone like Hopkins or Brunt. In fact, neither seems aware of the problem. Hopkins assumes that three ever-born children are meant,[116] and notes that this is well below the level of biological replacement—the figure, he says, should have been about twice that. Brunt, on the other hand, refers to three surviving children, a target he sees as "discouragingly high."[117] As far as I am aware, no attempt has ever been made to reach a definitive answer, nor indeed to even raise the question.

Our knowledge of the marriage legislation is imperfect, the sources are fragmentary. Many references to the *ius liberorum* merely state that three, four, or five children were required, without making it explicit whether these children had to be alive or not. The surviving evidence suggests, however, that the particular exemption applied for determined whether the children had to be living at the time. In the case of the capacity of husband and wife to exchange gifts between each other, the rule regarding the number of children is recorded explicitly in [Ulpian], *Epitome* 16.1a (cf. also the Flavian municipal law 56): "Libera inter eos testamenti factio est, si ius liberorum a principe impetraverint, aut si filium filiamve communem habeant, aut XIV annorum filium vel filiam XII amiserint, vel si duos tri-

mos vel tres post nominum diem amiserint, ut intra annum tamen et sex menses etiam unus cuiuscumque aetatis impubes
amissus solidi capiendi ius praestet." ("They [i.e., the husband
and wife] are free to take under each other's testaments, if they
have obtained from the emperor the *ius liberorum,* or if they
have a son or daughter born of their union, or have lost a son of
14 or a daughter of 12 years, or if they have lost two children 3
years of age or three after their naming-days, provided nevertheless that even one child lost at any age under puberty gives them
the right of taking the whole estate within a period of a year and
6 months.") In this situation it is the fact that the couple have
produced children that matters—they are in effect rewarded for
trying to do the right thing.

Although it is implied by some modern scholars that these
rules in regard to the husband and wife's right to exchange
property applied to the *ius* in general,[118] this is not true. In the
case of claims for the *ius liberorum* in order to gain exemption
from *munera,* particularly from acting as *tutor* or *curator,* the
legal evidence is far from ambiguous: cf. Justinian, *Inst.* 1.25.pr.:
children *superstites; Cod. Just.* 5.66.1 (A.D. 203); children *in-
columes; Cod. Just.* 10.52.5 (Diocletian and Maximian): five
children *superstites; Frag. Vat.* 247 (Paul): "qui tres pluresve
liberos habent superstites"; *Dig.* 27.1.2.4 (Modestinus): a *con-
stitutio* of the deified Severus to the effect that children must be
alive, and that those who died previous to an application for the
ius do not count, nor does it matter that some die subsequently;
cf. also *Dig.* 27.1.2.7; 27.1.2.8; 27.1.36.1; 50.4.3.6; 50.4.3.12;
50.4.4.pr.; 50.5.1.pr.; 50.5.1.3; 50.5.2.3; 50.5.2.5. Only those
who died in war could be counted among the number (cf. *Frag.
Vat.* 197, 199; *Dig.* 27.1.18, 50.5.14.pr.; Aulus Gellius, *Att.
Noct.* 2.15.4),[119] while dead, unborn, illegitimate, or adopted
children did not count (*Frag. Vat.* 196 [contrast 169]; *Dig.*
27.1.3, 27.1.6, 50.16.129; Justinian, *Inst.* 1.25.pr.); emancipated
sons and grandchildren born of one's sons could be, though the
latter could only count as one child (see *Dig.* 27.1.2.7, 50.5.2.5;
Cod. Just. 5.66.2, 10.52.3; *Frag. Vat.* 195, 198; Justinian, *Inst.*
1.25.pr.; the *lex Rom. Burg.* 36.6 actually states that only *mas-*

culi filii count). It is very revealing that cases of fraud apparently became common, with men coming forward with children not their own (*Cod. Theod.* 12.17.1, A.D. 324; cf. Juvenal 1.123–26 for fraud in the case of having a wife, *nota . . . arte*). If it had been the case that deceased children counted in such applications for the *ius liberorum,* we would expect rather that cases of fraud would have involved people claiming to have had children, since deceased, which they had never really had. If children were dead, how could one prove that they had ever existed? The point is that living children counted because there was the expectation that they could perform the duty at some time in the future on the father's behalf (cf. *Cod. Just.* 10.52.6; *Cod. Theod.* 12.17.1; *Frag. Vat.* 198), or because a man who had numerous children of his own to take care of could hardly be expected to act as the *tutor* or *curator* of still more. Relevant in this context is *P. Mich.* 14.625 (A.D. 241), the petition of a father of five children for exemption from a liturgy; in his petition, the father stresses the fact that he has *raised* the children, and by so doing has already performed a public service (cf. lines 15–18).

In direct contradiction to the rule that the children must be alive, however, [Paul], *Sent.* 4.9.1 and 9, states equally explicitly that for women to obtain the *ius liberorum* the children do *not* have to be alive, so long as they were born alive. There are, however, other inconsistencies between this passage and the bulk of the other evidence regarding the terms of the Augustan marriage laws (e.g., regarding triplets contrast *Sent.* 4.9.2 with *Dig.* 50.16.137, and regarding monstrous births, *Sent.* 4.9.3 with *Dig.* 50.16.135), and I am inclined for this reason to favor the interpretation that in general in the case of exemption from personal *munera* only living children counted.

But, as has already been seen, it was not the rule in every case of application for the *ius.* For example, for freedmen to be excused from *operae* to their patron they had to have fathered two children, even if they were dead at the time of application; alternatively, one child who had survived to the age of 5 years would suffice (*Dig.* 38.1.37.pr.–2; cf. Gaius, *Inst.* 3.44; [Ulpian], *Epit.*

29.3; *Cod. Just.* 8.57.1; and *Cod. Theod.* 8.16.1). Compare this, however, with the *anniculi probatio,* whereby a 1-year-old *living* child was the requirement for a Junian to qualify to become a full *libertus.*

In cases where the *ius liberorum* referred to three *living* children, then a gross reproduction rate of 2.5 or 3 (i.e., five or six live births) is implied, the sort of figure discussed in relation to the model life tables. One implication from this is that the Roman elite were failing to achieve such a figure on average, and therefore that the freeborn population was indeed in decline, or at least was perceived to be so.

Various ingenious attempts have been made to account for this apparent decline: the effects of hot baths on spermatozoa, for example, the effects of lead poisoning (again), or the effects of racial mixing or of a process of natural selection, where elite males married heiresses who by definition were the sole surviving children of their families and who thus inherited low fertility.[120] Venereal disease has also been mentioned in this context,[121] and one might add the fact that in a nuclear family structure a woman may have had too much housework to do to have time to produce many children (unless she had slaves to do the work for her)! All such theories are rather limited, both in scope and in evidence.

It is probably a more constructive practice to look at general social practices and expectations to understand why fertility declined to such an extent that legislation was thought necessary. The mentality that childlessness brought advantages was mentioned earlier and is something that is stressed in much of the literature of the Roman aristocratic circle. Various reasons may be adduced: The upper-class Roman, in a system of partible inheritance, may not have wanted to see his estate split up among too many children after his death and so may have attempted to limit the size of his family.[122] The father then ran the risk, of course, that what children his wife did bear may die at an early age, thus effectively terminating the family line.[123] Thus a desire to have some children, but not too many.

At the same time, however, there seems to have existed a trend toward having no children at all. Literary, moralistic references abound where such a practice is seen as disgraceful but, by implication, widespread, making the *orbi* the prey of the notorious *captatores*.[124] The picture painted by Dio of the majority of equestrians at Rome being unmarried and childless (or at least with no legitimate children) may not tell us the real extent of this practice, but it does stress the perceived reality, at least as it was believed several centuries after the event to have been perceived by contemporaries.[125] Pliny the Elder explicitly condemns *contemporary* morals, according to which *orbitas* occupies the place of highest *auctoritas* and *potentia,* and where legacy-hunting is ranked as the most "fertile" profession, in sharp contrast (so he would have us believe) to the "good old days."[126] In fact, of course, the Augustan legislation was attempting to correct an observed social practice of long standing,[127] and in the face of vocal and fierce opposition had little chance of success. The perceived reality, that the elite male class at Rome was on the whole failing to marry and produce legitimate children, may well have been a real one. We cannot measure the fall in fertility levels, but such an apparently widespread mentality of remaining unmarried and childless, combined with significant levels of natural infertility, will have made its presence felt through the decline in numbers of the propertied class over a long period.

Before we turn to consider the actual means of limiting fertility voluntarily, one might ask of the other levels of the population, since our discussion in the last few pages has inevitably focused on the elite to whom our sources relate and at whom the Augustan laws appear to have been especially directed. Augustus's legislation makes some references to freedmen and their families in the apparent hope of also increasing their fertility. The impression is that they too were believed to be failing to reproduce themselves. Treggiari has pointed out that freedmen's families would have been small because the childbearing years after manumission would generally be few.[128] Using inscriptional evidence, Treggiari argues that a family of more than two children ever-born would have been a rarity. But again there is the problem here that the inscriptions only record living children, and one must allow for high infant and child mortality rates.

When we turn our gaze to the "average" plebeian we are basically clutching at straws, or at least at impressions. The sources give us very little to go on, and it is dangerous to generalize from what we have. For the time of Tiberius, Tacitus refers to the vastly increased slave population at Rome as compared with the continual decline of the "plebs ingenua." [129] Even if the latter part of this reference is an accurate impression of reality (in hindsight, of course), such a decline could be due not only to lower fertility—and higher mortality in the *urbs*—but also to migration, a massive influx of slaves and possibly the emigration of the freeborn from Rome, though the corn dole was one reason for staying. [130]

Drawing demographic conclusions about the slave population of the Roman empire is even more difficult and uncertain. Figures for population numbers and life expectancy must remain highly conjectural. What is of more interest in a demographic context is whether slaves were usually born in *familiae* or were imported at adult ages as the primary source for slaves. [131] Could a slave population reproduce itself? Harris believes not, mainly on the basis of a male predominance—as he sees it—in slave households, though cases to the contrary have been seen. But what is probably most influential in this regard is the slave owner's wishes, or rather his pocket. The cost of rearing slaves might be greater than that of buying a fully grown slave, though not necessarily so. [132] For some specialized tasks a *verna* might be preferable to a new purchase, since one who grew up within the *familia* might be easier to train and perhaps to trust. But then again the owner ran the risk of losing at an early age through death a slave he had raised and invested in from infancy. In the mines, on the other hand, a bought, unskilled slave would probably prove a better short-term investment. One might also wonder whether an owner would cherish having a female slave off work during the later stages of pregnancy. Taking in an infant

121

foundling might have been one way of getting round both problems. Nevertheless, as Finley suggested, the level of slave breeding has probably been underestimated.[133]

Columella rewarded, albeit only for very high fertility, his slave women who produced children: a slave mother who gave birth to three *filii* (who presumably had to survive) gained *otium,* exemption from work, while a woman who produced more than this number was granted *libertas* as well. There is no indication, however, that such "generosity" was typical.[134] Nor is there any indication that many slave women were in a position to achieve such high fertility. Unlike cattle—however much some masters at the time may have seen the parallel with slaves—humans cannot be forced to breed. Columella offered some encouragement and was perhaps in a position to sustain the expense of rearing infant slaves. Other owners may not have had the means or the inclination to look so far ahead. At any rate a slave population is far from a natural one, and its demographic regime, which probably varied sharply over space and time, remains difficult to elucidate or even to make conjectures about.

To what extent the poor of the Roman empire had large families, whether through choice or by accident, is open to speculation, and we will return to this question briefly when we consider age at first marriage. The fact remains that our evidence centers almost exclusively on the elite class of Rome, and in what follows our attention will focus on this social class, about whom it was said some seventy years ago:

> C'est par la stérilité volontaire qu'a péri l'élite romaine; elle n'a pas été engloutie par la vague de fond surgie au nord-est de l'Europe des abîmes barbares d'une société superficiellement civilisée; elle a péri par le suicide.

> The Roman elite perished through voluntary childlessness: it was not swallowed up by the tidal wave that rose up in northeastern Europe from the barbarous depths of a society superficially civilized; it perished through suicide.[135]

A wonderful way of putting it, even if in reality the decline was rather less dramatic. We have mentioned the effects of a fall in fertility levels and the way that this fall was perceived and reacted to in attempts to increase fertility through legislation. That the decline was as real or as drastic as the traditional image would have us believe is less certain. It is our final task here to consider various demographic aspects of the factors by which fertility may have been enhanced or, more usually, restricted. Several of the individual aspects to be considered here have been discussed by others, so I shall proceed quickly.

The first point to consider is the actual reproductive period of the female, since obviously this is the primary natural factor setting the age limits for fertility. Menarche, the onset of menstruation, was generally perceived by the ancient sources to occur around the age of 14 years.[136] The age of menopause varies more widely, from the age of 40 or even 35, to 60 years.[137] It should be realized that menopause is a process, not an event, and so any single figure will be unsatisfactory. Whether reality accorded with these isolated literary and medical references is uncertain.[138] The age of menarche given is as low as today's figure for the Western world, though in reality it was clearly higher in the past century.[139] What is certain is that the age of both menarche and menopause is also to some extent influenced by environmental and dietary conditions, and it may vary over time and space. It needs to be noted, especially in the context of an early marriage age, that even after the onset of menstruation fecundity in females is generally very low, with irregular ovulation for several years in the early teens. Similarly, males do not achieve full sexual capacity in terms of sperm production until some time after puberty.[140] Also fecundity in women wanes as the onset of menopause approaches.[141] The reproductive period in females is, therefore, generally referred to as being some 29 years in duration, from the age of about 15 to 44 years.

This much is biology. The age at marriage, on the other hand, is based largely on social criteria, and the age at first marriage at Rome, the focus of quite considerable scholarly attention, is of demographic importance in terms of both mortality and fertility. Hopkins's study has long been the standard work on the subject, showing on the basis of inscriptional evidence that the average

age at marriage of Roman girls *of the upper classes* was "by our standards very young," around 14 years.[142] Shaw has provided convincing evidence that this can only be held to apply to the upper classes (as Hopkins himself suggested), and he points to a later average age among the lower classes, in the late 10s or early 20s.[143] His evidence for this, the age at which women at death tend to be commemorated by husbands rather than by parents on tombstone inscriptions, is attractive but not certain. Differences in commemorator may not always reflect differences in marital status. Nevertheless, that girls of the lower classes on average married in their late 10s, a few years after girls of the upper classes, is probably right,[144] but conclusive evidence one way or the other is sadly lacking.

In terms of fertility, it is obviously the age of the female at marriage rather than that of the male that matters most. Roman elite girls may have married around the age of puberty but, as mentioned, they would have achieved full fecundity only a few years later. By the terms of the Augustan social legislation a woman was expected to have given birth by the age of 20 years,[145] and this gap of some 6 years may reflect an awareness of the female reproductive capacity. The early age also reflects, not so much a supposed significant shortage of women, though such a perception is possible without it necessarily existing in reality,[146] as a general high mortality regime, where an early female age at marriage and an expectation that the majority of the eligible population will marry is necessary to maintain population size.[147] By marrying at a relatively very young age a woman does not necessarily significantly increase her fecundity (i.e., her physiological capacity to bear children). While a very late marriage age would markedly lower a woman's fecundity (Malthus's preventive check), a very early age such as was apparently the case among the Roman elite would increase the risk of childbirth complications, leading to sterility and possible mortality (of both infant and mother),[148] and to some extent lower fertility levels in the later years of marriage, due to the relative frequency of intercourse and the marriage duration effect. Together with sterility problems in later life, these factors should warn us against equating an early marriage age with an extended period of female fecundity, except that more women survived to age 14 than to age 18 years or whatever. The reproductive span would on average have remained much the same, whether women were marrying at age 14 or 18 years. The idea that the poor were marrying later primarily as a conscious method of avoiding large families is not, I think, feasible.[149]

The age of men at first marriage does have some demographic significance if there was a considerable age gap between marriage partners. This is a feature of the Mediterranean family pattern, as opposed to a western European pattern where men and women both tend to marry in their mid 20s and a significant proportion of women never marry, or the eastern European pattern, where both marry in greater proportion and in their mid to late 10s.[150] Saller has shown that Roman men tended to marry around the mid to late 20s.[151] Elite males, particularly those of the senatorial class, generally married earlier, around the early 20s.[152] As a result, an age gap emerges of some 8 to 10 years between spouses over broad social categories. Such an age gap, apart from its effect on the ages at which male and female children left the family home, would probably have had a negative effect on marital fertility levels, as historical cases indicate.[153] Few facts emerge from all this, however, only impressions. But it is at least worth pointing out the importance of consideration of marriage age of both males and females in terms of the effect on fertility and family size. The impression is that while a very early marriage age for elite Roman women would have meant more females were available for reproduction than if the marriage age was on average significantly higher, any potential increase in fertility levels that this may have produced would to some extent have been offset by the greater average age of the husband and in the long term by lessened fertility in later years.[154]

From considerations of biological and social factors influencing the reproductive span of females and their fecundity, we turn now to ways that fertility might be limited or enhanced, intentionally or otherwise, within this reproductive period. Modern demographic techniques enable us to measure age-specific fertility rates, the parity progression ratios for populations (i.e., the probability of a woman having another child after having already had a given number), and the average interval between each live birth. The data needed for such calculations, however, will never be available to the ancient demographer.[155] For the ancient world even crude birth rates can only be estimated on comparative evidence. What we can consider here, in relation to assumed family size and apparent desires to limit fertility, among the Roman elite at least, are the ways, both biological and social, that potential fecundity might not be realized. Factors involved here are the deliberate practices of contraception and abortion, and the effects of breast-feeding and the proportions of the population marrying.[156] The first two aspects have been dealt with at some length by others; the latter two are less easy to elucidate for the ancient world, and will require further study. Here we can give only an introductory overview.

The classic work on contraception in the Roman empire is that by Hopkins.[157] His study is deliberately confined to the upper classes, since—as usual—almost all our information is limited to this social level.[158] It emerges that contraceptive knowledge through the medical writers was quite widespread, but that techniques described were often totally ineffective, relying as much on magic as on medical methods, such as ivory amulets worn around the left ankle. Hopkins stresses that we cannot automatically assume factors that we today might take for granted; the practice of coitus interruptus, for example, is not as obvious an expedient as might be supposed.[159] Similarly, the apparent confusion between contraception and abortion in many of the sources,[160] together with an ignorance of the "safe period" in the menstrual cycle, further undermine the reliability of many contraceptive techniques available. Certainly some methods described in the medical sources would have been effective, but it is to be doubted whether the difference between the effective and the useless could have been tested or realized. All in all contraception, mention of which appears very rarely in the written sources as compared with abortion and infanticide or exposure as a means of limiting family size,[161] may have played a small but

significant role in the demographic regime of the Roman empire.[162] More exact knowledge of levels of contraceptive practice
and efficacy could be derived if we had knowledge (which we do
not) of birth intervals (if intervals are longer than naturally expected, contraception or abortion may be responsible), of the
average age of women at their last parturition (if under age 30,
something must be responsible for the next decade of infertility), or of age-specific fertility levels (if fertility is very low in the
20s and early 30s but increases thereafter, again contraception
may be responsible).[163]

For contraception to play a significant role in family limitation, as it does in the Western world today, the practice needs to
be acceptable, both morally and socially, as well as financially,
and needs to be available, wanted, and acknowledged as effective. It is very difficult to know if contraception was acceptable
in the eyes of Roman society, the references to it in literature are
so few and often so moralistic in tone. Literary moralizing, epit-
omized in Musonius Rufus, may not reflect everyday reality. Soranus and Pliny the Elder, with the Hippocratic Oath as their
mainstay, speak out against both contraception and abortion,[164]
but again theory is often different from practice. It was only
under Christianity that real and effective criticism came. The
main factor against the demographic significance of contraception in the ancient world was not its unacceptability but its in-
effectiveness, combined perhaps with a general lack of male interest.[165] The will for it to work may have been there, but that
alone is not enough. The results of abortion and infanticide were
more visible and more certain, though also presumably more
traumatic, physically and mentally, for all involved, so perhaps
contraception was considered as worth trying as a first line of
defense. But nobody would have been too surprised if pregnancy
resulted all the same.

From contraception to abortion, a much more widely attested
practice.[166] Abortion was regarded by classical Roman law as
criminal only if a woman usurped the father's right to decide the
fate of a future son or daughter, not because of any rights held
by the unborn fetus.[167] The implication is that abortion with the

127

father's consent was perfectly valid.[168] Again there is a mixture of effective and useless methods described in the sources.[169] But there is no doubt that successful abortions were carried out—"successful" in that they killed the unwanted fetus; their effect on the future fecundity or even the life of the mother can only be guessed at but was presumably often far from salutary. Whereas the wealthy may have been able to afford comparatively hygienic surroundings and relatively skilled doctors for such operations, the poorer classes, if indeed they turned to abortion as an alternative to exposure or infanticide, must have resorted to the ancient equivalent of back-street "clinics," if not indeed attempted home operations—the picture is far from a pleasant one.[170]

Ovid, perhaps rather surprisingly, is the first ancient author to be outspoken in his rejection of abortion, although his concern is the life not of the fetus but of the mother, Corinna.[171] On the whole, exposure may have been seen as a safer and more certain means of limiting family size than either contraception or abortion, especially for the poor. To us this may seem barbaric, but at the time it may have been considered practical or unavoidable: again the problem of another society and of unrecorded emotions. The sources speak often enough, in elite circles, of women practicing abortion and avoiding childbirth through motives of self-conceit and concern for physical beauty,[172] but such references should not be regarded as typical. Underlying this apparent selfishness lay social and economic realities, at all levels of society. The small size of families cannot be explained by mortality rates alone, but also by a limiting of fertility through both intention and circumstances. We have dealt with various factors on both sides: not only contraception, abortion, and exposure and infanticide as part of an apparent aversion to matrimony and child rearing, but also natural sterility. Other social factors, such as homosexuality and extramarital relationships, may also have had a part to play.

Marriage as depicted here is quite limited: *matrimonium iustum* or *iustae nuptiae* between legally recognized (i.e., free) partners who enjoyed rights of *conubium*, producing legitimate children. As Rawson has clearly shown, concubinage between partners where one or both was freed or of servile status appears to have been common in the empire, and offspring resulting from such unions were illegitimate and took the mother's status.[173] The extent of illegitimacy, however one defines that term, in the Roman world is another unknown factor. As Syme comments, "the class [of aristocratic bastards] must have been fairly numerous" but there is "a singular dearth of evidence" about them. Illegitimacy seems to have carried little of the modern-day connotations of shame, and perhaps for this reason it aroused little interest among Roman writers.[174] In Egypt illegitimacy has been estimated at about 10 percent of all live births, but this is based on inadequate evidence, and in any case Egypt cannot be regarded as typical of the empire as a whole.[175] Concubinage between free partners, on the other hand, was not—despite traditional assumptions—common,[176] and hence should not be assumed as a significant factor in the declining fertility of the elite through the postponement or discouragement of marriage. As discussed already, a general unwillingness to marry, in line with an image of celibacy, was more significant in this context.

One very important contraceptive factor (not considered by Hopkins) is the effect of breast-feeding. It has long been realized that "mother's milk" offers an easily digested and ideal diet for an infant, and indeed in preindustrial societies the feeding of an infant with unpasteurized milk from animals would have been tantamount to murder. Breast milk provides immunological protection from many common childhood diseases and remains uninfected in even the most unsanitary conditions.[177] The health not only during infant years but also in later life is greatly improved as a result of breast-feeding a baby.

These benefits seem to have been appreciated in the ancient world, but with one refinement: the infant should be fed by the mother, not by a wet nurse.[178] Soranus's comments in this regard are typical. He states that for the first month following childbirth a wet nurse should be employed because the mother's milk is bad. Otherwise, a mother should always feed her own baby, unless for some medical reason the mother is incapable or would suffer as a result.[179] Biologically, of course, it would make no difference whether the milk was that of the mother or of a wet nurse. Emotionally, however, it was felt, it might make considerable differences in terms of parent-child relationships, as well as being indicative of a certain degree of snobbery.[180] How long the period of breast-feeding was is difficult to determine; contracts from Egypt for wet nurses range from 6 months to 3 years, most being for 2 years.[181]

The other factor relating to breast-feeding that is of great interest in this context is its potential contraceptive effect, something that has only been widely recognized this century. After pregnancy there occurs a brief postpartum infertile or nonsusceptible period before full menstruation and ovulation are restored.[182] This period is usually of some 2 to 3 months in duration, even shorter if the pregnancy resulted in a stillbirth or the fetus was aborted. However, if the mother practices *frequent and prolonged* breast-feeding, the period of amenorrhea (i.e., of not menstruating) is substantially increased, up to a period of as much as 2 years. The precise mechanisms involved need not concern us here—nor indeed are they properly understood even now. But the contraceptive effect of lactation is extremely important, especially where contraceptive methods are lacking or inadequate.[183]

Rather surprisingly, there is some apparent awareness of this effect of lactation in the classical sources. Aristotle states that as a rule menstruation does not occur while a woman is breast-feeding. Soranus follows this, and adds elsewhere that a wet nurse should be employed in some circumstances, especially for the mother's benefit, "with a view to her own recovery and to further childbearing"—implicit in this is the idea that breast-feeding lowers the chances of pregnancy. A similarly implicit reference may be seen in a work traditionally ascribed to Plutarch, the *de Liberis Educandis,* where again mothers are urged to breast-feed their infants themselves rather than have them fed by wet nurses, unless "they are unable to do this, either because of bodily weakness (for such a thing can happen), or because they are in a hurry to have more children."[184] This is far from conclusive proof of knowledge in antiquity of the contraceptive effects of lactation; possibly the reference here may be to the fact that, as has already been seen, intercourse was commonly regarded as detrimental during the period when breast-feeding was taking place, the belief being that breast milk was in fact derived from menstrual blood and that intercourse might induce menstruation and result in pregnancy. Even if the contraceptive element is the implication from these few references, we cannot presume that such knowledge was widespread. Nevertheless, it is an important consideration in any analysis of ancient demography.

Breast-feeding appears to have been the norm in the ancient world, but was *maternal* breast-feeding? The arguments of Favorinus, Tacitus, and Soranus (already cited) would suggest that it was not, at least among the elite, and some epigraphic evidence bears this out, especially in the frequency of the mention of wet nurses and the special mention made of the apparently unusual cases of a *mater nutrix,* a mother feeding her own infant.[185] If it is true that most elite Roman mothers left the feeding of their infants to lower-class wet nurses, despite the moral denouncements of such a habit, then this would have automatically increased their fertility quite dramatically. It would therefore suggest that, if efficient contraceptive techniques were not being widely practiced, women would, in normal, marital circumstances, become pregnant again fairly soon after a birth. Whether women of the poorer classes breast-fed their own babies is obviously impossible to answer for certain. The expense of a wet nurse must be considered, but then again the busy mother may not have wanted to have been hampered by an infant to feed, especially if she was engaged in some form of work and had already lost time through pregnancy. In some circumstances a woman may have had to hire a wet nurse because she could produce no milk of her own.

Nevertheless, that wet-nursing was the norm among the lower classes cannot be assumed.[186] If maternal breast-feeding was the norm among poorer people in the Roman empire, then their fertility may have been significantly lower than that of their social "superiors" and, if abortion and exposure did not restore the balance, then the poor may have had smaller families, especially if they were also marrying at a later age on average than the upper classes. Slave *familiae* are another question again. Presumably one slave woman could feed all the slave infants, so that the other mothers could get on with their work (and their breeding?). Again, the owner's decision would have determined what happened.[187] A lot of questions remain about this particular demographic aspect of the ancient world, at all levels of the society. But it is an extremely important factor for its potential effects on levels of both mortality and fertility, though till now it has been overlooked by ancient social historians.

One final consideration regarding levels of fertility. It has been noted that in a high mortality regime, if fertility is to be high enough to sustain the population at a stationary let alone growing rate, marriage needs to take place at a fairly early age, and almost all the members of the population must marry.[188] A further factor influencing fertility levels is coital frequency,[189] but I doubt that such a factor could ever be measured for the ancient world. However, one other feature that can be considered is remarriage. Because of high mortality marriage duration would not on average have been long, with one partner dying at a relatively young age.[190] For demographic purposes it was important that widows remarry. In a society with a high divorce rate,[191] furthermore, remarriage was essential. Therefore, the tradition of the *univira*,[192] the woman who remained faithful to one man, even after his death, would seem to have undermined this demographic necessity. In fact, however, this image of the *univira* should be regarded as a traditional classical ideal rather than a commonplace reality. As Humbert has made clear in his excellent study of remarriage at Rome, the young widow or divorcée who remained single would have been a rarity.[193] Indeed, while by tradition a widow was expected to pass a period of 10 months in mourning before remarrying (or suffer *infamia* as a result), the Augustan legislation on marriage expected widows to remarry within 1 year, though this was subsequently increased to 2 years after some public pressure.[194] It was only in

Christian times that the remarriage of widows was actively discouraged,[195] and such an attitude, together with the encouragement of a celibate life-style, could certainly have had very real demographic consequences. In classical Roman society, however, a childless widow would have been in a singularly unenviable position when she grew old, with no form of state support, and so she would have had every reason to remarry while the opportunity was available. It would appear that most women at this time, of the elite class at any rate, did remarry and remain potentially productive throughout their childbearing years.[196]

The picture of fertility in the Roman empire, then, is something of a muddled one: many impressions, some contradictory, and lamentably few facts. In general, family size seems smaller than would be expected on the grounds of natural fertility. High mortality, particularly in infancy and early childhood, is one of the main reasons for this, but not the only one. Other factors have been discussed here, factors by which fertility was in various ways and to various degrees limited, whether intentionally or not. Fertility levels needed to be high if the population was to survive and to maintain its size. Some strata of Roman society appear to have failed to reproduce themselves naturally (though in the case of the senatorial and equestrian classes their numbers might be increased artificially), and as a result a gradual demographic decline set in, a decline that was in part perceived at the time and against which measures were taken, albeit unsuccessfully. Precise causes for the decline in fertility are not readily apparent, but a general mentality advocating the advantages of bachelorhood and childlessness seems to underlie it, a mentality that was put into effect consciously through practices of abortion and exposure, and to some extent of contraception, and which was augmented by significant levels of natural infertility, and by the practice of maternal breast-feeding among some sections of the society. It is to be hoped that further and more detailed analysis of the aspects of Roman society mentioned here will lead to an increased awareness of the factors influencing the fertility levels prevalent in Roman society.

Conclusion

This survey of the problems and possibilities involved in the study of ancient demography has perhaps raised more questions than it has answered. Yet I believe I am justified in the degree of caution and skepticism (some would call it pessimism) that I have felt it necessary to employ. The first half of this book, chapter 1, is an attempt to show that the various types of ancient source material traditionally utilized in attempts to "discover" some demographic features of the classical world are in fact not as reliable or as useful as many have too often supposed. Nor can literary references be taken at face value as definitive or reliable records of demographic variables such as population size or rates of population growth. Model life tables are available that enable the ancient historian, using the stable population theory, to gain a realistic awareness of the probable structure of an ancient population, and can also be used to test the validity or measure the effect of various assumptions one might make about such populations (chapter 2). For example, one can reasonably suppose that in Roman society those over the age of 60 years represented some 5 to 10 percent of the total population, the figure varying depending on the mortality, fertility, and growth rates one assumes to have operated at the time. Such models are very useful tools in analyzing such demographic features, but no model of this kind can be used to measure the effect of social pressures on a population. For such indications, we must rely both on the critical use of the sources and on a certain degree of demographic sense, to decide what is plausible or improbable (chapter 3).

This last area in particular requires a good deal of refinement and expansion. Various aspects that up till now have been rather isolated pockets of research—such as age at marriage, the extent of remarriage, and the use of contraceptive methods—need to be integrated into one, comprehensive picture, as I have tried to begin to do here. Other areas, such as the extent of maternal mortality, the effects of breast-feeding, and the prevalence of natural sterility within ancient populations, require further research. Some problems may never receive conclusive answers (the debate and confusion surrounding the question of infanticide and exposure will doubtless continue to grow in on themselves) but the questions are still worth asking.

Migration in particular requires careful consideration, though I cannot see how our knowledge of it will ever be so adequate in demographic terms as to make it possible to bring it into the basic equation for natural population growth.[1] For individual locations in the empire at particular times quite considerable detail may be achieved, but when considering national populations over several centuries the significance of migration in terms of population size and structure cannot be underestimated, nor for our period can it be easily or accurately measured. Probably the best indicator of migration levels within a population may be derived from figures for infants, since this group is the least likely to migrate. But as should be clear by now, infants are the group for whom information from the ancient world is most noticeably lacking, so no clue on migration is forthcoming. Migration rates may vary according to sex, age, time, and space. Generalizing over any one of these categories is misleading, over all four it is pointless. For the purposes of this book, in dealing with the general nature of the population of Roman society as a whole, the effects of migration have been regarded as secondary in comparison with the consequences of the levels of and changes in mortality and fertility, and over a vast population like this such a method is justified. But if further, more detailed analyses of different populations are to be made and are to be valid, migration will have to be taken into account.

In such future demographic analyses, attention should be focused not on the tombstone inscriptions or skeletons as the sole bases of inquiry, but on more general demographic factors and trends, looking at the society as it was rather than on the scattered pieces as they now remain. True, such a method will not tell us *precisely* how long on average a person lived, or *exactly* how many Romans lived to the age of 60 years. But any source that purports to give such information would be spurious anyway—such precision cannot be expected and would only be a misleading generalization. We may never achieve the detail possible for a study such as that made by Wrigley and Schofield of the population of England from 1541 to 1871, and that is to be regretted. But all is not lost. With an understanding of demographic methods and models, used in their right context and with due care, we can achieve a sufficient awareness of probable population structure to understand general demographic factors and to apply these features to our perceptions of the social, economic, and political reality of the ancient world.[2] The basic message, then, is optimistic, so long as our sights are not set too far distant.

I opened this study with Pliny and his clouds. In something like a similar manner to his, I have tried to put forward here various figures, different approaches, and some rather tangled problems. That demographic methods and models "never mislead" would be an exaggeration, and indeed the pursuit of precise figures for demographic variables in Roman society would be the mark of "an almost insane absorption in study." But conjectural calculations—or, better, plausible conjectures—based on what is demographically probable will help us to learn, not perhaps about the height of clouds above the earth, but certainly about something rather more useful in terms of ancient history, namely the population of the ancient world.

Appendix A

The Album of Canusium

Duncan-Jones discusses a further potential source of information on ancient life expectancy, and again it is an epigraphic one: the so-called album of Canusium, a complete list of the 100 members of the town council of A.D. 223 at Canusium in southern Italy.[1] To summarize Duncan-Jones's method and argument briefly: by assuming that the age of entry to the town council was normally 25 years (as quaestor) and because there are listed in the inscription 68 surviving office holders, Duncan-Jones works from the principle (that a regular intake of two magistrates per year at age 25 produced 68 survivors) that $e_{25} = 34$. From this he uses Coale-Demeny[2] Model South to work backward to find a value for e_0, and comes up with Model South Level 6 male, where $e_0 = 31.7$. A similar method may be used in regard to the senate at Rome.[2] Allowing for some distorting factors, he argues that this figure represents an indication that upper-class life expectancy at birth in Roman times was over 30 years.[3]

There are several problems here, however. For a start, Duncan-Jones shares the mistaken belief of many that only the "male" model life tables can be used; that this is not so has been shown already (note also that Duncan-Jones miscalculates infant mortality rates, see chapter 2, n. 20). So "female" tables might also be compared; similarly, Model West could be used. In such scenarios, quite a different e_0 figure may be derived, ranging from 30 to over 40 years (for the dangers in calculating childhood mortality rates from those of an adult population, see chapter 2). There is also the problem here (as always) that one must assume a stationary population.

Other distorting factors, of which Duncan-Jones is aware, are that the quaestorship may have been held before the age of 25 years; some individuals may have enjoyed faster promotion; and, more significantly, the case of Canusium in A.D. 223 cannot be considered representative—there were 68 surviving officeholders in this year in that place, but need that be typical? A difference in numbers would affect the e_{25} figure, which would in turn affect the e_0 figure to be derived from it. For example, to use only Model South male models, for 64 survivors, $e_{25} = 32$ and $e_0 = 27$; for 72 survivors, $e_{25} = 36$ and $e_0 = 36$.

In summary, while the method itself is a potentially useful one, the results derived can be considered of demographic value—and then rather limited—only in terms of the upper class of Canusium in A.D. 223 as represented in the inscription. If we had similar inscriptions for Canusium over an extended chronological scale we might be in a better position. As it is, the album of Canusium in A.D. 223 is unique not only for that town but also for the Roman empire as a whole.

Appendix B

List of Tables and Figures

Figures

Table 1
The Egyptian Census Data: Distribution by Age (in Years) and Sex

Age	No. (%) of Males		No. (%) of Females		Sex Ratio
0–9	68	(26.6)	51	(20.6)	133.3
10–19	40	(15.6)	53	(21.5)	75.5
20–29	42	(16.4)	47	(19.0)	89.4
30–39	34	(13.3)	41	(16.6)	82.9
40–49	30	(11.7)	24	(9.7)	125.0
50–59	20	(7.8)	14	(5.7)	142.9
60–69	10	(3.9)	11	(4.5)	90.9
70–79	11	(4.3)	6	(2.4)	183.3
80+	1	(0.4)	—	—	—
Total	256		247		103.6

Table 2
The Customary and Ulpianic Tables

Age of Legatee (x) (*years*)	Customary Forma	Ulpianic Forma
0–19	30	30
20–24	30	28
25–29	30	25
30–34	$60 - x \ (=30/26)$	22
35–39	$60 - x \ (=25/21)$	20
40–49	$60 - x \ (=20/11)$	$60 - x - 1 \ (=19/10)$
50–54	$60 - x \ (=10/6)$	9
55–59	$60 - x \ (=5/1)$	7
60+	0	5

Table 3
The Determination of Skeletal Age (in Years) and Sex:
Two Comparative Case Studies

	Test Cases by Acsádi and Nemeskéri		
Test Case No.	Estimated Age	Actual Age	Difference
1	26	23	+3
2	53.3	54	−0.7
3	71.8	75	−3.2
4	52	72	−20
5	68.8	45	+23.8

	The Late Roman Cemetery at Sopianae (Pécs, Hungary) (n = 134)			
Grave No.	Éry		Lengyel	
(L)	Sex	Age	Sex	Age
2a	F	48–54	F	20–30
5	?	1.5–2	F?	4–7
9	F	65–69	M	15–25
22b	F	43–49	F	20–30
24c	?	1.5–2.5	F?	10–20
26	?	1.5	F?	10–15
32	F	19–21	F	30–40
47c	?	1.5	F	25–35
52a	M	19–20	F	35–45
52b	F	55–59	F	30–40
70b	F	49–55	F	15–25
82	F	30–60	M	45–55
83b	M	16–17	M	45–55
88a	F	54–58	M	35–45
88b	M	65–71	M	35–45
88c	F	60–70	M	25–35
90	?	2.5–3	F	30–40
93	F	67–72	F	25–35

Table 4
Romano-British Cemetery, Trentholme Drive, York:
Breakdown of Sample by Age, n = 290

Age Group (*years*)	No.	%
0–5	5	1.72
5–10	5	1.72
10–15	14	4.83
15–20	20	6.90
20–25	29	10.00
25–30	46	15.86
30–40	116	40.00
40–50	50	17.24
50+	5	1.72

Table 5
Graeco-Roman Cemetery, Gabbari:
Breakdown of Sample by Age and Sex, n = 55

Age Group (*years*)	Male	Female	Sex Not Determined	% of Total
0–1	—	—	17	30.91
1–4	—	—	10	18.18
5–9	—	—	7	12.73
10–14	—	—	—	—
15–19	—	—	2	3.64
20–24	—	1	—	1.82
25–29	1	2	—	5.45
30–34	1	—	—	1.82
35–39	1	1	—	3.64
40–44	1	—	—	1.82
45–49	—	1	—	1.82
50–54	—	—	—	—
55–59	3	—	—	5.45
60–64	3	—	—	5.45
65–69	1	—	—	1.82
70+	1	—	—	1.82
Adult?	—	1	1	3.64

Table 6
Frier's Life Table for the Roman Empire:
Adapted from Frier (1982) table 5

x	q_x	d_x	l_x	$1000m_x$	L_x	T_x	e_x	C_x
0	0.3582	35822	100000	466.9	76716	2110730	21.107	3.63
1	0.2370	15210	64178	70.2	216573	2034014	31.693	10.26
5	0.0641	3140	48968	13.2	236990	1817441	37.115	11.23
10	0.0482	2210	45828	9.9	223615	1580451	34.487	10.59
15	0.0741	3233	43618	15.4	210008	1356836	31.107	9.95
20	0.0827	3338	40385	17.2	193580	1146828	28.397	9.17
25	0.0929	3443	37047	19.5	176628	953248	25.731	8.37
30	0.1056	3549	33604	22.3	159148	776621	23.111	7.54
35	0.1216	3654	30055	25.9	141140	617473	20.545	6.69
40	0.1424	3759	26401	30.7	122608	476333	18.042	5.81
45	0.1707	3865	22642	37.3	103548	353726	15.623	4.91
50	0.2114	3970	18777	47.3	83960	250178	13.324	3.98
55	0.2506	3711	14807	57.3	64758	166218	11.226	3.07
60	0.3278	3637	11096	78.4	46388	101461	9.144	2.20
65	0.4132	3082	7459	104.2	29590	55073	7.383	1.40
70	0.5278	2310	4377	143.4	16110	25483	5.822	0.76
75	0.6754	1396	2067	203.9	6845	9373	4.535	0.32
80	1.0000	671	671	265.4	2528	2528	3.768	0.12

Table 7
Different Mortality Levels in a Stationary Population:
Coale-Demeny[2] Model West Levels 1–5 Female

Age (years)	(1) e_x	C_x	(2) e_x	C_x	(3) e_x	C_x	(4) e_x	C_x	(5) e_x	C_x
0	20.00	3.81	22.50	3.48	25.00	3.21	27.50	2.98	30.00	2.78
1	30.32	10.50	32.61	9.98	34.85	9.53	37.04	9.12	39.21	8.75
5	36.59	11.24	38.35	10.87	40.06	10.53	41.75	10.21	43.40	9.91
10	34.30	10.55	35.92	10.27	37.50	10.00	39.05	9.74	40.58	9.50
15	31.23	9.87	32.75	9.66	34.24	9.46	35.70	9.26	37.13	9.07
20	28.52	9.06	29.93	8.94	31.31	8.81	32.67	8.68	34.00	8.55
25	26.14	8.18	27.43	8.15	28.69	8.10	29.93	8.04	31.14	7.97
30	23.83	7.29	25.00	7.34	26.14	7.36	27.25	7.37	28.34	7.37
35	21.61	6.42	22.64	6.53	23.65	6.62	24.64	6.69	25.61	6.75
40	19.34	5.59	20.25	5.76	21.13	5.91	22.00	6.03	22.84	6.13
45	16.92	4.82	17.71	5.04	18.48	5.22	19.23	5.39	19.97	5.53
50	14.26	4.06	14.96	4.30	15.64	4.52	16.30	4.71	16.94	4.89
55	11.80	3.26	12.40	3.52	12.99	3.75	13.56	3.97	14.11	4.17
60	9.43	2.41	9.94	2.67	10.44	2.91	10.93	3.14	11.40	3.35
65	7.55	1.58	7.96	1.80	8.37	2.03	8.76	2.25	9.13	2.46
70	5.80	0.88	6.13	1.05	6.45	1.23	6.75	1.41	7.05	1.59
75	4.39	0.37	4.64	0.47	4.88	0.58	5.11	0.70	5.33	0.83
80	3.22	0.10	3.40	0.14	3.57	0.19	3.73	0.25	3.89	0.31
85	2.31	0.02	2.43	0.03	2.54	0.04	2.66	0.07	2.76	0.09
BR/DR	50.00		44.44		40.00		36.36		33.33	
GRR	3.160		2.815		2.543		2.324		2.144	
Average age	25.49		26.41		27.27		28.09		28.87	
Dependency ratio	0.708		0.688		0.673		0.662		0.655	
	(1)		(2)		(3)		(4)		(5)	

Table 8
Different Mortality Levels in a Stationary Population:
Coale-Demeny[2] Model South Levels 1–5 Female

Age (years)	(1) e_x	(1) C_x	(2) e_x	(2) C_x	(3) e_x	(3) C_x	(4) e_x	(4) C_x	(5) e_x	(5) C_x
0	20.00	4.00	22.50	3.62	25.00	3.31	27.50	3.06	30.00	2.84
1	27.71	10.35	30.32	9.80	32.86	9.31	35.35	8.89	37.80	8.51
5	39.01	10.43	40.82	10.13	42.58	9.84	44.30	9.57	45.98	9.32
10	37.66	9.76	39.25	9.53	40.80	9.32	42.32	9.11	43.81	8.91
15	34.43	9.21	35.93	9.04	37.39	8.88	38.81	8.72	40.21	8.57
20	31.68	8.53	33.05	8.44	34.40	8.34	35.71	8.24	36.99	8.13
25	29.27	7.81	30.51	7.79	31.71	7.76	32.89	7.71	34.05	7.66
30	26.83	7.11	27.93	7.16	29.01	7.18	30.06	7.19	31.09	7.18
35	24.27	6.45	25.24	6.55	26.18	6.62	27.11	6.67	28.02	6.71
40	21.56	5.83	22.41	5.97	23.24	6.08	24.05	6.18	24.85	6.26
45	18.60	5.25	19.35	5.42	20.08	5.57	20.79	5.70	21.50	5.81
50	15.41	4.64	16.08	4.85	16.73	5.02	17.38	5.18	18.01	5.32
55	12.35	3.94	12.94	4.17	13.52	4.37	14.09	4.56	14.65	4.73
60	9.44	3.07	9.96	3.31	10.47	3.54	10.97	3.75	11.47	3.95
65	7.10	2.06	7.54	2.30	7.96	2.53	8.38	2.75	8.79	2.96
70	5.17	1.10	5.52	1.29	5.86	1.49	6.20	1.69	6.53	1.89
75	3.73	0.39	4.00	0.51	4.26	0.63	4.52	0.77	4.77	0.91
80	2.75	0.07	2.95	0.11	3.13	0.16	3.31	0.22	3.49	0.28
85	1.99	0.01	2.12	0.02	2.25	0.03	2.37	0.04	2.49	0.07
BR/DR	50.00		44.44		40.00		36.36		33.33	
GRR	3.282		2.920		2.635		2.406		2.218	
Average age	26.82		27.72		28.55		29.34		30.08	
Dependency ratio	0.702		0.684		0.671		0.662		0.656	
	(1)		(2)		(3)		(4)		(5)	

Table 9
Coale-Demeny[2] Model West Level 3 Female

x	q_x	d_x	l_x	$1000m_x$	L_x	T_x	e_x	C_x
0	0.3056	30556	100000	381.3	80139	2500000	25.000	3.21
1	0.2158	14988	69444	62.9	238224	2419861	34.846	9.53
5	0.0606	3300	54456	12.5	263206	2181638	40.062	10.53
10	0.0474	2424	51156	9.7	249963	1918431	37.502	10.00
15	0.0615	2998	48732	12.7	236465	1668468	34.237	9.46
20	0.0766	3503	45734	15.9	220261	1432003	31.312	8.81
25	0.0857	3617	42231	17.9	202472	1211742	28.693	8.10
30	0.0965	3728	38614	20.3	184121	1009269	26.138	7.36
35	0.1054	3677	34886	22.2	165603	825148	23.653	6.62
40	0.1123	3504	31208	23.7	147633	659545	21.134	5.91
45	0.1197	3315	27705	25.4	130566	511911	18.477	5.22
50	0.1529	3728	24389	33.0	112999	381345	15.636	4.52
55	0.1912	3950	20661	42.1	93828	268346	12.988	3.75
60	0.2715	4537	16712	62.4	72670	174518	10.443	2.91
65	0.3484	4241	12175	83.7	50695	101849	8.366	2.03
70	0.4713	3739	7934	121.8	30694	51154	6.448	1.23
75	0.6081	2551	4194	174.8	14596	20459	4.878	0.58
80	0.7349	1208	1644	254.1	4755	5864	3.567	0.19
85	0.8650	377	436	375.6	1004	1109	2.544	0.04
90	0.9513	56	59	551.9	101	105	1.784	0.00
95	1.0000	3	3	810.6	4	4	1.234	0.00

Table 10
Coale-Demeny[2] Model South Level 3 Female

x	q_x	d_x	l_x	$1000m_x$	L_x	T_x	e_x	C_x
0	0.2643	26433	100000	319.2	82819	2500000	25.000	3.31
1	0.3026	22263	73567	95.6	232801	2417181	32.857	9.31
5	0.0741	3799	51304	15.4	246073	2184380	42.577	9.84
10	0.0398	1892	47505	8.1	232984	1938307	40.802	9.32
15	0.0546	2490	45613	11.2	222089	1705323	37.387	8.88
20	0.0680	2931	43123	14.1	208581	1483234	34.395	8.34
25	0.0730	2935	40192	15.1	193915	1274653	31.714	7.76
30	0.0761	2836	37257	15.8	179478	1080738	29.008	7.18
35	0.0802	2759	34421	16.7	165482	901260	26.183	6.62
40	0.0817	2588	31662	17.0	152097	735778	23.239	6.08
45	0.0866	2519	29074	18.1	139323	583681	20.076	5.57
50	0.1122	2980	26555	23.7	125623	444358	16.733	5.02
55	0.1515	3572	23575	32.7	109302	318735	13.520	4.37
60	0.2405	4810	20003	54.4	88472	209433	10.470	3.54
65	0.3511	5335	15193	84.5	63163	120961	7.961	2.53
70	0.5101	5029	9858	135.1	37222	57798	5.863	1.49
75	0.6872	3319	4829	209.4	15849	20576	4.261	0.63
80	0.7900	1193	1510	297.2	4015	4727	3.130	0.16
85	0.9009	286	317	431.2	663	713	2.247	0.03
90	0.9674	30	31	622.5	49	50	1.590	0.00
95	1.0000	1	1	898.3	1	1	1.113	0.00

Table 11
Effect of Differing Gross Reproduction Rates on
a Stable Population: Coale-Demeny[2] Model West Level 3 Female: e_0 = 25

Age (years)	Population at Age x (%)				
	GRR = 2.00	GRR = 2.25	GRR = 2.50	GRR = 3.00	GRR = 3.50
0–1	2.52	2.84	3.15	3.73	4.26
1–4	7.65	8.54	9.39	10.93	12.30
5–9	8.78	9.63	10.40	11.76	12.90
10–14	8.70	9.34	9.91	10.84	11.57
15–19	8.58	9.03	9.40	9.96	10.34
20–24	8.34	8.60	8.78	9.01	9.09
25–29	8.00	8.08	8.10	8.04	7.89
30–34	7.59	7.50	7.39	7.10	6.78
35–39	7.12	6.90	6.66	6.20	5.76
40–44	6.62	6.28	5.96	5.37	4.85
45–49	6.11	5.68	5.29	4.61	4.05
50–54	5.52	5.02	4.59	3.87	3.31
55–59	4.78	4.26	3.82	3.12	2.59
60–64	3.86	3.37	2.97	2.35	1.90
65–69	2.81	2.41	2.08	1.59	1.25
70–74	1.78	1.49	1.26	0.93	0.71
75–79	0.88	0.72	0.60	0.43	0.32
80–84	0.30	0.24	0.20	0.14	0.10
85–89	0.07	0.05	0.04	0.03	0.02
90 +	0.01	0.01	0.00	0.00	0.00
Birth rate	31.29	35.40	39.34	46.69	53.42
Death rate	39.77	39.74	39.95	40.80	41.97
Growth rate	− 0.85	− 0.43	− 0.06	+ 0.59	+ 1.15
NRR	0.79	0.89	0.98	1.18	1.38
Average age	30.61	28.95	27.51	25.12	23.23
Age at death	31.61	28.29	25.45	20.92	17.56

Appendix B

Table 12
Effect of Differing Rates of Growth on a Stable Population:
Coale-Demeny[2] Model West Level 3 Female

Age (years)	Population at Age x (%)				
	r = −1.0%	r = −0.5%	r = 0	r = +0.5%	r = +1.0%
0–1	2.40	2.79	3.21	3.65	4.12
1–4	7.33	8.40	9.53	10.71	11.94
5–9	8.47	9.49	10.53	11.57	12.61
10–14	8.45	9.24	10.00	10.72	11.39
15–19	8.41	8.96	9.46	9.89	10.25
20–24	8.23	8.56	8.81	8.98	9.08
25–29	7.96	8.07	8.10	8.05	7.94
30–34	7.61	7.52	7.36	7.14	6.87
35–39	7.19	6.94	6.62	6.27	5.88
40–44	6.74	6.34	5.91	5.45	4.98
45–49	6.27	5.75	5.22	4.70	4.19
50–54	5.70	5.10	4.52	3.97	3.45
55–59	4.98	4.34	3.75	3.21	2.73
60–64	4.05	3.45	2.91	2.43	2.01
65–69	2.97	2.47	2.03	1.65	1.33
70–74	1.89	1.53	1.23	0.98	0.77
75–79	0.95	0.75	0.58	0.45	0.35
80–84	0.32	0.25	0.19	0.14	0.11
85–89	0.07	0.05	0.04	0.03	0.02
90+	0.01	0.01	0.00	0.00	0.00
Birth rate	29.85	34.72	40.00	45.65	51.63
Death rate	39.85	39.72	40.00	40.65	41.63
GRR	1.92	2.21	2.54	2.93	3.36
Average age	31.24	29.21	27.27	25.44	23.71
Dependency ratio	0.59	0.62	0.67	0.73	0.81
Age at death	32.86	28.81	25.00	21.51	18.39

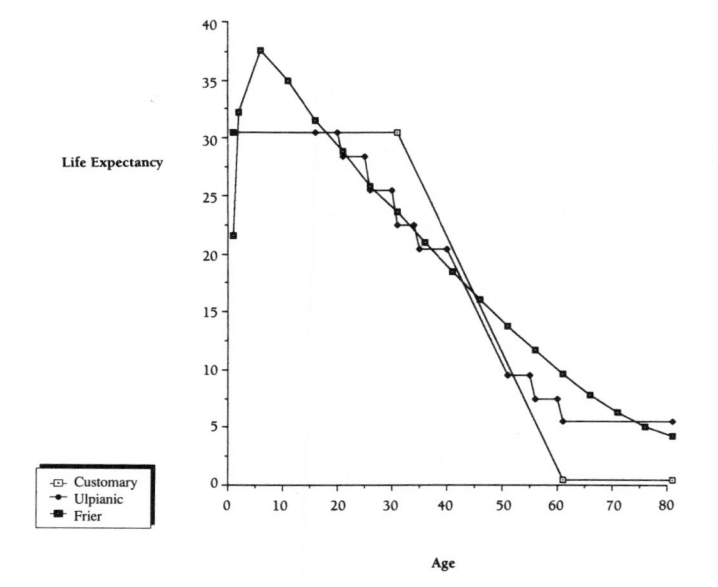

Figure 1. Median life expectancy according to the Ulpianic and customary tables, and average life expectancy according to Frier's life table.

Appendix B

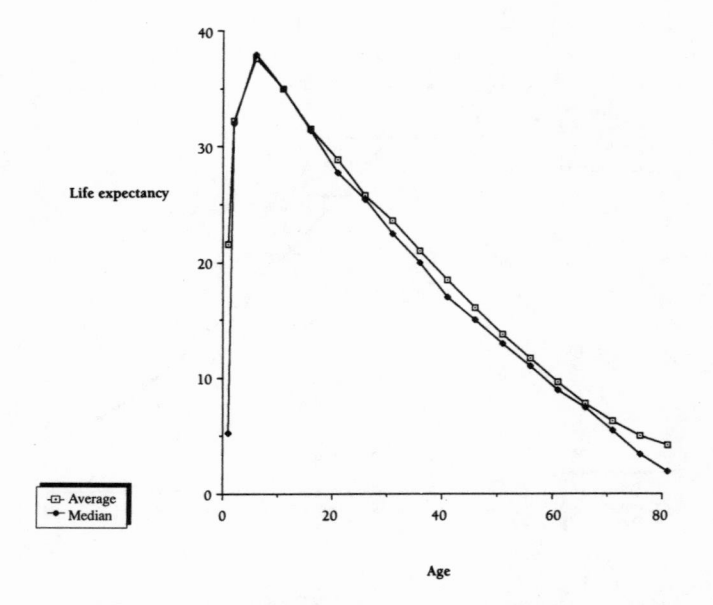

Figure 2. Average and median life expectancy according to Frier's life table.

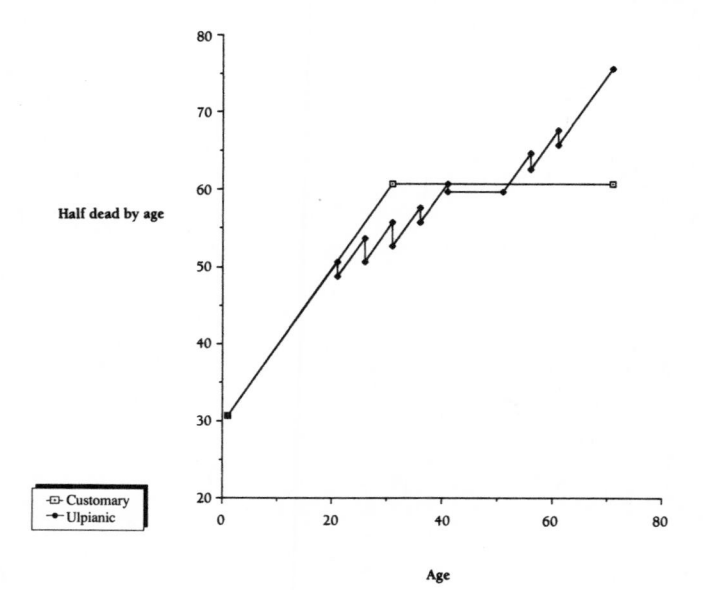

Figure 3. Age by which half a cohort of age x may be expected to be dead, according to the Ulpianic and customary tables.

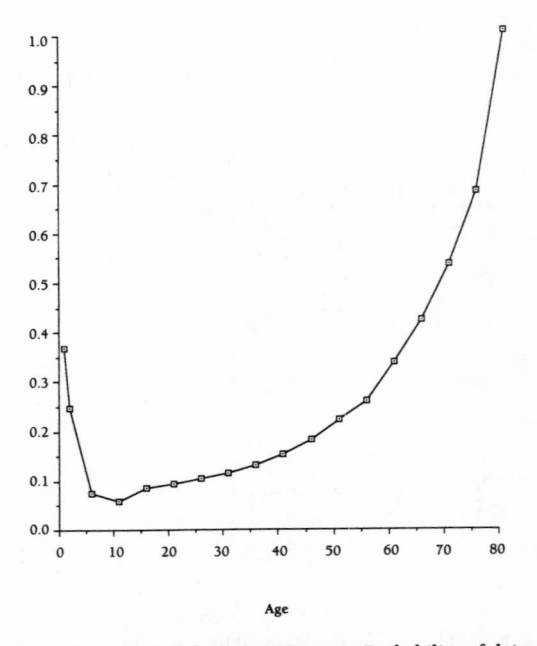

Figure 4. Frier's life table for the Roman Empire: Probability of dying between age x and age x + n [q_x].

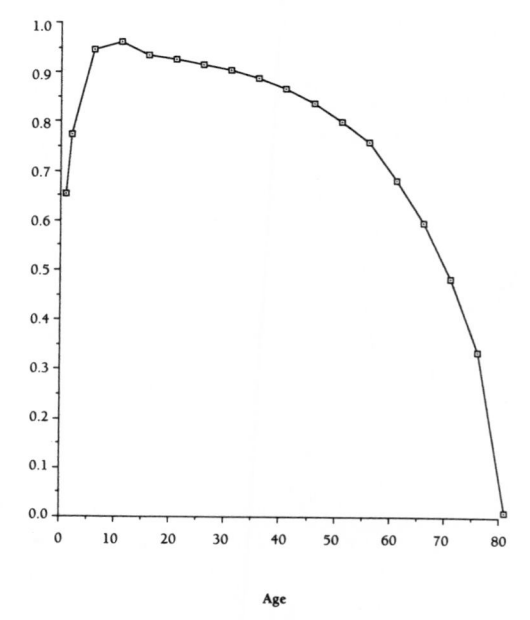

Figure 5. Frier's life table for the Roman Empire: Probability of surviving from age x to age x + n [p_x].

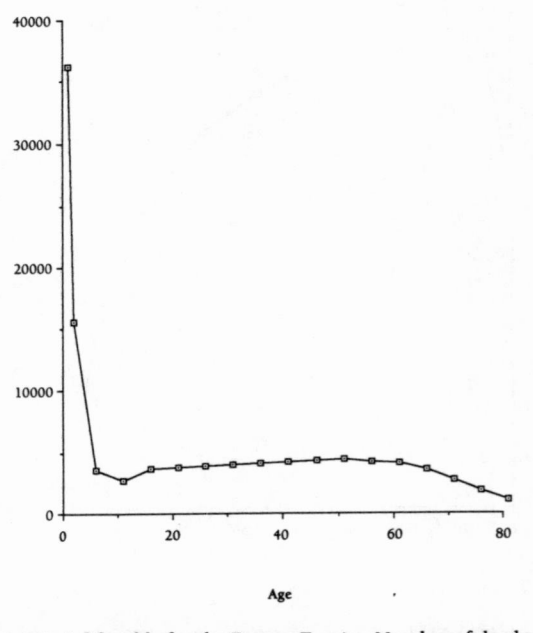

Figure 6. Frier's life table for the Roman Empire: Number of deaths between age x and age x + n [d_x].

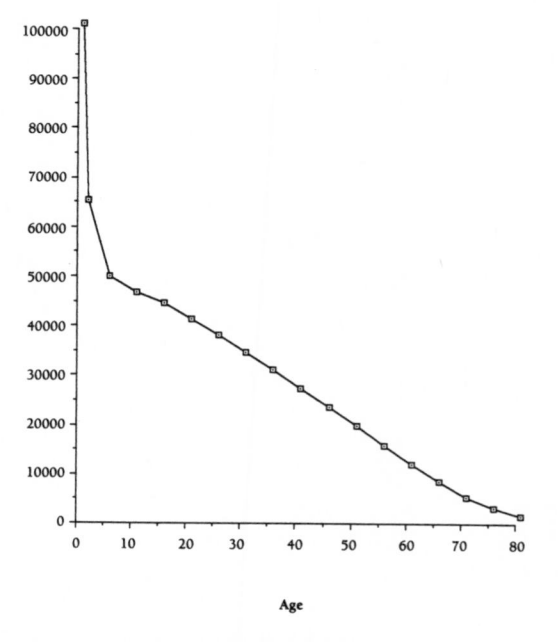

Figure 7. Frier's life table for the Roman Empire: Survivors at exact age x from an original cohort of 100,000 [l_x].

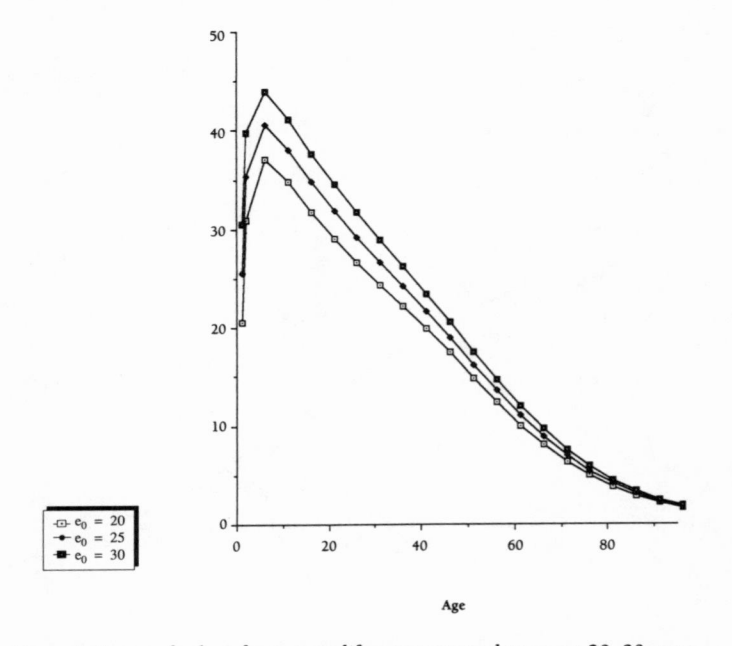

Figure 8. Range of values for average life expectancy where e_0 = 20–30 years. Coale-Demeny[2] Model West Female Levels 1–5.

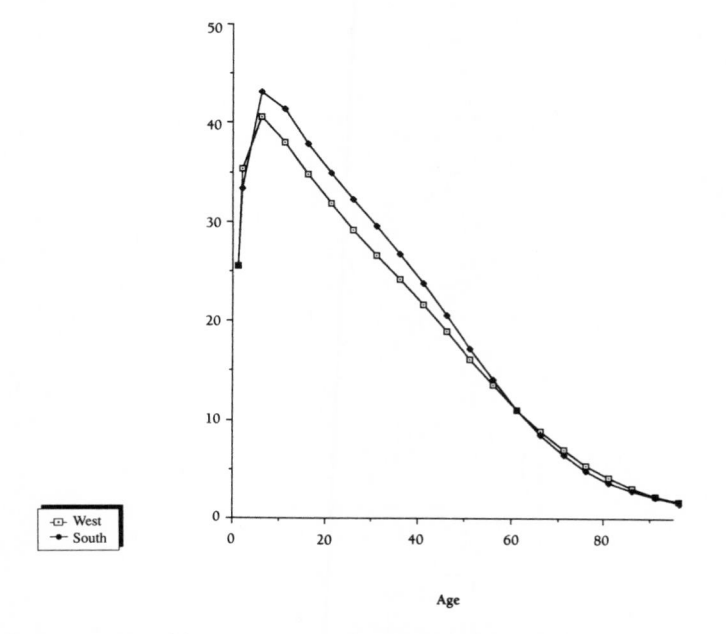

Figure 9. Average life expectancy e_0 = 25. Coale-Demeny[2] Level 3 Female Models West and South.

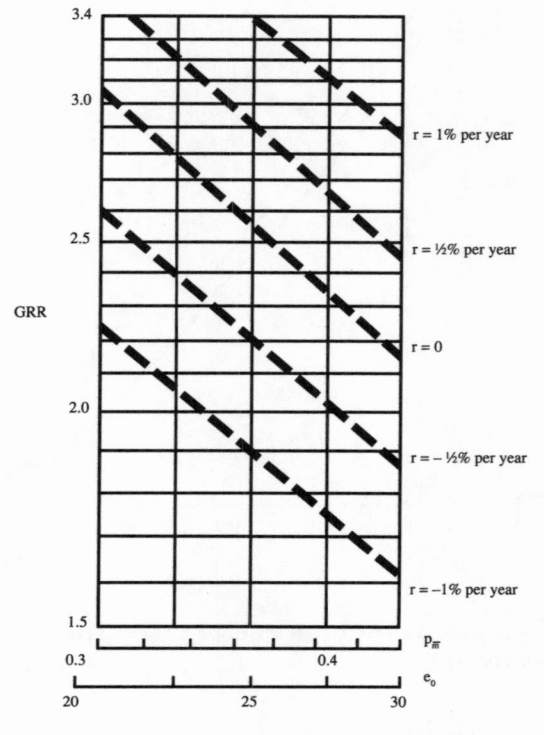

Figure 10. The relative importance of changes in GRR and e_0 in influencing rates of growth in a stable population. Adapted from Wrigley and Schofield [1981] figure 7.10, using values from Coale-Demeny[2] Model West.

Notes

Introduction

1. *Nat. Hist.* 2.21.85 (tr. H. Rackham): "Inconperta haec et inextrica-
   bilia, sed prodenda quia sunt prodita, in quis tamen una ratio geo-
   metricae collectionis numquam fallacis possit non repudiari, si cui
   libeat altius ista persequi, nec ut mensura (id enim velle paene de-
   mentis otii est) sed ut tantum aestumatio coniectandi constet an-
   imo."
2. To quote Brunt (1971) 3, "What does a statement about the Romans
   mean, if we do not know roughly how many Romans there were?"
3. See especially Wrigley and Schofield (1981), Flinn (1981). Flinn's
   comments (p. 6) on the benefits accrued from such methods are
   instructive; they are also a source of some envy for the ancient demographer: "In one important respect . . . the reconstitution and
   aggregation studies possess a supreme virtue. They register facts,
   not hypotheses; and their facts relate to whole populations, not just
   to selected social groups within them. In this area of history, as in
   almost no other, we can penetrate the opacity of history and the
   inarticulateness of the peasant to discern how the common man behaved as accurately and comprehensively as we are able to discern
   how a ruling class behaved." While it must be admitted from the
   outset that such a degree of illumination is not available in the study
   of ancient demography, the same may be said to be true of most
   aspects of investigation into the ancient world, and this fact alone
   should not deter us from the attempt. New methods of handling old
   evidence often bear fresh fruit.
4. Suder's bibliography of Roman demography (1988a) appeared too

late to be of any use in my research, but it certainly gives an idea of the quantity of material available; again, this does not assume quality.

5. See, e.g., de Ste. Croix (1981) 243–49, 509–18; Bradley (1987a) 45 and n. 9, on this point. Examples of mass enslavements were certainly demographically significant cases of migration into the empire.

One. Ancient Evidence

1. Beloch (1886) remains the standard work still for such population estimates of the Roman world; for Athens, see Gomme (1933), together with Hansen (1986).
2. See Salmon (1974), chs. 2 and 3; in fact David Hume, in his eighteenth-century essay *Of the populousness of ancient nations,* had much to say of relevance on the subject; his caution in the face of ancient "statistics" remains instructive, and many modern scholars could benefit from reading his study.
3. Maier (1953–54), still the most thorough introduction to the subject as a whole; cf. also Bernardi (1977) and Duncan-Jones (1982) 259–87, and, in most detail, Brunt (1971).
4. Cf. Salmon (1974) 11–22; Hopkins (1978) 96–98. Russell (1958) 63–68, (1985) 8–25, however, gives a figure as ludicrously low as under 200,000; this gives some indication of the state of our knowledge.
5. Cf. Beloch (1886) 436; Brunt (1971) 124; Hopkins (1978) 68–69. See also Jongman (1988) 65–76.
6. Beloch (1886, 507) gives 54 million, accepted by Hopkins (note, however, that in 1899 Beloch increased this figure substantially); cf. Russell (1958) 7 and Salmon (1974) 23–39 for a range of estimates. More detailed discussion of the sources and problems for these and other figures for population size in antiquity may be found in Brunt (1971) and Hermansen (1978), as well as Maier (1953–54). As Deevey (1960, 197) comments in regard to population estimates in history before about A.D. 1650, "one suspects that writers have been copying each other's guesses."
7. Beloch (1886); Harkness (1896); and Macdonnell (1913). Cf. Étienne (1955, 1959, 1978); Étienne and Fabre (1970); Szilágyi (1959, 1961, 1962, 1963, 1965–67).
8. Szilágyi, whose work represents the most detailed study in this area, used some 43,000 individual ages.
9. See especially the well-known paper by Hopkins (1966–67), together with his more recent contribution (1987). The largely over-

looked study by Éry (1969) adds much that is worthwhile; cf. also Kajanto (1968), Clauss (1973), Suder (1975), and Salmon (1974) 76–112 (of which Salmon [1987] is little more than a repetition). Levison (1898) was already aware of some of the problems with the inscriptional evidence, as indeed was Beloch in 1886. The demographer Louis Henry (1957, 1959, 1960), writing partly in response to Étienne, was the first to highlight clearly the biases produced in using epitaphs as sources for mortality estimates, by discussing the example of the cemetery of Loyasse at Lyon (early nineteenth century).

10. Cf., e.g., Beloch (1886) 50.
11. Using the figures of Macdonnell (1913), who collected 10,697 ages at death from Roman Africa (p. 379, table 1), one finds that 2,835 give ages of 70 years or more (i.e., 26.50%), 317 of 100 years or more (2.96%), and 27 of 120 years or more (0.25%). In the case of Rome, of 9,849 inscriptions from *CIL* 6 that give age at death (5,905 male, 3,944 female), 435 (7.37%) males and 151 (3.83%) females are recorded as dying at or over the age of 60 years; of these 49 males and 10 females are said to be at least 90 years of age.
12. Such as Macdonnell (1913) 375–77, Berelson (1934) 82, and Étienne (1959) 419, finding support in Sallust, *Bell. Iug.* 17.6. Cf. also Pliny, *Ep.* 5.6.5–6, on the healthy air in Tuscany, conducive to long life, and Amm. Marc. 27.4.14 on the long life of the Thracians, due to such factors as "aurae purioris dulcedo." Brogan (1962, 371–72) cites several cases of individuals recorded as dying as centenarians in Roman Africa, and concludes that "Africans of the second and third centuries, by and large, found that life was worth living." Rowland (1971–72) is another striking example of a modern scholar placing too much credence in ancient evidence, in this case inscriptional as regards mortality levels in Roman Sardinia. It is worth noting that Berelson (1934) was so convinced by the demographic information he derived from tombstone inscriptions in *CIL* 6 that he concluded with confidence (pp. 67, 84) that life expectancy at age 60 was higher in ancient Rome than in Rome or the United States of his own day.
13. E.g., Wilcox (1938): 15–89 year olds; Burn (1953): from age 15, (1965): from age 10; Russell (1958): from age 5; Durand (1959–60): males aged 15–42. Hopkins (1987, 123) comments in this context that "this massage of the data is only cosmetic; massaging slightly improves their looks without removing the basic flaws."
14. Hopkins (1966–67) 246.
15. See Suder (1983a) for an idea of the extent of the bibliography.
16. Clauss (1973) table X.
17. Kajanto (1968) 9, with amended figures given here.

18. Russell (1958); Blumenkranz (1961).
19. Hombert and Préaux (1945, 1946). Mummy labels were assumed to be of similar value, though perhaps related to a lower social class. Particular attention is paid here, as elsewhere in this book, to Roman Egypt, both because of the special nature of the evidence from that province and because Roman Egypt has formed a particular focus of my research into age.
20. 34.27 years for males, 29.13 for females; Willcox (1938) used the same method on a sample of 141 mummy labels and produced similar results.
21. Of the sample of 813 ages, only 61 (7.5%) were under the age of 5 years, and only 172 (21.2%) under 15 years. The sex ratio in the sample is 183.65 males for every 100 females.
22. Hombert and Préaux (1946) 95–96; Willcox (1938).
23. Hooper (1956); males = 36.89, females = 28.49 years.
24. Though this too is open to doubt: see now Boyaval (1977b, 1977c, 1986).
25. Hooper calculated a ratio of 83 males to 82 females, but in fact subsequent examination, with a slightly larger sample, gives a ratio of 92 males to only 80 females; cf. Boyaval (1976) 223.
26. I note from a review in *Revue des études grecques* 100 (1987) 501–3 that a further sample of 173 epitaphs has come to light from Kom Abou Billou, so no doubt we can shortly expect to see a further analysis of data for demographic purposes.
27. Boyaval (1976).
28. Abydos: $e_0 = 13.6$ (n = 5!); Hawara in the Fayoum: $e_0 = 45$ (n = 17, none of which is less than 10 years of age but 2 of which are more than 70). See Boyaval (1977a) 346.
29. Éry (1969) 60; Greek inscriptions from Rome (n = 822) collected in Szilágyi (1959) 45–47.
30. Kajanto (1968) 21.
31. It is interesting to note, for example, that Aristotle, *de Long. et Brev. Vit.* 1.465a, states that people have different life-spans in different places, due to climatic differences; his theory is that people live longer the warmer the climate. Seasonal differences in mortality are also worth consideration: hot summers and cold winters tend to take their toll, especially on the very young and old. Autumn was regarded as a particularly lethal period (cf., e.g., Mayor on Juv. 4.56). See further Boyaval (1981a); Duncan-Jones (1980) 78 n. 52, (1990) 104 n. 31, and also chapter 3, n. 86.
32. Cf. Éry (1969) 56–60.
33. Cf. Saller and Shaw (1984) 127–28.
34. On evidence for slave mortality levels from tombstone inscriptions, cf. also Suder (1983b).

35. To be fair, Étienne (1987, 65–66) recognizes some of "mes erreurs de jeunesse."
36. There is much of interest in Sippel (1987).
37. Clauss (1973) 398–402; cf. Finley (1981) 158 and Duncan-Jones (1990) 103–4.
38. Cf., e.g., Burn (1965), who notes an apparent increase in expectation of life from the Christian inscriptions of the fourth to sixth centuries. See now Hopkins (1987) 119.
39. Clauss (1973) table X; Éry (1969) 62–63.
40. See especially Duncan-Jones (1977).
41. *CIL* 8.28082 = *ILA* 1.2831. Cf. the use of the words "p⟨lus⟩ m⟨inus⟩" in many statements of age on epitaphs; e.g., *CIL* 6.3450. For another instance of conflicting statements of age, cf. *CIL* 6.21303a and 21319: in one case the man is said to have been 80 years and 3 months old, the woman 60 years and 8 months; in the other, the same man was 80 years and 8 months, the same woman 63 years and 8 months.
42. Shryock and Siegel (1976) 128: "There is a notable tendency, in particular, to report an age over 100 for persons of very advanced age, stemming from a desire to share in the esteem generally accorded extreme old age or from a gross ignorance of the true age." They go on to observe that even in modern censuses, data for those over the age of 85 years are considered as "not too meaningful." See also Acsádi and Nemeskéri (1970) 17–24.
43. In Szilágyi's overall sample of 42,909 ages, 25,585 (59.63%) relate to males and 17,324 (40.37%) to females, an apparent sex ratio of 147.69 males to 100 females. For discussion of sex ratios and related topics, see further chapter 3.
44. Cf. Hopkins (1966–67) 261; Éry (1969) tables 4 and 5.
45. See Éry (1969) table 3.
46. See, e.g., Burn (1953) 10–13.
47. Hopkins (1966–67) 260–63, and cf. Hopkins (1987) 125.
48. Boyaval (1978), against Hombert and Préaux (1945) 144.
49. Szilágyi (1962) 297; Clauss (1973) 406–9.
50. Cf. Étienne and Fabre (1970), a study of the *officiales* of Carthage, which they regard as one body of evidence belonging to "certains cas privilégiés" where the epigraphic material does, they insist, reflect reality; but the point is that, while the figures may appear plausible enough overall, we have no way of knowing whether they reflect reality. For the use of median life expectancy (i.e., the age to which half the population may be expected to survive), see, e.g., Burn (1953). For manipulation of figures, cf. Aguilella Almer, Lopez Cerda, Montes Suay, and Pereira Menaut (1975).
51. Most notably Lassère (1977) on the African epigraphic material

(cf. Lassère [1987], incorporating skeletal evidence from Africa also); cf. also Garcia Merino (1975) for the extensive (and in my view misguided) demographic use of a limited body of epigraphical testimony for a limited geographical area over a vast span of time. Frier (1982, 235–38) notes that inscriptional evidence from around Cirta in North Africa provides data that appear strikingly similar to population statistics from Mauritius for 1942–46 and are, therefore, demographically plausible (exactly what "demographically plausible" means we shall further discuss in chapter 2). This much is true, at least when considering figures for those deceased from the ages of about 5 to 50 years (see Frier [1982] table 2 column B). But as Frier himself notes (236 n. 58), this inscriptional evidence will only have any demographic significance if we are dealing with a stationary population (i.e., the rates of birth and death are equal, and there is no distorting effect from migration levels), and if the evidence suffers from no biases in terms of age, sex, and class differences. Frier himself notes that "all this is highly unlikely." In other words, from picking and choosing among the evidence we may find cases that appear demographically reasonable—even strikingly so—but in which no certain confidence can be placed. Some bodies of evidence may *support* demographic conclusions or impressions that are reached, but such evidence cannot be used on its own to *prove* such conclusions. See further Hopkins (1987) 121–26. The brief summary of the demographic picture of the Roman world by Minois (1989, 78–81) shows what little progress has been made.

52. For the use of a different type of inscription to calculate mortality levels, see my appendix A.

53. Parkin (1992) ch. 5.

54. Parkin (1992) ch. 5.

55. Hombert and Préaux (1952) 156–57: for males (n = 256) e_0 = 27.23, for females (n = 247) e_0 = 26.39.

56. Pliny, *Nat. Hist.* 7.49.162–64; Phlegon, *FGH* 2.257.37.

57. I calculate that the total extant today, about 320 in number, represents only 0.0008 percent of the total ever produced.

58. Hopkins (1980) 320.

59. Hopkins (1980) 318–20.

60. By Hombert and Préaux's sample, 103.64 males per 100 females, or, as calculated by Hopkins (1980), 107.24:100. See also chapter 3.

61. I note from the *American Philological Association Abstracts* for 1990 (p. 188) that Bruce Frier and Roger Bagnall are conducting a demographic study of the census returns from Roman Egypt; the preliminary report by Frier states that life expectancy at birth on

the basis of this evidence appears to be between 23 and 24 years, with male life expectancy at over 27 years and female at just under 20 years (Frier suggests that the female figure is accurate, the male an exaggeration due to migration).

62. *P.Princ.* 1.8 of ca. A.D. 40/41.
63. Though more than Szilágyi's 75 mentioned earlier.
64. Samuel, Hastings, Bowman, and Bagnall (1971). It might be said that this is the closest we may ever get in ancient history to the demographic method of family reconstitution, albeit in a very primitive form.
65. Ibid., 19.
66. Ibid., 63–75.
67. Ibid., 29–47; he does express some doubts (p. 38).
68. P. S. Derow and E. O. Derow in *Phoenix* 27 (1973) 80–88.
69. Numbers used here refer to the list in Samuel, Hastings, Bowman, and Bagnall (1971) 63–75.
70. Ibid., 39–43.
71. By my calculations, of the 160 individuals for whom money tax receipts are extant, 112 have 3 or less such receipts. The 3 individuals for whom more than 20 receipts for taxes are extant are numbers 79, 85, and 90.
72. Cf., e.g., numbers 30, 33, 44, 45, 71, 73, 75.
73. Some of which the editors themselves are aware of: Samuel, Hastings, Bowman, and Bagnall (1971) 22–24; at p. 43, Hastings also notes the "small amount of data."
74. The authors argue on plausible grounds (ibid., 23–24) that migration was relatively negligible anyway.
75. In fact it was A. DeMoivre in 1725 (*Annuities on Lives: Or, the Valuation of Annuities Upon Any Number of Lives; as also, of Reversions,* London) who suggested an arithmetic progression in mortality rates between the ages of 12 and 86 years (the latter being what he considered as the maximum potential life-span). The English actuary Benjamin Gompertz in 1825 realized, however, that the probability of dying increases exponentially with age ("On the nature of the function expressive of the law of human mortality," *Philosophical Transactions of the Royal Society* 27 [1825] 513–85), and this realization was refined in 1860 to produce the Gompertz-Makeham formula for calculating the rate of mortality at various ages. It is now realized, however, that even this approach oversimplifies reality, since a mathematical formula describing the relationship between age and mortality risk takes no account of social and economic factors, which may also significantly affect the chances of surviving from one year to the next. A graph of a typical survivorship curve in a high mortality regime may be seen in figure 5, discussed in chapter 2.

76. Samuel, Hastings, Bowman, and Bagnall (1971) 25 for the quotation, 23 and 25 for the qualification.
77. Ibid., 46–47.
78. Boyaval (1975, 60, and 1977b, 263) misunderstands and assumes average life expectancy *at birth* to be 29.4 years (i.e., 15 + 14.4), which is certainly not what the editors here say or mean.
79. Samuel, Hastings, Bowman, and Bagnall (1971) 25.
80. Its precise meaning and the problems involved in its interpretation will be considered in chapter 2.
81. *Dig.* 35.2.68pr.; for the other fragments of Macer's work preserved in the *Digest,* see Lenel's *Palingenesia* I.570–71. The text quoted here is that of Mommsen's edition.
82. Cf. Gaius, *Inst.* 2.227; Justinian, *Inst.* 2.22; and *Dig.* 35.2.1pr., in which Paul quotes the law.
83. From as early as the eighteenth century: see *Index Interpolationum* II.322, and Lenel, *Palingenesia* I.571 n.4.
84. Though it is strange that Mommsen makes no mention of it in his edition of the *Digest.* Duncan-Jones (1990, 96 n. 10) defends the reading of *Falcidia.*
85. Cf. Stein (1962) 341.
86. This problem occupies Frier (1982) at some length (pp. 220–24), and his discussion—though at times rather circuitous—provides some plausible conjectures.
87. Frier (1982, 217) rightly stresses that Macer does not say that Ulpian actually devised the table, only that he "writes" it; for convenience's sake we will continue to refer to it as the Ulpianic table.
88. Despite the assumptions of Frier (and also of Hopkins [1987] 120), the only argument for believing that the customary table predates the Ulpianic is that it is cruder in form. It may be the case that "Ulpian" refined an earlier, simplistic table, but equally it may be that the customary table arose later (as in fact Appleton [1920, 6–7] took for granted) as an easier form to work with than that described by Ulpian. *Solitum est* may mean "it has been customary" or "it is customary" (I am not convinced by Frier [1982] 219 n. 11 against the latter translation).
89. *Basilika* 47.1.67.
90. Ferrini, writing in 1889; cited by Stein (1962) 343 n. 34.
91. Parkin (1992) ch. 4 and 7.
92. As discussed in Parkins (1992) ch. 4.
93. E.g., Hombert and Préaux (1946) 91, 95, 97; Russell (1958) 24 (mentions the Ulpianic table but makes no use of it); Étienne (1959) 419–20; Degrassi (1964) 90; Éry (1969) 62–64; Acsádi and Nemeskéri (1970) 215; Lassère (1977) 563.
94. Victor (1987) 69. Further delusions may be seen in Minois (1987, 119) who, while arguing that the Ulpianic table is "un document

d'une valeur inestimable," unfortunately dates it to the third century B.C. I note that the English translation of 1989 amends the error.

95. Greenwood (1940). Cf. Hopkins (1966–67) 264 n. 32 (though some more detail in Hopkins [1987] 120–21; Brunt (1971) 132 n. 2.

96. Which Frier (1982, 224 n. 30, and 229 n. 40) fails ever really to confront. Greenwood's ideas were later developed by Stein (1962).

97. Frier himself assumes that infant mortality was high. Hombert and Préaux (1946, 97) state that the creator of the Ulpianic table was a Roman "non au courant de la démographie—et particulièrement incapable d'apprécier la gravité de la mortalité infantile"; incapable of measuring it precisely, perhaps, but anyone intelligent enough to have constructed a table as complex as this could hardly have been unaware of how serious a factor infant mortality was in the population. On infant mortality, see chapter 3.

98. Which was entitled to enjoy the usufruct for 100 years: *Digest* 33.2.8.

99. Frier (1982) 221–22.

100. Hendriks (1852) 224; Roby (1884) 190.

101. Stein (1962) 335–36.

102. Thus Greenwood (1940) 248; Stein (1962) 345.

103. Frier (1982). His life table is given in slightly amended form here in table 6. Frier has brought to the subject of Roman demography a level of sophistication previously only displayed by Keith Hopkins. While I question in some detail here many of Frier's assumptions, I in no way wish to give the impression that I question his demographic expertise—far from it. And in the case of the Ulpianic table, Frier's expertise in Roman law is equally obvious. Less detailed defense of the Ulpianic table by other authors adds little to Frier's arguments; cf. most recently Jacques (1987) 1296–97, with references to earlier literature. Note also Duncan-Jones (1990) 96–101, who compares the Ulpianic figures with the Coale-Demeny tables (on which see my chapter 2) and concludes that the Ulpianic *forma* either reflects a population (perhaps servile) in decline with a very low average life expectancy at birth, or is not based on accurate demographic observation, or reflects a population whose demographic experience was significantly different from any other population, real or theoretical. I would favor the second option.

104. Frier (1982) 219–20. I note that Appleton (1920, 5) made the same suggestion. Dupâquier (1973, 1067) states that the Ulpianic figures correspond "sans doute à la durée de vie probable (inter-

valle au bout duquel a disparu la moitié de l'effectif d'une génération), et non à l'espérance de vie proprement dite (ou durée de vie moyenne . . .)." Jacques (1987) 1296, in believing that the Ulpianic figures imply "une connaissance pragmatique de la démographie romaine," states that "les espérances de vie reflètent sans doute plutôt un optimum qu'une moyenne."

105. For comparison, I have drawn in figure 2 curves derived from Frier's own life table of values for average life expectancy as compared with those of median life expectancy. It may be seen from this that while the two are very close from the age of 5 years, average life expectancy at birth is over 21 years while median life expectancy is under 5 years. So in fact the Ulpianic figure of 30 years at birth is closer to an average life expectancy value here than to a median one.

106. Roby (1884) 190–91; Stein (1962) 343.

107. Cf. also Hume (1777) 443; Milne (1837) 513; Trenerry (1926) 151–52.

108. On which see *RE* iv (1900) 726–59.

109. Cf. Hopkins (1983) 211–17; on burial clubs, see now Flambard (1987).

110. Hombert and Préaux (1946) 91–92; Levison (1898) 80.

111. See Parkin (1992) chs. 5 and 6; specifically on death notices, cf. Schulz (1951) 75: "Registration of deaths was unknown to Roman legislation"; Kaser (1971) I.273: "Der Tod wird nicht amtlich registriert, aber die Tatsache häufig beurkundet."

112. Cf. Parkin (1992) ch. 6.

113. Frier (1982) 228.

114. Cf. Suetonius, *Nero* 39.1, and other sources cited in *RE* xiii (1926) 113–14 (Latte) and Daremberg-Saglio 3.2.1221–22 (Hild).

115. And I am not dismissing the possibility, though the ancients seem to have been more interested in longevity than in life expectation.

116. *Dig.* 35.2.55.

117. Duncan-Jones (1990, 100–101) states, however, that "in many cases, probably the majority, the subjects of Ulpian's calculation can only have been slaves or ex-slaves."

118. The source of which is, as noted previously, never discussed but is presumed to be statistical: Frier (1982) 226.

119. Frier (1982) 229.

120. Frier (1982) 214, 228.

121. Frier (1982) 251.

122. Frier (1983) 343.

123. Éry (1969) 51, 62.

124. Hollingsworth (1969) 43–44. The only example I am aware of where an ancient historian expresses any pessimism about the

usefulness of the skeletal data as regards demographic studies is the brief mention by Hopkins (1987) 121.

125. To avoid any possible confusion, I should perhaps stress that by the phrase "skeletal age" I mean in this context the age of the individual at death, not the length of time that the skeleton has been buried, and by "aging of skeletons" the determination of the age at death of the individual.

126. A stationary population is one with a zero rate of growth and with no significant level of migration, or at least where immigration and emigration rates are balanced for the various age classes and for both sexes; see chapter 2.

127. Cf. the case of the skeletons of 175 newborn babies or fetuses, together with those of 100 dogs, 1 adult, and 1 older child, being found in a single well in Athens, probably dating from the first century B.C. (the Sullan siege of Athens in 84 B.C.?); the cause of death is thought to be starvation or plague (Angel [1945] 311, 330). In *Archaeologia* 21 (1921) 150 A. H. Cocks describes the excavation of a Romano-British "homestead" in Buckinghamshire where the skeletons of 97 mostly newborn babies were found in one area (cited by Harris [1980] 123). Slim (1983) describes an infant burial site in Roman Africa where the oldest skeleton found is said to be that of a 15-year-old and where most appear to be under the age of 5 years—the average age is given as 25 months, and Slim (p. 177) notes the different practices carried out in the case of the funeral of a young person in the Roman world. It is tempting but ill-advised to see in such collections of young burials evidence of the practice of child exposure: see chapter 3 for a discussion of the mentality governing the burial (or nonburial) of young children.

128. The following are the main works I have consulted for details on the aging and sexing of skeletons: Vallois (1960); Genovés (1969); Acsádi and Nemeskéri (1970) ch. 3; Cornwall (1974) 218–37; Ubelaker (1978) 41–67; Brothwell (1981); Molleson (1981); Boddington, Garland, and Janaway (1987). New sophistication continues to be brought to the subject, as well as an increased awareness of the difficulties in accurate and precise evaluation of age and sex. Morris (1987, 57–62) has a useful discussion of Attic cemeteries (cf. his appendix 1), but he feels safe only in an age classification of skeletons in two classes: adult/youth and child/infant. In what follows it should become apparent that such a loose classification is in fact the best we can hope for, but it is not adequate for proper demographic analysis.

129. Weiss (1972) detects a 12 percent bias toward the sexing of skeletons as male.

130. For whatever reason: cf. chapter 3.

131. Ubelaker (1978) 46.
132. Humerus, radius, ulna, femur, tibia, and fibula.
133. On the age of puberty in antiquity, see chapter 3.
134. This method was used, for example, by Angel (1947) for skeletons from ancient Greece; the article is still widely cited as authoritative. More detailed treatment of skeletal remains, together with an awareness of the problems, is given by Angel (1971) in his study of the prehistoric skeletal remains from Lerna (modern Myloi, in the plain of Argos).
135. See Ubelaker (1978) 59–60.
136. Cf. Acsádi and Nemeskéri (1970) 123, 126–27; Ubelaker (1978) 53–59.
137. Cf. Ubelaker (1978) 64–66.
138. See Acsádi and Nemeskéri (1970) 135–37; cf. Parkes (1986, 122–23) on aging a skeleton by the level of amino acids present in tooth enamel.
139. See now papers by J. Henderson and T. Waldron in Boddington, Garland, and Janaway (1987) 43–64.
140. Weiss (1973) 59.
141. Cf. Reece (1988) 85: "it now seems certain, and studies in progess will probably document this, that you cannot suggest an absolute age for a skeleton from any presently known characteristics"; also T. Waldron (1989) 65: "the methods which are used to age the skeleton are highly subjective and thus prone to much error. . . . ten year intervals are probably the finest divisions that can be made and many anthropologists and paleopathologists prefer to place skeletons into descriptive categories—young, mature and old adults, for example."
142. From Acsádi and Nemeskéri (1970) 133–34, whose study is widely regarded still as the fundamental work on the subject.
143. I. Lengyel in 1971 and K. Éry in 1973. The two sets of figures are conveniently tabulated in Fülep (1984), excursus 2, pp. 177–79.
144. Frier uses the description and life tables produced by Acsádi and Nemeskéri (1970) 227–28, 296–301. It should be pointed out that Acsádi and Nemeskéri use both skeletal and inscriptional evidence as equally valid sources of data.
145. Though one is immediately struck by the very low infant mortality rate recorded at Keszthely-Dobogo, which is typical of most cemetery sites and which is demographically unrealistic.
146. Clarke (1979) 24–94, 123–27, 342 (skeletal report by Mary Harman).
147. Ibid., 123: "of the 185 people who survived until they were about 20, only 52 definitely died when older than 30."
148. Ibid., 124–25, table 4.

149. Wenham (1968) 2:111–76: skeletal report by R. Warwick.
150. For the method, see chapter 2.
151. McWhirr, Viner, and Wells (1982); burial report by C. Wells, pp. 134–202.
152. Harman, Molleson, and Price (1981).
153. Hawkes and Wells (1983).
154. Subsequent differences of opinion also seem to have surfaced regarding the age and sex classifications: ibid. 31–34.
155. Figures in table 5 were collected and corrected from information given in Dzierzykray-Rogalski (1983).
156. In fact it is about what we would expect for the time on the basis of comparative evidence: cf. chapter 3.
157. Hurst and Raskams (1984) 222–28; report on human remains by J. H. Schwartz and D. C. Dirkmaat.
158. Partridge (1981) 277–304 (especially 284–86), report by C. Wells, sample size of 92; Millett (1986), sample size of only 7.
159. Cf. Gejvall (1969) 468–79 and Morris (1987) 61–62.
160. Hirst (1985) 33–35.
161. Evison (1987) 123–29, 197–201; specialist report by R. Powers and R. Cullen. Passages quoted are from p. 123 (by D. Brothwell) and p. 128.
162. As, e.g., on lead content—see my chapter 3 and cf. Waldron (1989).
163. Cf. Acsádi and Nemeskéri (1970) 58; Ubelaker (1978) 97; Boddington, Garland, and Janaway (1987) 180. There may be some hope for the future, as with the large skeletal sample available for analysis at Pompeii (cf. Russell [1985] 1–8), but great care must be taken both with the methods of determining age and sex, and with the conclusions reached as to whether the sample is representative and not distorted by biases of one kind or another. The skeletons at Pompeii offer us a unique opportunity to glimpse the demography of a "living" ancient population, and it is to be hoped that such an opportunity will receive the care and objectivity it deserves. See also Bisel (1988) on the skeletons of Herculaneum.
164. Cf. Finley (1985a) 27–31, quoting A. H. M. Jones's 1948 London Inaugural Lecture: "it is unlikely that I shall long be able to conceal the ignominious truth, that there are no ancient statistics."
165. Cf. the very apposite comments by Whittaker (1976), reviewing Salmon (1974).
166. Frézouls (1977, 109–10) has some useful remarks concerning the lack of awareness in antiquity of demographic variables and he makes the comment—obvious but sometimes forgotten—that such lack of awareness does not necessarily mean that no such population problems existed.

167. Tertullian, *de Anima* 30.1–4, written at the beginning of the third century A.D. J. H. Waszink, in his edition (Amsterdam, 1947), gives the date of composition as ca. 210–13. See further T. D. Barnes, *Tertullian: A Historical and Literary Study* (Oxford, 1971), especially p. 219. Hume (1777, 459) had this to say on the passage at hand: "The air of rhetoric and declamation which appears in this passage, diminishes somewhat from its authority, but does not entirely destroy it"; in the 1752 edition of his essay, he made the added comment that "a man of violent imagination, such as Tertullian, augments everything equally; and for that reason his comparative judgments are the most to be depended on."

168. *De Anima* 30.2: "invenimus autem apud commentarios etiam humanarum antiquitatum [perhaps of Varro: cf. Waszink's comments] paulatim humanum genus exuberasse" ("we find, however, among the records of human antiquities, that the human race has gradually grown abundantly").

169. *De Anima* 30.4: "revera lues et fames et bella et voragines civitatum pro remedio deputanda, tamquam tonsura inolescentis generis humani" ("Indeed pestilence, famine, wars, and earthquakes must be regarded as a remedy for nations, as a means of pruning the burgeoning human race").

170. See the papers in *Arethusa* 8, no. 2 (1975) on classical Greek population theory. Plato, *Laws* 5.740–41, provides some particularly interesting ideas on population theory, for example on family size in the ideal population.

171. *Ad Demetrianum* 3; as Duncan-Jones (1980, 79–80) notes, Cyprian was writing in the same province and probably in the same town as Tertullian some 40 years earlier.

172. Cf., e.g., Boak (1955) (together with Finley [1958]); Rostovtzeff (1957) ch. 8 and 11; Jones (1964) 1040–45; Finley (1968) 153–61; Salmon (1974) 114–79.

173. For a valuable collection of contemporary views, see Géza Alföldy, "The crisis of the third century as seen by contemporaries," *Greek, Roman and Byzantine Studies* 15 (1974) 89–111, especially pp. 101–2.

174. Duncan-Jones (1980) 75.

175. Including *anachoresis;* cf. p. 23 above.

176. Cf. Wrigley and Schofield (1981) 457–66.

177. M. M. Sage, *Cyprian* (Philadelphia, 1975), 275.

178. Eusebius, *Hist. Eccl.* 7.21.9–10.

179. Over how long a time period? It is not specified, but perhaps was very short, if in fact the corn dole had only recently been intro-

duced to Alexandria; cf. J. R. Rea in *The Oxyrhynchus Papyri*, vol. 40 (London, 1972), 1–2.

180. These rough calculations are based on model life tables: cf. chapter 2.

181. Dionysius's depiction of an aging population actually suggests a fall in fertility, rather than a rise in mortality, over the long term, unless age-specific mortality (i.e., specific to the young) on a dramatic scale is responsible.

182. Pliny, *Nat. Hist.* 6.30.122.

183. Josephus, *de Bell. Jud.* 2.16.4.385. As Russell (1987, 76) notes, one should perhaps allow a fair degree of exaggeration in Herod's calculation, since he is trying to dissuade the Jews from revolting.

184. Diodorus Siculus 1.31.8—perhaps Josephus's source?

185. Diodorus Siculus 17.52.6.

186. Philo, *In Flacc.* 43; Lewis (1983, 31) incorrectly takes this to mean the Jewish population of Alexandria alone. On the population of Egypt, cf. Walek-Czernecki (1938); Finley (1985a) 63; Bowman (1986) 17–18; and Delia (1988).

187. Appian, *Gallic History* 1.2; Diodorus Siculus 5.25.1; Hume (1777) 454. Multiplying by four to allow for women and children is simple and simplistic but is justifiable as an approximation, on the basis that adult males in a high mortality and fertility regime comprise about one-quarter of the whole population; for such assumptions (with minor variations), cf. Brunt (1971) 59, 117, 261 n. 4; Duncan-Jones (1963) 87 n. 24, (1982) 264 n. 4; Hobson (1985) 219–20; Engels (1990) 83. Caesar, *de Bell. Gall.* 1.29, seems to make just such a calculation. In the Coale-Demeny tables (on which see chapter 2), in a stationary population where average life expectancy at birth is 25 years, males and females aged between 15 and 44 years represent 46.26 percent of the population.

188. The figures from 508 B.C. to A.D. 14 are conveniently set out in Brunt (1971) 13–14, who also gives the best critical analysis of the figures. For the early period, see now Ward (1990).

189. Cf. the figures for 209/8 and 194/93 B.C., which seem to be out by 1 million.

190. The growth in numbers from 86 to 70 B.C. may be a reflection of the granting of citizenship to Italians over the period, though one might have expected the increase to have been evident already in 86. Cf. Brunt (1971) 91–99.

191. Compare Brunt (1971) for his central thesis that the freeborn population was in decline.

Two. Ancient History and Modern Demography

1. Mention should also be made of the work by M. H. Hansen on Athens in the fifth and fourth centuries B.C.
2. Oldenziel (1987) 93, 98, 99.
3. Hopkins (1974) 78. Cf. Hopkins (1987) 121 on the study of skeletons for demographic purposes: "The ratio of hard work to intellectual reward is lamentably meagre. Perhaps that is the masochism of our profession."
4. Cf. Flinn (1981) 1, and see also my introduction, n. 3.
5. Cf. the debate between Den Boer (1974) and Hopkins (1974).
6. Howell (1976) 25–28; cf. Bocquet and Masset (1977), and Reece (1988) 84.
7. Cf. Reece (1988) 84 for a rather more straightforward statement of basically the same idea: "Either we say that man has not changed that much in 1600 years, so modern death patterns are representative of the human population over the past 30,000 years. Or we say from our evidence the Romans were physically quite distinct from us in their patterns of life and death. I follow the first course without any doubts at all because the evidence is totally against any such observable and absolute changes in the human machine over the past 30,000 years."
8. Den Boer (1973) 34.
9. The precise relationship (if indeed there is any relationship at all) between mortality and fertility levels is still not perfectly understood, especially in terms of the demographic transition. We will return briefly to this problem.
10. I rely principally on Cox (1976), Shryock and Siegel (1976), and Newell (1988).
11. Migration is of particular demographic importance in dealing with an urban population and should not be underestimated in terms of age and sex structure.
12. Cf. Weiss (1975). I disagree with Hansen (1985, 173–76) on this point.
13. Shaw (1987b) 36.
14. Newell (1988) 120.
15. As indeed they are used at various points by Shaw and Saller: e.g., Saller and Shaw (1984) 130 n. 27, 136 n. 49; Saller (1986) 21 n. 35, (1987a) 31 n. 27, etc.
16. Frier (1982); his life table is given here in table 6 in slightly amended form: Some incorrect figures are revised, a d_x column is added, and his FB_x column is omitted.
17. For the sake of conciseness, p_x is not given in the life table. As stated above, $p_x = 1 - q_x$.

18. This number will obviously be smaller than the number of the population of that age at the beginning of the year (the number used in calculating the q_x value) since some of the cohort will die during the course of the year.

19. In this case, 76,716; i.e., L_0.

20. Frier (1982) 249. The same mistake in reading the IMR is made by Duncan-Jones (1990) 94.

21. A birth rate of 50/1000—$e_0 = 20$ in a stationary population—is regarded as about the highest possible in any society over the long term.

22. Use has been made of them, e.g., by Hopkins, Saller and Shaw, Hansen, Duncan-Jones, Engels, Golden, and Harris—see my bibliography.

23. Cf., e.g., E. Badian in *Journal of Roman Studies* 72 (1982) 165, reviewing Hopkins (1978).

24. Frier's suggestion (1982, 244) that "Ulpian's life table . . . should be used to criticise the Coale-Demeny models, rather than the reverse" strikes me as ridiculous.

25. Yet Hopkins for some reason for a long time insisted on still referring to them, and Rawson (1986) 245, whose brief bibliographical discussion on demography is clearly influenced by Hopkins, mentions only the 1956 U.N. tables. See now Hopkins (1987) 116 n. 9; while it is true that any well-constructed life table is valid for Roman historians, it seems better (as I shall argue) to make use of the wider applicability offered by the Coale-Demeny tables. It should be noted that the United Nations issued a new set of model life tables in 1982, based entirely upon 72 empirical life tables from developing countries: cf. Newell (1988) 139–40. However, it is difficult to assess their applicability to ancient demography, and at this stage the Coale-Demeny tables are to be preferred.

26. Including by some ancient historians, notably Saller and Shaw, as well as Frier.

27. The method is described in the second edition of the Coale-Demeny tables (1983) pp. 9–28. Henceforth all references will be to this second edition and will be cited as Coale-Demeny².

28. Cf. Frier (1982) 251 n. 84, whose dismissal of the South tables is unjustified; cf. Brunt (1987) 719. Saller and Shaw seem undecided between the two regions and employ one or the other in various places.

29. For different q_x values, cf. Coale-Demeny², p. 26. The two tables, West and South Level 3 female, are given in my tables 9 and 10.

30. Hollingsworth (1969) 343.

31. Cf. Zubrow (1976) 1–25 for an introduction to the links between demography and anthropology.

32. Cf. Weiss (1973) 44–45.
33. Hall (1978). Similarly Moore, Swedlund, and Armelagos (1975) discussed in detail particular problems involved in the use of life tables (such as levels of infant mortality, allowance for growth and short-term fluctuations) and concluded that such problems, while still very real, are not so serious as to prevent the effective use of life tables and the stable population theory in the study of high mortality populations.
34. Cf. Frier (1982) 244–46.
35. Hopkins (1980, 318) certainly seems to think so: "if we know death rates among the young, we can predict death rates among the old and vice versa."
36. Ohlin (1974, 66) states that in populations where e_{15} is the same, e_0 can vary by up to 10 years. Schofield and Wrigley (1979), in analyzing data for English parishes in the sixteenth and seventeenth centuries, have highlighted the fact that in the first 10 years of life levels of mortality can vary sharply within the same national population and that the infant and childhood mortality rates may be much higher or lower than would be expected from the adult mortality levels in that population when related to model life tables (cf. especially their tables 6 and 22). They therefore suggest (p. 95) "splicing" life tables to match infant/child with adult mortality levels (e.g., for their eight English parishes the closest fit is Model West Level 12 up to age 10 years, then Level 7 for the remaining age groups).
37. This point, little appreciated even by many demographers, it would appear, is made clear by Newell (1988) 138.
38. And I believe that it is, though perhaps a little on the low side. It is certainly demographically possible, however: Coale-Demeny[2] West Level 2 (male and female combined) gives an e_0 of 21.42 years.
39. The article by Deevey (1960) still holds some sway, it would seem, but without good reason. His estimation of "life-span" in classical Roman times of 32 years (35 years for classical Greece) is based on skeletal evidence, and is too high because of the marked underrepresentation of juveniles in his sample (Deevey himself, p. 202, admits this, and he adds the sweeping generalization that "it is fair to guess that human life-expectancy at birth has never been far from 25 years—25 plus or minus five, say—from Neanderthal times up to the present century"). Cf. Weiss (1973) 48–51, who estimates a range of e_0 values for classical and medieval times of 22 to 29 years.
40. Cf. Durand (1959–60) 372; Hopkins (1966–67) 263–64, (1983) 70–71.
41. Cf. Acsádi and Nemeskéri (1970) 45; Wrigley (1987) 136.

42. In tables 9 and 10 are given Coale-Demeny[2] Models West and South Level 3 female, where e_0 = 25 years.
43. For the method of calculating such figures, basically by the equation 69.31/r, see Shryock and Siegel (1976) 216–17. I say "in theory" because in reality no growth rate is so constant as to lead to such precise timing.
44. As Wrigley and Schofield (1981), from whom figure 10 is adapted, state, the mean age of maternity varies very little over populations: the reproductive capacity of females is primarily a biological function largely independent on a natural level of the constraints of society (though differences in the average age at first marriage for females may affect the $p_{\dot{m}}$ value). Fertility levels themselves, however, may be greatly influenced by society's expectations and demands, as will be seen in chapter 3.
45. The same is true of a change from stationariness to a negative growth rate: in the case where e_0 = 25 years, from a GRR of 2.543 to one of 2.208 for a growth rate of -0.5 percent per year, or from an e_0 of 25 years to one of around 21.5 years where the GRR remains the same.
46. Some of these questions, among others, are discussed in demographic terms in, e.g., Hopkins (1983) chs. 2 and 3 (on which see also Jacques [1987]; Hahn and Leunissen [1990]), and Saller (1986), as well as in Parkin (1992).

Three. Demographic Impressions

1. In what follows reference will also be made to ancient Greek (in particular Athenian) society and literature. For the assumption that the demographic regimes of classical Greece and Rome were comparable, cf. Jones (1957) 82; Hopkins (1966–67) 250 n. 14; Finley (1981) 157; Hansen (1986) 11; Golden (1990) 111.
2. Cf. Wrigley and Schofield (1981) 228–36 for England.
3. Cf. Wrigley (1987) 133–50. The point is that mortality levels are not *always* of greater importance than fertility levels in dictating the dynamics of a population; the situation may vary between different populations.
4. Wrigley (1987) 133. He also allows for the minimilization of migration as a demographic factor in this context, which "for very large units of area or population . . . is a defensible simplification" (p. 146 n. 1).
5. Cf. Lassère (1977) 545–56 and Corvisier (1985) 145–55 for attempts. For some causes of death recorded on epitaphs, see Berelson (1934) 87–88.

6. See especially the graphic descriptions in Scobie (1986), which is an explicit attempt to account for the low expectation of life at birth in the Roman world; cf. also Yavetz (1958); Brunt (1966), (1971) 385–88; Syme (1980) 20–25, (1986) 15–31; Ramage (1983); Waldron (1989); Engels (1990) 74–76. On food shortages, see especially Garnsey (1988) and Halstead and O'Shea (1989). On the secondary role of medicine in determining mortality levels, cf. Bresson (1985) 23–25. See Wrigley (1987) 147 n. 12 for literature on urban mortality. In effect urban centers in past history have been net consumers of population: mortality levels tend to outweigh fertility levels, with the deficit being made up by in-migration from rural areas; cf. Flinn (1981) 22–23.

7. On which cf. Gilfillan (1965), H. A. Waldron (1973), A. T. Hodge (1981), Phillips (1984), Scobie (1986) 423–24; for the skeletal evidence, cf. T. Waldron (1982) 203–4, (1983) 172–82, (1989) 68–70.

8. Cf. Pliny, *Nat. Hist.* 7.50.170: "namque et universis gentibus ingruunt morbi et generatim modo servitiis modo procerum ordini aliosque per gradus" ("for diseases attack not only entire nations but also particular classes, sometimes the slaves, sometimes the nobility, and likewise other grades"). Contrast Tacitus, *Ann.* 16.13 (A.D. 64).

9. Cf. Burn (1953) 14; Hopkins (1966–67), (1983) 225. For more recent historical examples from Europe, in the range of 150–250 per 1,000 live births, cf. Flinn (1981) 16–17 and table 10 (where it may be seen, for example, that in York before 1750 the rate was as high as 480).

10. The IMR in England and Wales, 1985, e.g., was 9.36 per 1,000. Cf. Cleland and Scott (1987) 862–81 on childhood mortality in general.

11. Cf. Étienne (1976) 150–52 on childhood illnesses in antiquity, and Bradley (1986) 219.

12. Neonatal mortality (i.e., death within the first month of life) accounted for some 57.5 percent of infant deaths in England and Wales in 1985, and 80.8 percent of these deaths occurred within the first week of life. For an awareness of such mortality risks in antiquity, cf. Aristotle, *Pol.* 2.6.12.1265b, [Aristotle], *Hist. An.* 7.588a, and Finley (1981) 158; as Brunt (1971, 564) points out, the Augustan legislation on childbearing recognizes high infant mortality rates. Compare also Vergil, *Aen.* 6.426–29. Étienne (1976) comments that in the face of childhood illnesses up to the age of puberty medicine would have been a mere spectator.

13. Cf. Lassère (1977) 557–60.

14. Six boys and six girls—alternately, according to Pliny, *Nat. Hist.*

7.13.57 (though on the meaning of this see Moir [1983]); cf. Plutarch, Mor. 312c–d. The number of children seems to get confused
by modern scholars, though not by the ancient sources: cf. Burn
(1953) 8 (says 10 children) and Dixon (1988) 30 (says 11 children).

15. Cf., e.g., Cicero, de Inv. 1.49.91; also Pliny, Nat. Hist. 34.14.31.
16. This means a lot of births in a short time and has worried and
    occupied the minds of many scholars (cf. especially Carcopino
    [1967] 47–83 and Moir [1983]), but if Cornelia's children were
    really this numerous, I see no reason why multiple births cannot
    be considered a factor. On the other hand, it would be of interest to
    know if Cornelia breast-fed her children; if she did not, it is feasible
    that she might have conceived very shortly after each birth. The
    literary sources do not tell us whether Cornelia breast-fed her chil-
    dren or not; one might assume that she did, following the tradi-
    tional notion, though Cicero, Brutus 211, might suggest otherwise
    (cf. also Tacitus, Dial. 28).
17. Plutarch, Tib. Gracch. 1.2; Pliny, Nat. Hist. 7.13.57; Seneca, ad
    Marc. 16.3, ad Helv. 16.6; cf. Carcopino (1967) 77.
18. Suetonius, Gaius 7; Quintilian, Inst. Or. 6 pr. 2–11; Corbier (1987)
    1272. Cf. Étienne (1976) for details of childhood mortality among
    the imperial families in the first and fourth centuries A.D.; see also
    Étienne (1987), Wiedemann (1989) 17–25.
19. Cf. Burn (1953) 14.
20. On this interesting but unanswerable question, the literature is be-
    coming extensive. Cf. first the interesting material on mors imma-
    tura discussed in Vrugt-Lentz (1960), especially pp. 65ff., together
    with the more specialized study by E. Griessmair, Das Motiv der
    Mors Immatura in den griechischen metrischen Grabinschriften
    (Innsbruck, 1966), and for various reflections on the question of
    the response to young deaths, see Lattimore (1942) 184–91; Finley
    (1981) 159; Hopkins (1983) 217–26; Néraudau (1984) 379–89;
    Garland (1985) 77–88; Bradley (1986) 216–20; Néraudau (1987);
    Saller (1987b) 87 n. 82; Dixon (1988) 23–25; and, most recently,
    Golden (1988) and (1990) 82–100, with valuable comparative ma-
    terial (to which add P. Crawford in Continuity and Change 1
    [1986] 23–51, on seventeenth-century England).
21. Cf. Oldenziel (1987).
22. Cf., e.g., Brunt (1971) 148. Boswell (1984) gives some useful defi-
    nitions, and shows that exposure could be an alternative to infan-
    ticide, even though the result might end up the same, as a means
    of avoiding direct responsibility. Boswell (1988) is now the author-
    itative work on the subject in later history, and has much of value
    to say for the ancient historian. See also Motomura (1988), who

argues for a high level of survivorship from exposure—contrast [Quintilian], *Decl. Min.* 306.22: "rarum igitur est ut expositi vivant."

23. Cf. Brunt (1971) 148–54 and Den Boer (1973) 36–40, both of whose conjectures on the subject are plausible enough but who reach totally different conclusions.

24. As argued by Golden (1981; cf. Golden [1990] 86–87) and Harris (1982), against Engels (1980) and (1984); cf. also Bresson (1985) 14–17. Engels makes the mistake of adding the infanticide rate to the crude death rate, whereas in fact of course it was a part of it and not separate.

25. Patterson (1985).

26. Cf. Schmidt (1983–84). Soranus, *Gynaec.* 2.6.10, provides some strict rules of thumb from a medical standpoint. It is worth pointing out that if only, or in most cases, medically infirm infants were exposed, ones who might be expected to have died shortly anyway, this may have had a *positive* effect on fertility, since mothers would not then be breast-feeding and, as will be seen, would therefore be more likely to conceive in the immediate future.

27. Patterson (1985) 115–21.

28. Cf. Boswell (1984) 18. Plutarch, *Mor.* 497e, certainly implies that poverty was seen by some (though not necessarily the poor) as a reason for exposing an infant; cf. Musonius Rufus 15b.

29. Cf. Harris (1986).

30. Dionysius of Halicarnassus, *Rom. Ant.* 2.15.1–2.

31. Dionysius of Halicarnassus, *Rom. Ant.* 9.22.2.

32. Compare Engels (1980, 1984) with Golden (1981) and Harris (1982) again for a start.

33. Cf. Harris (1980) 123; Boswell (1984) 13–14; Motomura (1988). Saller (1987b, 69) quotes Justin the Martyr (second century A.D.), *Apol.* 27 in this context: "we see that almost all so exposed (not only the girls, but also the males) are brought up to prostitution."

34. *Cod. Theod.* 9.14, A.D. 374.

35. Cf. *Dig.* 25.2.4 (Paul), and [Quintilian], *Decl. Min.* 306.22 (see n. 22 above), with Eyben (1980–81) 19.

36. Cf. Seneca, *Controv.* 10.4.13–14, for the (hypothetical) case of a man who crippled exposed children and forced them to beg; the comment is made that "non in censu illos invenies, non in testamentis." Of course the practice of exposure may have been commented on for the very reason that it was a rarity and therefore all that more striking when it did occur.

37. Pomeroy (1986); cf. the modern Italian surname of Esposito.

38. Aristotle, *Hist. An.* 9.608a; Xenophon, *Lac. Const.* 1.3; cf. Golden (1990) 94. For skeletal evidence, cf. Wells (1975) 1247–48. For

interesting comparative material, cf. Klapisch-Zuber (1985) ch. 5, esp. 101–6, and Miller (1981).

39. Cf. Duncan-Jones (1982) 288, 301; on this whole question, cf. Pomeroy (1975) 184, 202; (1983) 208.
40. Cf., e.g., Shryock and Siegel (1976) 109. Brunt (1971) 151, "more girls normally survived infancy than boys," is not, however, logical.
41. This is normally regarded as biologically determined; cf. Siegel (1980) 350.
42. Newell (1988) 30, and cf. also Miller (1981). Probably the first factor had more to do with it than the second. Note that regional variations also occur within India itself, especially between Hindu and Islamic areas.
43. As may be seen, e.g., in Hopkins's computation of a sex ratio of 135 from Macdonnell's data; cf. Degrassi (1964) 85–86.
44. See table 1.The total sample size for the figures in this table is 503 individuals, with 5.5 percent of the sample unidentifiable by sex. Hopkins (1980, 316–17) arrives at similar figures, with a sample size of 802, with another 9 percent of undetermined sex, and an overall sex ratio of 107.2. Interestingly enough, the slave population recorded in the Egyptian census returns gives a ratio of 68.1, suggesting that females outnumbered males quite significantly (cf. similarly Hopkins [1978] 138–40 for the Delphic figures). But it must be remembered that we are not dealing here with natural populations; depending upon his requirements, a slave owner would purchase or retain male or female slaves, and an imbalance is thus perhaps to be expected. In an urban area female slaves might have been considered of more use for domestic chores, while in a rural household male slaves to work the land may have been the primary requirement. See further Bradley (1987a). Female slaves retained for breeding purposes will be considered shortly.
45. Duncan-Jones (1982, 301) provides the most plausible reasoning in this regard.
46. Pomeroy (1986) 161. Cf. also Gallo (1984b); Golden (1990) 23, 94–97, 135.
47. Two especial favorites are lines from the comic poet Posidippus (frag. 11K; ca. 300 B.C.): "Everyone raises a son, even if he's poor; but a daughter is exposed [*ektithēsi*], even if he's rich"; and *P.Oxy.* 4.744, which records that in 1 B.C. one Hilarion wrote from Alexandria to his wife (and sister?) to say: "If you happen to bear a child, if it's a boy, that's fine, if it's a girl, throw it out [*ekbale*]"; cf. Ovid, *Met.* 9.669–81.
48. Cf. Pomeroy (1983) 209–18 and Brulé (1990).
49. Cassius Dio, *Roman History* 54.16.2.
50. As Duncan-Jones (1980, 68) points out. Dio is not strictly talking

only of the aristocracy, however, but of all the freeborn at Rome, though perhaps the aristocracy is all that really interests him.

51. Dio 56.1–10.

52. Dio was, it should be remembered, writing some 200 years after the events he records here.

53. As indeed the literary sources often allege to have been the case in the early empire, as with Dio and the speech he has Augustus make to the *equites* in A.D. 9. See further Brunt (1971) 560; Hopkins (1983) 94–97; Dixon (1988) 92–97. Marriage patterns, especially in regard to age gaps between partners, are also relevant here, as will be discussed.

54. Cf. Vatin (1970) 232–33 for Hellenistic Greece: "La cause de l'abandon des filles est sans mystère: le régime dotal en est responsable"; Hopkins (1983, 77) states that "we also know that dowries in the Roman upper classes were large, and that daughters were considered expensive." For a similar view in the case of Roman Egypt, cf. Lewis (1983) 55.

55. Saller (1984b); quotation from p. 205. Golden (1990, 132–35) has since argued that dowries in Athens may not have been all that substantial either.

56. Cf. *CIL* 6.12307, 26901; Lattimore (1942) 187–91; Hopkins (1983) 219 (with Bradley's review comments in *Classical Philology* 81 [1986] 266–67); Dixon (1988) 148. Also see Parkin (1992), ch. 8.

57. Cf. Newell (1988) 138.

58. It is of interest, though of dubious demographic value, that there emerges in antiquity the idea that women age more quickly than men, a feature attributed in particular to childbirth; cf. Aristotle, *Gen. An.* 4.6.775a; *Hist. An.* 7.1.582a, 7.3.583b; Pliny, *Nat. Hist.* 7.4.37, 9.48.89, 16.51.118; Hippocrates, *On the Fetus of Eight Months* 9.6 (7.450L); Galen, *Comm. III in Hipp. Epid. Lib. II* 31 (17.1.445K). Aristotle, *de Long. et Brev. Vit.* 5.466b and 6.467a, states that as a rule in the animal kingdom males live longer than females, due to the fact that the male is warmer than the female. However, he goes on to say, men who work hard age more quickly because work brings dryness and old age is cold and dry (cf. 5.466a). Cf. Garland (1990) 248.

59. Dixon (1988) 30, and cf. 6 ("women who survived the dangers of reproduction were likely to outlive their husbands"), 32 ("The fact that childbirth was so dangerous also meant that many Romans grew up without a natural mother from birth or early childhood"), and 31, 179, and 182 for the same argument.

60. The idea goes back at least as far as Beloch (1886) 41–54.

61. Burn (1953) 10, 13.

62. As well as Dixon, it is assumed by, e.g., Berelson (1934) 89; Hombert and Préaux (1945) 144; Pomeroy (1975) 84, 164, 168; Gardner (1986a) 40 (with some caution); Bradley (1986) 202, 210, (1987a) 58.

63. Appleton (1920) 16–22; cf. Beloch (1886) 49.

64. Cf. Eyben (1980–81) 12: "The number of women who failed to survive an abortion must have been great"; Gourévitch (1984) 214–16, 262–63. Saint Basil, *Letters* 188.2 (A.D. 374) argues that a woman who destroys her fetus may be guilty of a double murder, since not only does she kill the unborn child but she also puts her own life at risk, "since women in most cases die from such attempts"; compare Hippocrates, *Mul.* 1.72 (8.152 Littré).

65. Cf. Hopkins (1966–67) 260–63 and (1987) 125. Suder (1988b) remains unconvinced.

66. For Greece, cf. Corvisier (1985) 161–66; for Rome, Lassère (1977) 560–62, Gourévitch (1984) 169–93 and (1987). In some preindustrial societies the early age of female marriage and of first childbearing may also be a factor, as Aristotle for one realized: cf. *Pol.* 7.16.7.1335a.

67. Schofield (1986) 256, table 9.6; similar results (11.5 per 1,000 births) and conclusions are reached for eighteenth-century France (with significant variations over time and space) by Gutierrez and Houdaille (1983). Bullough and Campbell (1980) provide useful comparative material on anemia and its relation to maternal mortality (as they say, women require more iron than men because of the loss of iron in the menstrual flow, while pregnant women require more iron because of fetal needs), but I am unconvinced by their conclusion that anemia-related maternal deaths "would be enough to explain the predominance of men over women in the early medieval population" (p. 323), or, for that matter, in ancient populations.

68. The rate today in the modern industrial world is much lower, around 0.1 per 1,000, but in Bangladesh today, for example, it remains around 17 per 1,000. French (1986, 69) states that, "if we retroject the worst mortality rates of the modern world back into the Greco-Roman one, we would estimate that . . . among every 20,000 women giving birth, five would die." If this is what she really means—a maternal mortality rate of 0.25 per 1,000—then her figures have become rather confused and misleading. Her article on maternity care in the Roman world is, however, very useful.

69. For one instance of maternal mortality (of two sisters), cf. Pliny, *Ep.* 4.21. For difficult births, cf. the name "Agrippa," and Aulus Gellius, *Att. Noct.* 16.16 and Pliny, *Nat. Hist.* 13.37.117 for superstitions.

70. See also Wells (1975) for the lack of convincing skeletal evidence. One may ask, if maternal mortality was not such a statistically significant event, why it was perceived as such a great danger. Richard Saller has pointed out to me a reference from Shostak (1981). While childbirth was perceived to be dangerous among the !Kung bushmen, Shostak's informant did not know of a single case among her over 400 female acquaintances who had died in childbirth—another good example, perhaps, of the unreliability of impressions in relation to demographic realities. Pollock (1990, 47–49) points out that while a society may experience a low maternal mortality rate, there may still exist among women of that society a great dread of childbirth as "a very conspicuous *single* cause of mortality and a fate which a prospective mother had several long months to contemplate."

71. As part of the uniformitarian theory; Howell (1976) 33. It is true, however, that in very recent years average life expectancy figures at advanced ages (70, 75 years) have begun to make quite significant increases.

72. Cf. Acsádi and Nemeskéri (1970) 16–17, and our African centenarians again. Of the approximately 10,000 tombstone inscriptions from Rome contained in *CIL* 6, the oldest person recorded died, it is said, at the age of 113 years (6.6835); nine individuals in all are recorded as dying at 100 years of age or more.

73. Pliny, *Nat. Hist.* 7.48.153–49.164. For Pliny's sources, see G. Ranucci in *Athenaeum* 54 (1976) 131–38. Cf. Saint Augustine, *de Civ. Dei* 15.12.

74. Most sources give 150 years (e.g., Phlegon, [Lucian], Censorinus—all misquoting Herodotus), but Herodotus and Cicero say he lived 120 years, and Valerius Maximus (quoting Asinius Pollio) says 130. At any rate, Arganthonius was traditionally believed to have lived a long time, and the exact figure probably was of little more than pedantic concern.

75. E.g., Epimenides of Crete was traditionally said to have lived for 157 years—57 (but Varro says 50) of which were spent asleep in a cave—though some sources give 154, and another, apparently the Cretans themselves, 299 years! Cf. Diogenes Laertius 1.111; Phlegon, *FGH* 2.257.38; Pliny, *Nat. Hist.* 7.48.154, 7.52.175; Varro, *de Ling. Lat.* 7.3; Valerius Maximus 8.13.Ext.5; Plutarch, *Mor.* 784a. Another good example of pedantic squabbling for the sake of spurious accuracy.

76. E.g., Myson, 97 years; Pittacus, variously 70 to 100; Solon, usually 80, though [Lucian] (*Macr.* 18) says 100; Thales, 78, 90, or 100 years.

77. Galen, *de Remediis Parabilibus* book 3, 14.56 K; cf. Diogenes Laertius 8.44 for more "established" figures.
78. Cf. *American Journal of Philology* 21 (1900) 59–60.
79. Cf. *L'Année Épigraphique* (1972) 174.
80. Pliny, *Nat. Hist.* 11.63.167. An abundance of teeth, incidentally, was taken as a sign of longevity (cf., e.g., Hippocrates, *Epidem.* 2.6.1 [5.132L]; Aristotle, *Hist. An.* 2.3.501b; Pliny, *Nat. Hist.* 11.114.274), whereas old age was traditionally associated with toothlessness.
81. Cf. Aulus Gellius, *Att. Noct.* 3.10, 15.7; Censorinus, *de Die Nat.* 14. Seneca, *de Brev. Vit.* 3.5, states, to suit his argument, that *pauci* survive beyond the age of 50 or 60 years; cf. Cicero, *de Sen.* 19.67: "pauci veniunt ad senectutem."
82. Pliny, *Nat. Hist.* 7.49.161, for the astronomical view of the school of Aesculapius that "longiora tempora" are "rara."
83. Pliny, *Ep.* 1.12.11; Solon, frag. 27.17–18 (= Philo, *de Opif. Mund.* 104: 70 years); Diogenes Laertius 1.60–61 (Mimnermus, frag. 6: 60 years; Solon, frag. 20: 80 years), and cf. Herodotus 1.29–33, 3.22, Dio Chrysostom 17.20, and Psalms 90.10.
84. Hesiod: Ausonius, *Ecl.* 5 (cf. *Idyll* 2.4–6 for 81 years, i.e., 9 times 9); Plutarch, *Mor.* 415c. 100 years: Pliny, *Nat. Hist.* 11.70.184 for the Egyptian tradition; Plato, *Rep.* 10.615b; Cf. Diodorus Siculus, 1.26.4; Varro, *de Ling. Lat.* 6.11; Seneca, *de Brev. Vit.* 3.2.
85. Cf. Censorinus, *de Die Nat.* 17.7–15, for the most detail, and also Varro, *de Ling. Lat.* 6.11: "seclum [sic] spatium annorum centum vocarunt, dictum a sene, quod longissimum spatium senescendo-rum hominum id putarunt" ("A *saeculum* was what they called the space of 100 years, named from *senex*, 'old man,' because they thought this the longest stretch of life for aging men"). Generally *saeculum* refers to a life-span, *aetas* to a generation (i.e., the time a man takes to be born and to reproduce himself, usually taken in classical times to be between 27 and 40 years), though the two were frequently confused: cf. Pliny, *Nat. Hist.* 16.95.250; Juvenal 10.248–49; Stein (1962); Den Boer (1979) 118–19, 123.
86. Pliny, *Nat. Hist.* 7.49.160, for 112 years, the view of Epigenes, and more than 116, that of Berosus; cf. Censorinus, *de Die Nat.* 17.4; Servius, *in Aen.* 8.51. The 124 figure belongs to Petosiris and Necepsos, the "Theory of the Quarters," says Pliny. For 120 years, cf. Censorinus, *de Die Nat.* 17.4; Servius, *in Aen.* 4.653; *Script. Hist. Aug., Claudius* 2.4; Tacitus, *Dial.* 17.4; and for the old age of Britons *beginning* at 120 years (because they live in a colder climate, as opposed to the Ethiopians, who, because of the heat of the sun, grow old in their 30th year), cf. [Galen], *de Hist. Philosoph.* 133

(19.344–45K = Diels, *Dox. Graec.* p. 648) and [Plutarch], *Plac. Philosoph.* 5.30 (*Mor.* 911b; Diels pp. 443–44), and contrast Herodotus 3.22–23 (the Ethiopians live to be 120).

87. For illustration of this, see figure 4.

88. Cf. Flinn (1981) 18–19. Note that whether infants are breast-fed or not could have a very significant effect on infant mortality.

89. Frier (1982, 228 n. 26) quotes Cox (1976, 137) to support his argument that "class differences are small when mortality is very high." This is true enough, but only relates to mortality levels; as regards fertility, significant differences may occur.

90. See again figure 10, discussed in chapter 2.

91. For useful introductions to Hutterite society, see J. A. Hostetler, *Hutterite Society* (Baltimore, 1974); and K. A. Peter, *The Dynamics of Hutterite Society: An Analytical Approach* (Alberta, 1987), esp. 133–70 on demographics.

92. Cf. Laslett (1983) 116–17.

93. As may be seen from the model life tables discussed in chapter 2.

94. Rawson (1986) 8; cf. Salmon (1974) 55–60. On the myth of the large preindustrial family, cf. Mitterauer and Sieder (1982) 24–47, Laslett (1983) 90–105; on the nuclear family in Roman society, see especially the various papers by Saller and Shaw, and also Bradley (1987b), together with Bradley's contribution in Rawson (1991).

95. Cf., e.g., Raepsaet (1973). Carcopino (1956, 72) mentions "Martial's estimate of an average of five mouths per family"; Carcopino's evidence for this (Martial 13.12), however, is only a statement that 300 *modii* from the harvest of a Libyan *colonus* will maintain a *suburbanus ager*. Carcopino uses this statement to suggest 60 *modii* per person in a family per year, hence a family size of five—tentative, to say the least!

96. Vielrose (1976).

97. Hombert and Préaux (1952) 154–55; cf. Hopkins (1980) 328–29, Hobson (1985) 217–20 (7.34 persons in the average household). This includes some very large households, in one case of 24 individuals. Note, on the other hand, that adult children who had left the household would not have been included in the census declaration for that house.

98. Cf. Aristotle, *Gen. An.* 773a–774b; Pliny, *Nat. Hist.* 7.11.48–49; cf. Garland (1990) 35–36 and, in greater detail, Lienau (1971).

99. For the fecundity of Egypt, cf., e.g., Pliny, *Nat. Hist.* 8.17.42 (with Aristotle, *Hist. An.* 606b), 10.75.153, 16.33.81, 16.50.115, etc. Apparently drinking the water of the Nile was supposed to bring fecundity (7.3.33), rather surprising for anyone who has seen the river in its present state! For five births, cf. [Aristotle], *Hist. An.*

7.4.584b; Phlegon, de Mir. 28; Antigonus, Hist. Mir. 119, and cf. 110.1; Pliny, Nat. Hist. 7.3.33 mentions seven.

100. Pliny, Nat. Hist. 7.3.34 (cf. Dig. 5.4.3, 34.5.7pr.; Script. Hist. Aug., Pius 9.3); Aulus Gellius, Att. Noct. 10.2; and, discussed previously, Pliny, Nat. Hist. 7.48.158. In applications for exemption due to the ius liberorum, some fathers claim to have as many as 16 children: cf. Dig. 50.6.6.2; Cod. Iust. 10.13.24 (Cod. Theod. 12.1.55).

101. Again, especially in Egypt: cf. [Aristotle], Hist. An. 7.4.584b; Aulus Gellius, Att. Noct. 10.2; Columella, de Re Rust. 3.8; Seneca, Quaest. Nat. 13.25.

102. Martial 10.63.

103. Cf. Pliny, Nat. Hist. 7.43.139–40, where to leave many children is counted as one of the ten "maximae res optumaeque in quibus quaerendis sapientes aetatem exigerent" ("greatest and highest objects in the pursuit of which wise men pass their lives").

104. Cf. Pliny, Ep. 4.15.3, 8.10, and 8.11.

105. Hence the frequent recourse to adoption; cf. Rawson (1986) 12, Dixon (1988) 96.

106. Cf. Lucretius 4.1233–77, rejecting superstitions; Garland (1990) 36–41 on Greece; Salmon (1974) 59–60 and Gourévitch (1984) 142–48 on Rome.

107. Aulus Gellius, Att. Noct. 4.3, 17.21.44; Valerius Maximus 2.1.4; Plutarch, Thes. et Rom. 6.3 (cf. S. F. Bonner, Roman Declamation [Liverpool, 1969], 122–24). The date of Carvilius's divorce is confused in the sources; see L. Holford-Strevens, Aulus Gellius (London, 1988), 187. Cf. A. Watson in Tijdschrift voor Rechtsgeschiedenis 33 (1965) 38–50, for a discussion of the evidence.

108. Cf. the aes uxorium, a tax on celibacy (see Festus 519L), and Valerius Maximus 2.9.1 ("Camillus et Postumius censores aera poenae nomine eos, qui ad senectutem caelibes pervenerant, in aerarium deferre iusserunt"; "The censors C. and P. ordered that those who had reached old age without having married pay money by way of a penalty into the treasury"); Plutarch, Cam. 2.4; with Humbert (1972) 138.

109. Cf. also Aristotle, Pol. 2.1265b.

110. Cf. Ulpian, Digest 1.7.15.2; Cicero, de Domo Sua 13.34–14.38; Aulus Gellius, Att. Noct. 5.19.4–6. The general assumption appears to have been that it was the woman's fault if a couple was infertile—that the man may have been responsible is rarely conceded (I have come across only Isaeus 2.7, where infertility is linked to old age, Plutarch, Solon 20.2, and Seneca, Controversiae 2.5.14).

111. Pliny, *Nat. Hist.* 14.22.117, 16.46.110, 16.95.251; cf. Plutarch, *Rom.* 21.5, and Ovid, *Fasti* 2.425–26, for the Lupercalia, during which young married women were struck with leather thongs in order to promote fertility.

112. Brunt (1971), and cf. also Hopkins (1983) ch. 2. Brunt's statement (p. 133) that life expectancy at birth of the free population may therefore have fallen below 20 years, however, confuses mortality with fertility. The whole point is that the population declined (if indeed it did decline) not through heightened mortality but through decreased fertility.

113. Pliny, *Nat. Hist.* 7.45.149. Cf. also Aulus Gellius, *Att. Noct.* 1.6.6 for the speech *de ducendis uxoribus* by the censor of 102 B.C., Metellus Numidicus, where the comment is made that Metellus, "quod fuit rerum omnium validissimum atque verissimum, persuasit civitatem salvam esse sine matrimoniorum frequentia non posse" ("persuaded them of something that was the soundest and truest of all principles, that the state cannot survive without numerous marriages").

114. The most useful modern discussions are in Brunt (1971) appendix 9, Nörr (1977), and Wallace-Hadrill (1981).

115. My special thanks to Richard Saller for his comments on this section.

116. Hopkins (1965–66) 126 and (1983) 95. The same assumption is made by Csillag (1976) 83, 123, and Rawson (1986) 19. Gardner (1986a, 77), talks of the "production" of legitimate children; cf. E. Badian's comment in *Philologus* 129 (1985) 89.

117. Brunt (1971) 563.

118. Cf., e.g., *CAH* 10.451 (Last); Astolfi (1986) 78–79.

119. Brunt (1971) 563.

120. Hot baths: Krenkel (1975)—the same idea is put forward, apparently independently, by Devine (1985). Lead poisoning: See my previous discussion. Natural selection: Last (1947); this ignores infant mortality, however—a sole surviving daughter may originally have had several brothers and sisters.

121. Needleman and Needleman (1985) reject lead poisoning as a cause of sterility among the elite in the early Roman empire, and replace it with gonorrhea.

122. Cf. Musonius Rufus 15b (though Musonius's views can hardly be held to be typical); Seneca, *ad Helviam* 16.3. Polybius 36.17.5–8 is explicit for Hellenistic Greece.

123. Cf. Brunt (1971) 141–42, and Hopkins (1983) ch. 3, for the disappearance of families, due not just to poverty or political retirement.

124. Cf. Hopkins (1983) 96–97, who rightly warns against regarding

literary references in this context as representative of general reality. A. R. Mansbach, in her unpublished doctoral thesis "'Captatio': Myth and Reality" (Princeton, 1982), argues that the evidence for *captatio* is literary, not historical, and that the idea was more a literary topos than a historical reality. This may be true, but what is important here is that some of the elite class at Rome at least thought *captatio* was a real threat (or promise) in old age. For literary references, cf. Mansbach 118–35.

125. Cassius Dio 56.1.
126. Pliny, *Nat. Hist.* 14.1.2–7.
127. Cf. Brunt (1971) appendix 9, with Humbert (1972) 138.
128. Treggiari (1969) 213–14. Incidentally, this would also make the *ius liberorum* virtually impossible to attain, since only children born after manumission counted. Brunt (1971, 143–46) argues that freedmen would have kept their families small through choice, though his calculation of the proportion of freedmen in the population may be exaggerated. Den Boer (1973, 42), on the other hand, argues against Brunt that freedmen would have wanted large families as a status symbol. Perhaps this was a real motive, but for many freedmen economic factors probably tempered this ambition in reality.
129. Tacitus, *Ann.* 4.27, of A.D. 24, and cf. *Ann.* 10.27 (A.D. 56).
130. Cf. Appian, *Bell. Civ.* 2.120; Duncan-Jones (1980) 72.
131. On numbers cf. those given by Harris (1980); also Brunt (1971) 121–30, 702–3, and most recently Dumont (1987) 41–82, with a review of the scholarly literature. On the question of home as opposed to bought slaves cf. Treggiari (1976) 92, (1979); Gardner (1986a) 157, 206–9. The question had already been considered by David Hume (1777) 386–98.
132. Harris (1980) 118, and cf. p. 183 n. 44 above. On the cost of rearing, cf. Bradley (1978) 247 and n. 22, (1986) 211–12, quoting Treggiari; de Ste. Croix (1981) 226–37, especially 231–33; Duncan-Jones (1982) 50.
133. Finley (1985b) 86, *pace* Den Boer (1973) 41. Cf. also Bradley (1978, 1979), with Dalby (1979), and see now Bradley (1987a), who stresses the interplay between, rather than the exclusiveness of, "breeding" and intake. Note *Dig.* 5.3.27 (Ulpian): "non temere ancillae eius rei causa comparantur ut pariant" ("slave girls are not acquired solely in order that they may breed").
134. Columella 1.8.19. *FIRA*² ii, p. 629, a fragment of a law *de iure fisci* of the second century A.D., records an apparent reward for "ancilla Caesaris quae quinque liberos habuerit" ("a slave woman of Caesar who had five children"), but the context is uncertain.
135. Appleton (1920) 22.

136. Cf., e.g., Soranus, *Gynaec.* 1.8, 33, and Amundsen and Diers (1969) for an uncritical collection of the sources. Eyben (1972), however, is an excellent discussion of antiquity's view of puberty; on questions of age, see pp. 695–97, though his analysis focuses primarily on males.
137. Cf. Amundsen and Diers (1970), again unsatisfactory, and Diers (1974) for a rather more critical approach to the sources. The average age of a woman at the birth of her last child is a demographically useful figure (tending to be around 40 years of age; cf. Flinn [1981] 3, 29, 128–29) but one that cannot even be estimated from ancient testimony.
138. See further Hopkins (1964–65) 310–13.
139. Cf., e.g., Laslett (1973) and Denker-Hopfe (1986).
140. As the ancients themselves were aware: cf. Aristotle, *Gen. An.* 2.4.739a; *Hist. An.* 5.14.544b, giving 21 years as the male age for sexual maturity; 7.1.582a.
141. Cf. [Aristotle], *Hist. An.* 7.5.585a.
142. Hopkins (1964–65). The median is about 15.5 years, including some remarriages presumably. On the marriage of *impuberes,* cf., besides Hopkins, Durry (1970), Ruggiero (1981), Gardner (1986a) 38–41.
143. Shaw (1987b).
144. As Brunt (1971, 137–40) had suggested as an impression on economic grounds (though Den Boer [1973] 34–41 disagreed).
145. [Ulpian], *Epitome* 16.1.
146. Cf. Brunt (1971) 138.
147. Later marriage ages are a feature of populations with lower mortality levels at early ages, where e_0 is over 30 years.
148. Claudian, *de Raptu Pros.* 1.123–24, is of interest.
149. Cf. Flinn (1981) 28.
150. Cf. the classic paper by Hajnal (1965), together with Hajnal and Laslett in Wall, Robin, and Laslett (1983), and the comments of Goody (1983) 8–12.
151. Saller (1987a), using the same method as Shaw (described earlier); cf. Saller and Shaw (1984).
152. Cf. Syme (1987). By the age of 25 years elite males were, by the terms of the Augustan marriage legislation, expected to have fathered a legitimate child.
153. E.g., in the later Byzantine empire, southern Europe in the sixteenth century, Ireland in the late nineteenth century; in the Asiatic/Russian pattern the age gap was as large as 20 years (which is, incidentally, the sort of difference in ages Aristotle recommends for the ideal state: *Pol.* 7.16.5.1335a). On age gaps in marriage, cf. Wrigley (1969) 103–6; Laslett and Wall (1972) 52–

53, 272, 380; Cleland and Scott (1987) 755. The age gap in Roman Egypt (cf. Hombert and Préaux [1952] 161–63 and Hopkins [1980] 333–34) appears—from the available census evidence—much smaller, only about 3 years on average, with a later average age of marriage for women. But an apparently different family pattern here from that prevalent in the Roman empire as a whole is not as surprising as Hopkins indicates; cf. Hobson (1985).

154. Cf. Laslett (1977) 106–7. Also relevant in this regard is the attitude toward the remarriage of women, since in many societies constraint *not* to remarry is put upon women who may still be of fertile age but whose husbands, because of the large age gap, have died. For the situation in ancient Rome, see subsequent discussion.

155. On parity progression ratios, cf. Shryock and Siegel (1976) 291–93. Historically birth intervals tend to increase after each birth (cf. Flinn [1981] 30–33). Golden (1985, 10 n. 8) uses in the context of Athenian family life a figure of 2.5 years between each birth, with a completed family size of six—for a general model as good a rough estimate as any.

156. And remarrying, together with the proportion who are fertile.

157. Hopkins (1965–66), to which subsequent work adds little, though Fontanille (1977) has much of value. Eyben (1980–81) is a useful collection of material, particularly for attitudes among the Christian writers, but Patlagean (1969) and (1977) 145–55 is better for this period and beyond; cf. also Shaw (1987a) 45–46.

158. Though there survives on papyrus an advertisement for one contraceptive which is "probably aimed beyond the upper classes" (Hopkins [1965–66] 141 n. 51).

159. Hopkins (1965–66) 142–49, though that it was *not* widely used cannot be proved either. Fertility control, being regarded by males in the ancient world as a concern for females, was rarely talked about by males—hence references in the medical literature to the woman *after intercourse* ensuring that the semen is discharged (cf., e.g., Hippocrates, *Genit.* 5 [7.476 Litt.], *Nat. Puer.* 13 [7.490 Litt.]), or indeed to the *woman* drawing back during intercourse (Lucretius 4.1269–77; Soranus 1.19.61). There may be a reference to coitus interruptus, on the male's initiative, in Archilochus (seventh century B.C.), frag. 196W (*P.Köln* 2.58, the "Cologne epode," first published in 1974), lines 13–16 and 35. Cf. Gourévitch (1984) 204–6; Garland (1990) 48–50.

160. Cf. Soranus, *Gynaec.* 1.19.60–65.

161. Though this need not mean that it was not popular, only that it was not talked about, perhaps through a sense of decency or again because males left it up to females to worry about such things.

162. Hopkins's hypothesis (1965–66, 149–50) that the use of contraceptives declined in the later empire may be true but is unconvincing as it stands. Cf. Patlagean (1969) 1354, who stresses not only the use of contraceptives in this period but also complete abstention from intercourse.
163. Cf. Flinn (1981) 43–44.
164. Cf., e.g., Pliny, *Nat. Hist.* 29.27.85.
165. Cf. Vatin (1970) 236–67; Pomeroy (1975) 167; Eyben (1980–81) 7–10.
166. Cf. the vast collection of references in Nardi (1971).
167. Cf. Cicero, *Pro Cluentio* 11.32; Nero's charge against Octavia, Tacitus, *Ann.* 14.63; *Dig.* 25.3.4 (Paul), 48.8.8 (Ulpian). Étienne (1976, 133–34) rightly stresses not only the rights of the father but also those of the state in this regard.
168. Or even presumably at his command: cf. Domitian forcing his niece Julia to have an abortion: Juvenal 2.32–33; Pliny, *Ep.* 4.11.6; Suetonius, *Dom.* 22.
169. Pliny, e.g., gives a wide range, though his descriptions are tinged with moralizing—he regarded abortion as a female invention, the ultimate crime against nature (*Nat. Hist.* 10.83.172).
170. Cf. Eyben (1980–81) 12.
171. *Amores* 2.13, 14.
172. Cf., e.g., Seneca, *Cons. ad Helv.* 16.3, and [Quintilian], *Decl. Min.* 277.10, for children being an unwanted sign of one's age.
173. Cf. Rawson (1966, 1974); Treggiari (1981); Rousselle (1984); Weaver (1986) 145–69; Gardner (1986a) 56–60.
174. Cf. Syme (1960), Brunt (1971) 150–51, Rawson (1986) 178–79. See now Rawson (1989); while not discussing demographic aspects of illegitimacy at any length, this paper greatly increases our understanding of illegitimacy in the Roman world, particularly in its analysis of inscriptional evidence.
175. Calderini (1953) 363. More generally, cf. Weiss in *RE* ii.3.2.1889–91, Rawson (1986), and, for general discussion of illegitimacy in history, Laslett (1977) and Laslett, Oosterveen, and Smith (1980).
176. As Rawson (1974) shows.
177. Cf. Knodel (1977) on death rates among those artificially fed being considerably higher than among breast-fed infants. See also Wrigley (1987) 138–39, 145, on the effect of breast-feeding on lowering the infant mortality rate.
178. Cf. Favorinus *ap.* Aulus Gellius, *Att. Noct.* 12.1 (Favorinus wrongly assumes that the aristocratic woman will feed her own child); Soranus, *Gynaec.* 2.11.17–18; Tacitus, *Dial.* 28–29, *Germ.*

20. Beaucamp (1982) collects useful comparative material for the Byzantine period.

179. "For fear she grows prematurely old, having spent herself through the daily suckling"; cf. 2.12.19–20, with [Plutarch], *de Lib. Educ.* 3.5, for the very careful selection of a wetnurse (it is worth noting that Plutarch wrote a work entitled *Tittheutikos* [Lamprias, cat. 114]). The fear seems to have been that a lowly wet nurse might adversely influence the infant in terms of character and speech: cf., e.g., Cicero, *Tusc. Disp.* 3.1.2; Aulus Gellius, *Att. Noct.* 12.1.17–20. For cosmetic reasons for not breast-feeding, cf. Aulus Gellius 12.1.8. For concoctions to promote breast milk, cf., e.g., Pliny, *Nat. Hist.* 30.43.125 (worms in honey wine) and 32.46.132 (boiled crabs).

180. See Bradley (1986), the best detailed study of wet-nursing at Rome; see further Étienne (1976) 147–50; Joshel (1986); Fildes (1988) 1–25 (rather simplistic but part of a valuable history of the subject); and Dixon (1988) 120–29. For an interesting view on the links between an infant and the person who breast-feeds it, see E. E. Filsonger and R. A. Fabes, "Odor communication, pheromones and human families," *Journal of Marriage and the Family* (May 1985) 349–59.

181. Bradley (1980) and (1984) 70. The sample is, however, very small; for a collection of 39 wet-nursing contracts and receipts from the Roman period, see now M. M. Masciadri and O. Montevecchi, *I contratti di baliatico, Corpus Papyrorum Graecarum* I (Milan, 1984). Celibacy, on superstitious and bogus medical grounds, was also required from the wet nurse (cf. Soranus 2.19; Fildes [1988] 8–9). For weaning at the age of around 2 years, cf. Fildes (1986) 12, 35–41, 60–61.

182. Cf. Wilson (1986) 219–26.

183. Cf. Knodel (1977); McLaren (1978) and (1979); Anderson (1983); Wilson (1986) 219–26; Cleland and Scott (1987) 753–54, and 778: "one month less of breast-feeding subtracts 0.4 months from the length of the birth interval." Cf. Flinn (1981) 31–32, 42–43 (noting geographical differences), and Klapisch-Zuber (1985) 132–64, for historical contexts, with Knodel. On the demographic effects of lactation, see now S. Thapa, R. V. Short, and M. Potts, "Breast-feeding, birth spacing and their effects on child survival," *Nature* 335 (October 1988) 679–82.

184. Aristotle, *Gen. An.* 4.8.777a, and cf. *Hist. An.* 7.587b; Soranus, *Gynaec.* 1.3.15, 2.11.17–18; [Plutarch], *de Lib. Educ.* 3d.5. Cf. also Shaw (1987a) 42, 44, for possible evidence from Saint Augustine.

185. Cf. Treggiari (1976) 88–89; Bradley (1986); Dixon (1988) ch. 5. Gardner (1986a, 242) cites *P.Lond.* 3.951v, where a mother-in-law actually tells a husband off for forcing his wife to breast-feed!

186. *Pace* Bradley (1986) 201. Juvenal (6.592–93) implies that it was not the norm, in contrast with the situation among the upper classes: cf. Dixon (1988) 123. But then would Juvenal have really known or cared?

187. Cf. Bradley (1986) 210–13. Varro, *Res Rust.* 2.10.8, implies that slave mothers normally fed their own infants.

188. As is clearly recognized in the Augustan marriage legislation; cf. also Plato, *Laws* 6.773–74.

189. Cf. Wilson (1986) 212–19; Cleland and Scott (1987) 797.

190. Hopkins (1965–66) suggests, on the basis of the U.N. model life tables, that half of elite females' first marriages would have lasted about 18 years (assuming that e_0 = 25 years, and that girls married on average at age 15, males at 25 years; cf. also Salmon [1974] 61 n. 97). This is about right: the Coale-Demeny[2] model life tables give a similar figure, and exact figures are not as important as a realization of the fact that widows (and, to a lesser extent, widowers) were a common feature of ancient society (cf. Dixon [1988] 31). Marriages of extremely long duration did, however, exist, to be sure: cf., e.g., *CIL* 6.8684, 12388, 18137, 18758, 19008, 20241, 21303a, 21319, 25697, 25905, 33087, 34407, 34706.

191. Though not necessarily as high as is often assumed: Cf. I. Kajanto, "On divorce among the common people of Rome," *Mélanges M. Durry, Revue des études latines* 47 bis (1970) 99–103, and S. M. Treggiari, "Divorce Roman style: how easy and how frequent was it?" in Rawson (1991) 31–46.

192. Cf., e.g., Humbert (1972) 62–75.

193. Humbert (1972) 76–112; cf. also Rawson (1986) 31–32.

194. The *tempus lugendi* is discussed by Humbert (1972) 113–31. Under the terms of the Augustan legislation, divorcées were expected to remarry after 6 months, though this figure too was increased to 18 months. Cf. [Ulpian], *Epitome* 14; Humbert (1972) 146–53.

195. Though cf. *Nov. Maj.* 6, A.D. 458.

196. On the question of remarriage among the lower classes, a question open to speculation but lacking in any real evidence, compare the arguments of Penta (1980) and Gardner (1986a) 56. As to Roman Egypt where the evidence probably relates to a broad social spectrum, Hopkins (1980, 334, figure 5) detects a significant proportion of women remaining unmarried in later life (i.e., widowed or divorced); but again this is atypical of the empire as a

whole and should perhaps be regarded as indicative of a different marriage and family pattern (cf. p. 193 n. 153 above).

Conclusion

1. The equation for natural increase, namely the difference between mortality and fertility rates, *plus* net migration.
2. Care must be taken, however, to avoid what Whittaker (1976) 234 (in his criticism of Salmon [1974]) calls the mistaken belief "that an accumulation of impressionistic evidence drawn from ancient writers plus a consensus of modern opinions will in the end approximate towards the truth and that, in spite of the absence of clear answers, the study in itself heightens our perception of reality." To a certain extent I may at times in the present work be held to be guilty of the same belief. But when modern demography cannot illuminate the social realities of the ancient past, impressionistic evidence and common sense may still yield results. Cf. Willigan and Lynch (1982) 429: "The focus of historical demographic inquiry is by definition the study of population processes. However, it is clear that an understanding of the causes and consequences of these processes can occur on many levels and from a wide variety of perspectives. No one set of sources, analytical techniques or causal models is likely to help answer the large number of research questions brought to the study of historical demography by scholars from the different disciplines. What is needed . . . is the integration of the skills of sensitive source criticism with increasingly sophisticated techniques of data analysis and the capacity to go beyond narrow demographic analysis to the construction of explanatory sketches or models."

Appendix A

1. Duncan-Jones (1990) 93–96. *CIL* 9.338; *ILS* 6121. See also Jongman (1988) 317–29.
2. Cf. Hopkins (1983) 147.
3. Duncan-Jones (1990) 103–4.

Bibliographic References

Acsádi, G., and Nemeskéri, J. (1970). *History of Human Life Span and Mortality.* Tr. K. Balás. Budapest.

Aguilella Almer, J., Lopez Cerda, M. A., Montes Suay, F., and Pereira Menaut, G. (1975). "Determination de la représentativité des inscriptions latines grace à la statistique inférentielle. *Antiquités Africaines* 9: 115–26.

Amundsen, D. W., and Diers, C. J. (1969). "The age of menarche in classical Greece and Rome." *Human Biology* 41: 125–32.

Amundsen, D. W., and Diers, C. J. (1970). "The age of menopause in classical Greece and Rome." *Human Biology* 42: 79–86.

Anderson, P. (1983). "The reproductive role of the human breast." *Current Anthropology* 24: 25–45.

Angel, J. L. (1945). "Skeletal material from Attica." *Hesperia* 14: 279–363.

Angel J. L. (1947). "The length of life in ancient Greece." *Journal of Gerontology* 2: 18–24.

Angel, J. L. (1954). "Human biological changes in ancient Greece." *Yearbook of the American Philosophical Society* 98: 266–70.

Angel, J. L. (1969). "The bases of palaeodemography." *American Journal of Physical Anthropology* 30: 427–37.

Angel, J. L. (1971). *The People of Lerna: Analysis of a Prehistoric Aegean Population.* Princeton.

Angel, J. L. (1972). "Ecology and population in the Eastern Mediterranean." *World Archaeology* 41: 88–105.

Appleton, C. (1920). *La longévité et l'avortement volontaire aux premiers siècles de notre ère.* Lyon.

Astolfi, A. (1986). *La lex Julia et Papia*^{2}. Padua.

Beaucamp, J. (1982). "L'allaitement: mère ou nourrice." *Jahrbuch der Österreichischen Byzantinistik* 32, no. 2 (*XVI. Internationaler Byzantinistenkongress, Akten* II no. 2): 549–58.

Beloch, K. J. (1886). *Die Bevölkerung der griechisch-römischen Welt.* Leipzig.

Berelson, L. (1934). "Old Age in Ancient Rome." Unpublished dissertation, University of Virginia.

Bernardi, A. (1977). "Sul popolamento dell'Italia antica." *Athenaeum* 55: 88–106.

Bisel, S. (1988). "The skeletons of Herculaneum, Italy." In *Wet Site Archaeology*, ed. B. A. Purdy, 207–18. Cardwell, N.J.

Blumenkranz, B. (1961). "Quelques notations démographiques sur les Juifs de Rome des premiers siècles." *Studia Patristica* 4: 341–47.

Boak, A. E. R. (1955). *Manpower Shortage and the Fall of the Roman Empire in the West.* Ann Arbor.

Bocquet, J.-P., and Masset, C. (1977). "Estimateurs en paléodémographie." *L'Homme* 17, no. 4: 65–89.

Boddington, A. (1982). "The Methods of Palaeodemography: A Case Study of Later Anglo-Saxon England." Unpublished paper.

Boddington, A., Garland, A. N., and Janaway, R. C. (1987). *Death, Decay and Reconstruction: Approaches to Archaeology and Forensic Science.* Manchester.

Boswell, J. E. (1984). "*Expositio* and *oblatio*: the abandonment of children and the ancient and medieval family." *American Historical Review* 89: 10–33.

Boswell, J. E. (1988). *The Kindness of Strangers: The Abandonment of Children in Western Europe from Late Antiquity to the Renaissance.* New York.

Bowman, A. K. (1986). *Egypt after the Pharaohs, 332 B.C.–A.D. 642.* London.

Boyaval, B. (1975). "Remarques à propos des indications d'âges des etiquettes de momies." *Zeitschrift für Papyrologie und Epigraphik* 18: 49–74.

Boyaval, B. (1976). "Remarques sur les indications d'âges de l'épigraphie funéraire grecque d'Egypte." *Zeitschrift für Papyrologie und Epigraphik* 21: 217–43.

Boyaval, B. (1977a). "Tableau général des indications d'âge de l'Egypte gréco-romaine." *Cahiers d'Egypte* 52: 345–51.

Boyaval, B. (1977b). "Démographie différentielle et épigraphie funéraire grecque d'Egypte." *Zeitschrift für Papyrologie und Epigraphik* 26: 262–66.

Boyaval, B. (1977c). "Epigraphie antique et démographie: problèmes de méthode." *Revue du Nord* 59: 163–91.

Boyaval, B. (1978). "Surmortalité et fécondité féminines dans l'Egypte gréco-romaine." *Zeitschrift für Papyrologie und Epigraphik* 28: 193–200.

Boyaval, B. (1981a). "La mortalité saisonnière dans l'Egypte gréco-romaine." In *Livre du centenaire 1880–1980 de l'Institut français d'Archéologie orientale du Caire*, Mém. publ. par les membres de l'Inst. CIV, ed. Jean Vercoutier, 281–86. Cairo.

Boyaval, B. (1981b). "Quelques remarques démographiques sur les nécropoles de Mirgissa." *Cahier de Recherches de l'Institut de Papyrologie et d'Egyptologie de Lille* 6: 191–206.

Boyaval, B. (1986). "Documentation funeraire et sociologie." *Anagennesis: A Papyrological Journal* 4, no. 2: 153–63.

Bradley, K. R. (1978). "The age at time of sale of female slaves." *Arethusa* 11: 243–52.

Bradley, K. R. (1979). Reply to Dalby (1979). *Arethusa* 12: 259–63.

Bradley, K. R. (1980). "Sexual regulations in wet-nursing contracts from Roman Egypt." *Klio* 62: 321–25.

Bradley, K. R. (1984). *Slaves and Masters in the Roman Empire*. Brussels.

Bradley, K. R. (1986). "Wet-nursing at Rome: a study in social relations." In Rawson (1986) 201–29.

Bradley, K. R. (1987a). "On the Roman slave supply and slavebreeding." In Finley (1987) 42–64.

Bradley, K. R. (1987b). "Dislocation in the Roman family." *Historical Reflections* 14: 33–62.

Bresson, A. (1985). "Démographie grecque antique et modèles statisques." *Revue: Informatique et statistique dans les sciences humaines* (Université de Liège) 21: 7–34.

Brogan, O. (1962). "A Tripolitanian centenarian." *Hommages à Albert Grenier. Collection Latomus* 58, no. 1: 368–73.

Brothwell, D. R. (1981). *Digging Up Bones: The Excavation, Treatment and Study of Human Skeletal Remains*[3]. London.

Brothwell, D. R., and Higgs, E. (1969). *Science in Archaeology: A Survey of Progress and Research*[2]. London.

Brulé, P. (1990). "Enquête démographique sur la famille grecque antique. Étude de listes de politographie d'Asie mineure d'époque hellénistique (Milet et Ilion)." *Revue des études anciennes* 92: 233–58.

Brunt, P. A. (1966). "The Roman mob." *Past and Present* 35 (1966). Reprinted in *Studies in Ancient Society*, ed. M. I. Finley, 74–102. London, 1974.

Brunt, P. A. (1971). *Italian Manpower, 225 B.C.–A.D. 14*. Oxford. Reissued with postscript, 1987.

Brunt, P. A. (1987). Postscript to reissued edition of *Italian Manpower, 225 B.C.–A.D. 14*. Oxford.

Bullough, V., and Campbell, C. (1980). "Female longevity and diet in the Middle Ages." *Speculum* 55: 317–25.

Burn, A. R. (1953). "*Hic breve vivitur*: a study in the expectation of life in the Roman empire." *Past and Present* 4: 2–31.

Burn, A. R. (1965). Review of *Biometrical Notes*, by H. Nordberg. *Journal of Roman Studies* 55: 253–57.

Calderini, A. (1953). "*Apatores*." *Aegyptus* 33: 358–69.

Carcopino, J. (1956). *Daily Life in Ancient Rome*. Tr. E. O. Lorimer. Harmondsworth.

Carcopino, J. (1967). *Autour des Gracques: études critiques*². Paris.

Carrier, N. H. (1958–59). "A note on the estimation of mortality and other population characteristics given deaths by age." *Population Studies* 12: 149–63.

Chiang, C. L. (1984). *The Life Table and Its Applications*. Florida.

Clarke, G. (1979). *The Romano-British Cemetery at Lankhills. Winchester Studies 3, Pre-Roman and Roman Winchester, Part II*. Oxford.

Clauss, M. (1973). "Probleme der Lebensalterstatistiken aufgrund römischer Grabinschriften." *Chiron* 3: 395–417.

Cleland, J., and Scott, C. (eds.) (1987). *The World Fertility Survey: An Assessment*. Oxford.

Coale, A. J., Demeny, P. G., and Vaughan, B. (1983). *Regional Model Life Tables and Stable Populations*². New York.

Corbier, M. (1987). "Les comportements familiaux de l'aristocratie romaine (IIe siècle avant J. C.–IIIe siècle après J. C.)." *Annales: Économies, Sociétés, Civilisations* 42: 1267–85.

Cornwall, I. W. (1974). *Bones for the Archaeologist*³. London.

Corvisier, J. N. (1985). *Santé et société en Grèce ancienne*. Paris.

Cowgill, G. (1975). "On causes and consequences of ancient and modern population changes." *American Anthropologist* 77: 305–25.

Cox, P. R. (1976). *Demography*⁵. Cambridge.

Csillag, P. (1976). *The Augustan Laws on Family Relations*. Budapest.

Dalby, A. (1979). Critique of Bradley (1978). *Arethusa* 12: 255–59.

Deevey, E. S. (1960). "The human population." *Scientific American*, 203, no. 3: 194–205.

Degrassi, A. (1963). "Dati epigrafici in iscrizioni cristiane di Roma." *Rendiconti dell'Accademia Nazionale dei Lincei*, ser. 8, vol. 18: 20–28. Reprinted in *Scritti vari di Antichità* 3 (Trieste, 1967): 243–53.

Degrassi, A. (1964). "L'Indicazione dell'eta nelle iscrizioni sepolcrali latine." In *Akte des IV internationalen Kongresses für griechische und römische Epigraphik*, 72–98. Vienna. Reprinted in *Scritti vari di Antichità*, 3 (Trieste, 1967): 211–41.

Delia, D. (1988). "The population of Roman Alexandria." *Transactions of the American Philological Association* 118: 275–92.

Den Boer, W. (1973). "Demography in Roman history: facts and impressions." *Mnemosyne* 26: 29–46.

Den Boer, W. (1974). "Republican Rome and the demography of Hopkins." *Mnemosyne* 27: 79–82.

Den Boer, W. (1979). *Private Morality in Greece and Rome: Some Historical Aspects. Mnemosyne*, suppl. 57. Leiden.

Denker-Hopfe, H. (1986). "Menarcheal age in Europe." *Yearbook of Physical Anthroplogy* 29: 81–112.

Devine, A. M. (1985). "The low birth-rate in ancient Rome: a possible contributing factor." *Rheinisches Museum für Philologie* 128: 313–17.

Diers, C. J. (1974). "Historical trends in the age of menarche and menopause." *Psychological Reports* 34: 931–37.

Dixon, S. (1988). *The Roman Mother.* London.

Dumont, J. C. (1987). *Servus. Rome et l'esclavage sous la République. Collection de l'école française de Rome* no. 103. Rome.

Duncan-Jones, R. P. (1963). "City population in Roman Africa." *Journal of Roman Studies* 53: 85–90.

Duncan-Jones, R. P. (1977). "Age-rounding, illiteracy and social differentiation in the Roman empire." *Chiron* 7: 333–53.

Duncan-Jones, R. P. (1980). "Demographic change and economic progress under the Roman empire." *Tecnologia, economia e società nel mondo romano, Atti del Convegno di Como,* ed. E. Gabba, 67–80. Como.

Duncan-Jones, R. P. (1982). *The Economy of the Roman Empire: Quantitative Studies*[2]. Cambridge.

Duncan-Jones, R. P. (1990). *Structure and Scale in the Roman Economy.* Cambridge.

Dupâquier, J. (1973). "Sur une table (prétendument) florentine d'espérance de vie." *Annales: Économies, Sociétés, Civilisations* 28: 1066–70.

Durand, J. D. (1959–60). "Mortality estimates from Roman tombstone inscriptions." *American Journal of Sociology* 65: 365–73.

Durry, M. (1970). "Le mariage des filles impubères à Rome." *Mélanges Marcel Durry, Revue des études latines* 47 bis: 17–24.

Dzierzykray-Rogalski, T. (1983). "Aspects paléo-démographiques et paléo-pathologiques de l'influence de l'entourage sur la population de Gabbari-Alexandrie." In *Das römisch-byzantinische Ägypten, Akten des internationalen Symposions,* 205–7. Main am Rhein.

Engels, D. (1980). "The problem of female infanticide in the Greco-Roman world." *Classical Philology* 75: 112–20.

Engels, D. (1984). "The use of historical demography in ancient history." *Classical Quarterly* 34: 386–93.

Engels, D. (1990). *Roman Corinth: An Alternative Model for the Classical City.* Chicago.

Éry, K. K. (1969). "Investigations on the demographic source value of tombstones originating from the Roman period." *Alba Regia* 10: 51–67.

Étienne, R. (1955). "A propos de la démographie de Bordeaux aux trois premiers siècles de notre ère." *Revue historique de Bordeaux et du département de la Gironde* 4, no. 3: 189–200.

Étienne, R. (1959). "Démographie et épigraphie." In *Atti del Terzo Congresso Internazionale di Epigrafia Greca e Latina,* 415–24. Rome.

Étienne, R. (1964). "La démographie de la famille d'Ausone." *Études et Chroniques de démographie historique* (Paris): 15–25.

Étienne, R. (1976). "Ancient medical conscience and the life of children." *Journal of Psychohistory* 4: 131–61. First published as "La conscience médicale antique et la vie des enfants." *Annales de démographie historique* 9 (1973): 15–46.

Étienne, R. (1978). "La démographie des familles impériales et sénatoriales au IVe siècle après J. C." In *Transformation et conflits au IVe siècle après J. C.* (Colloque de la F.I.E.C., Bordeaux, 1970), 133–67. Bonn.

Étienne, R. (1987). "Les morts que l'on compte dans la dynastie flavienne." In Hinard (1987) 65–90.

Étienne, R., and Fabre, G. (1970). "Démographie et classe sociale: l'exemple du cimetière des *officiales* de Carthage." In *Recherches sur les structures sociales dans l'antiquité classique, Caen,* ed. C. Nicolet, 81–97. Paris.

Evison, V. I. (1987). *Dover: The Buckland Anglo-Saxon Cemetery.* London.

Eyben, E. (1972). "Antiquity's view of puberty." *Latomus* 31: 677–97.

Eyben, E. (1980–81). "Family planning in Graeco-Roman antiquity." *Ancient Society* 11–12: 5–82.

Fildes, V. A. (1986). *Breasts, Bottles and Babies: A History of Infant Feeding.* Edinburgh.

Fildes, V. A. (1988). *Wet-nursing: A History from Antiquity to the Present.* Oxford.

Finley, M. I. (1958). Review of *Manpower Shortage and the Fall of the Roman Empire in the West,* by A. E. R. Boak. *Journal of Roman Studies* 48: 156–64.

Finley, M. I. (1968). *Aspects of Antiquity: Discoveries and Controversies.* London.

Finley, M. I. (1981). "The elderly in classical antiquity." *Greece and Rome* 28: 156–71.

Finley, M. I. (1985a). *Ancient History: Evidence and Models.* London.

Finley, M. I. (1985b). *The Ancient Economy*². London.

Finley, M. I. (ed.) (1987). *Classical Slavery*. London.

Flambard, J.-M. (1987). "Éléments pour une approche financière de la mort dans les classes popularies du haut-empire. Analyse du budget de quelques collèges funéraires de Rome et d'Italie." In Hinard (1987) 209–44.

Flinn, M. W. (1981). *The European Demographic System, 1500–1820*. Baltimore.

Fontanille, M.-T. (1977). *Avortement et contraception dans la médecine gréco-romaine*. Paris.

French, V. (1986). "Midwives and maternity care in the Greco-Roman world." In *Rescuing Creusa: New Methodological Approaches to Women in Antiquity, Helios*, n.s. 13, no. 2, ed. M. Skinner, 69–84. Lubbock, Tex.

Frézouls, E. (1970). "Démographie et urbanisation." In *Atti del convegno di studi sulla città etrusca e italica preromana*. Istituto per la storia di Bolgona, 397.

Frézouls, E. (1977). "En marge de *La vie quotidienne à Rome à l'apogée de l'empire*: questions de demographie antique." In *Hommage à la mémoire de Jérôme Carcopino*, 109–17. Paris.

Frier, B. W. (1982). "Roman life expectancy: Ulpian's evidence." *Harvard Studies in Classical Philology* 86: 213–51.

Frier, B. W. (1983). "Roman life expectancy: the Pannonian evidence." *Phoenix* 37: 328–44.

Fülep, F. (1984). *Sopianae: The History of Pécs during the Roman Era and the Problem of the Continuity of the Late Roman Population*. Budapest.

Gallo, L. (1979). "Recenti studi di demografia greca (1970–78)."*Annali della Scuola Normale Superiore di Pisa* 9: 1571–1646.

Gallo, L. (1984a). *Alimentazione e demografia della grecia antica*. Salerno.

Gallo, L. (1984b), "Un problema di demografia greca: le donne tra la nascita e la morte." *Opus* 3: 37–62.

Garcia Merino, C. (1974). *Analisis Sobre el Estudio de la Demografia de la Antiguedad y un Nuevo Metodo para la Epoca Romana*. Valladolid.

Garcia Merino, C. (1975). *Poblacion y Poblamiento en Hispania Romana: El Conventus Cluniensis*. Valladolid.

Gardner, J. F. (1986a). *Women in Roman Law and Society*. London.

Gardner, J. F. (1986b). "Proofs of status in the Roman world." *Bulletin of the Institute of Classical Studies* 33: 1–14.

Garland, R. (1985). *The Greek Way of Death*. London.

Garland, R. (1990). *The Greek Way of Life*. London.

Garnsey, P. (1988). *Famine and Food Supply in the Graeco-Roman World: Responses to Risk and Crisis*. Cambridge.

Gejvall, N.-G. (1969). "Cremation." In Brothwell and Higgs (1969): 468–79.

Genovés, S. (1969). "Sex determination in earlier man" and "Estimation of age and mortality." In Brothwell and Higgs (1969) 429–39, 440–52.

Germain, L. R. F. (1969). "Aspects du droit d'exposition en Grèce." *Revue historique de droit français et étranger* 47: 177–97.

Gilfillan, S. C. (1965). "Lead poisoning and the fall of Rome." *Journal of Occupational Medicine* 7: 53–60.

Golden, M. (1981). "Demography and the exposure of girls at Athens." *Phoenix* 35: 316–31.

Golden, M. (1985). "'Donatus' and Athenian phratries." *Classical Quarterly* 35: 9–13.

Golden, M. (1988). "Did the ancients care when their children died?" *Greece and Rome* 35: 152–63.

Golden, M. (1990). *Children and Childhood in Classical Athens.* Baltimore.

Gomme, A. W. (1933). *The Population of Athens in the Fifth and Fourth Centuries B.C.* Oxford.

Goody, J. (1983). *The Development of the Family and Marriage in Europe.* Cambridge.

Gourévitch, D. (1984). *Le mal d'être femme: la femme et la médecine dans la Rome antique.* Paris.

Gourévitch, D. (1987). "La mort de la femme en couches et dans les suites de couches." In Hinard (1987) 187–93.

Greenwood, M. (1940). "A statistical mare's nest?" *Journal of the Royal Statistical Society* 103: 246–48.

Grmek, M. D. (1983). *Les maladies à l'aube de la civilisation occidentale: recherches sur la réalité pathologique dans le monde grec préhistorique, archaïque et classique.* Paris.

Gutierrez, H., and Houdaille, J. (1983). "La mortalité maternelle en France au XVIIIe siècle," *Population* 38: 975–94.

Hahn, J., and Leunissen, P. M. M. (1990). "Statistical method and inheritance of the consulate under the early Roman empire." *Phoenix* 44: 60–81.

Hajnal, J. (1965). "European marriage patterns in perspective." In *Population in History,* ed. D. V. Glass and D. E. C. Eversley, 101–43. London.

Hall, R. L. (1978). "A test of paleodemographic models." *American Antiquity* 43: 715–29.

Halstead, P., and O'Shea, J. (eds.) (1989). *Bad Year Economics: Cultural Responses to Risk and Uncertainty.* Cambridge.

Hansen, M. H. (1985). "Demographic reflections on the number of

Athenian citizens, 451–309 B.C." *American Journal of Ancient History* 7: 172–89.

Hansen, M. H. (1986). *Demography and Democracy: The Number of Athenian Citizens in the Fourth Century BC*. Herning, Denmark.

Hansen, M. H. (1988). *Three Studies in Athenian Demography*. The Royal Danish Academy of Sciences and Letters, *Historisk-filosofiske Meddelelser* 56. Copenhagen.

Harkness, A. G. (1896). "Age at marriage and at death in the Roman empire." *Transactions of the American Philological Association* 27: 35–72.

Harman, M., Molleson, T. L., and Price, J. L. (1981). "Burials, bodies and beheadings in Romano-British and Anglo-Saxon cemeteries." *Bulletin of the British Museum of Natural History (Geology)* 35, no. 3: 145–88.

Harris, W. V. (1980). "Towards a study of the Roman slave trade." In *The Seaborne Commerce of Ancient Rome: Studies in Archaeology and History*, ed. J. H. D'Arms and E. C. Kopff, *Memoirs of the American Academy at Rome* 36: 117–40.

Harris, W. V. (1982). "The theoretical possibility of extensive infanticide in the Greco-Roman world." *Classical Quarterly* 32: 114–16.

Harris, W. V. (1986). "The Roman father's power of life and death." In *Studies in Roman Law in Memory of A. Arthur Schiller*, ed. R. S. Bagnall and W. V. Harris, 81–95. Leiden.

Hassan, F. A. (1981). *Demographic Archaeology*. New York.

Hawkes, S. C., and Wells, C. (1983). "The inhumed skeletal material from an early Anglo-Saxon cemetery in Worthy Park, Kingsworthy, Hampshire, South England." *Paleobios* 1, nos. 1–2: 3–36.

Hendriks, F. (1852). "Contributions to the history of insurance, &c. . . ." *Assurance Magazine* 2: 222–58.

Henry, L. (1957). "La mortalité d'après les inscriptions funéraires." *Population* 12: 149–52.

Henry, L. (1959). "L'âge au décès d'après les inscriptions funéraires." *Population* 14: 327–29.

Henry, L. (1960). "Développements récents de l'étude de la démographie du passé." In *XIe congrès international des sciences historiques*, Rapports I: 89–96. Stockholm.

Hermansen, G. (1978). "The population of imperial Rome: the regionaries." *Historia* 27: 129–68.

Hinard, F. (ed.) (1987). *La mort, les morts, et l'au-delà dans le monde romain. Actes du colloque de Caen*. Caen.

Hirst, S. M. (1985). *An Anglo-Saxon Inhumation Cemetery at Sewerby, East Yorkshire*. York.

Hobson, D. W. (1985). "House and household in Roman Egypt." *Yale Classical Studies* 28: 211–29.

Hodge, A. T. (1981). "Vitruvius, lead pipes and lead poisoning." *American Journal of Archaeology* 85: 486–91.

Hodge, W. B. (1857). "On the rates of interest for the use of money in ancient and modern times, I." *Assurance Magazine* 6: 301–33.

Hollingsworth, T. H. (1969). *Historical Demography*. London.

Hombert, M., and Préaux, C. (1945). "Note sur la durée de la vie dans l'Egypte gréco-romaine." *Cahiers d'Egypte* 20: 139–46.

Hombert, M., and Préaux, C. (1946). "A propos des chances de survie dans l'empire romain." *Latomus* 5: 91–97.

Hombert, M., and Préaux, C. (1952). *Recherches sur le recensement dans l'Egypte romaine. Papyrologica Lugduno-Batava* 5. Leiden.

Hooper, F. A. (1956). "Data from Kom Abou Billou on the length of life in Graeco-Roman Egypt." *Cahiers d'Egypt* 31: 332–40.

Hopkins, M. K. (1964–65). "The age of Roman girls at marriage." *Population Studies* 18: 309–27.

Hopkins, M. K. (1965–66), "Contraception in the Roman empire," *Comparative Studies in Society and History* 8:124–51.

Hopkins, M. K. (1966–67). "On the probable age structure of the Roman population." *Population Studies* 20: 245–64.

Hopkins, M. K. (1972). Review of *Italian Manpower, 225 B.C.–A.D. 14*, by P. A. Brunt. *Journal of Roman Studies* 62: 192–93.

Hopkins, M. K. (1974). "Demography in Roman history." Reply to Den Boer (1974). *Mnemosyne* 27: 77–78.

Hopkins, M. K. (1978). *Conquerors and Slaves*. Cambridge.

Hopkins, M. K. (1980). "Brother-sister marriage in Roman Egypt." *Comparative Studies in Society and History* 22: 303–54.

Hopkins, M. K. (1983). *Death and Renewal*. Cambridge.

Hopkins, M. K. (1987). "Graveyards for historians." In Hinard (1987) 113–26.

Howell, N. (1976). "Toward a uniformitarian theory of human paleodemography." In Ward and Weiss (1976) 25–40.

Humbert, M. (1972). *Le remariage à Rome: étude d'histoire juridique et sociale*. Milan.

Hume, D. (1777). "Of the populousness of ancient nations." In *Essays Moral, Political, and Literary*. Published in 17 editions from 1741 to 1777, cited here from the 1777 edition, ed. E. F. Miller, 377–464. Indianapolis, 1987.

Humphreys, S. C., and King, H. (eds.) (1981). *Mortality and Immortality: The Anthropology and Archaeology of Death*. London.

Hurst, H. R., and Raskams, S. P. (1984). *Excavations at Carthage: The British Mission, vol. 1.1: The Avenue du President Habib Bourguiba, Salammbo—The Site and Finds Other Than Pottery*. Sheffield.

Jacques, F. (1987). "L'ethique et la statisque. A propos du renouvellement du sénat romain (Ier–IIIe siècles de l'empire)." *Annales: Économies, Sociétés, Civilisations* 42: 1287–1303.

Jones, A. H. M. (1957). *The Athenian Democracy.* Oxford.

Jones, A. H. M. (1964). *The Later Roman Empire 284–602: A Social, Economic and Administrative Survey.* Oxford.

Jongman, W. (1988). *The Economy and Society of Pompeii.* Amsterdam.

Joshel, S. R. (1986). "Nurturing the master's child: slavery and the Roman child-nurse." *Signs: Journal of Women in Culture and Society* 12: 3–22.

Kajanto, I. (1968). *On the Problem of the Average Duration of Life in the Roman Empire.* Helsinki.

Kaser, M. (1971–75). *Das römische Privatrecht.* 2 vols. Munich.

Klapisch-Zuber, C. (1985). *Women, Family and Ritual in Renaissance Italy.* Tr. L. Cochrane. Chicago.

Knodel, J. (1977). "Breast-feeding and population growth." *Science* 198: 1111–15.

Krenkel, W. A. (1975). "Hyperthermia in ancient Rome." *Arethusa* 8: 381–86.

Laslett, P. (1973). "Age at menarche in Europe since the eighteenth century." In *The Family in History,* ed. T. K. Rabb, 28–47. New York.

Laslett, P. (1977). *Family Life and Illicit Love in Earlier Generations: Essays in Historical Sociology.* Cambridge.

Laslett, P. (1983). *The World We Have Lost³.* London.

Laslett, P., Oosterveen, K., and Smith, R. M. (eds.) (1980). *Bastardy and Its Comparative History.* London.

Laslett, P., and Wall, R. (eds.) (1972). *Household and Family in Past Time: Comparative Studies in the Size and Structure of the Domestic Group Over the Last Three Centuries.* Cambridge.

Lassère, J.-M. (1977). *Ubique Populus: Peuplement et mouvements de population dans l'Afrique romaine de la chute de Carthage à la fin de la dynastie des Sévères (146 a.C.–235 p.C.).* Paris.

Lassère, J.-M. (1987). "Difficultés de l'estimation de la longévité: questions de méthode." In Hinard (1987) 91–97.

Last, H. M. (1947). "Letter to N. H. Baynes." *Journal of Roman Studies* 37: 152–56.

Lattimore, R. (1942). *Themes in Greek and Latin Epitaphs.* Urbana, Ill.

Levison, W. (1898). "Die Beurkundung des Civilstandes im Altertum. Ein Beitrag zur Geschichte der Bevölkerungsstatistik." *Bonner Jahrbücher* 102: 1–82.

Lewis, N. (1983). *Life in Egypt under Roman Rule.* Oxford.

Lienau, C. (1971). "Die Behandlung und Erwähnung von Superfetation in der Antike." *Clio Medica* 6: 275–85.

Macdonnell, W. R. (1913). "On the expectation of life in ancient Rome, in the provinces of Hispania and Lusitania, and Africa." *Biometrika* 9: 366–80.

Maier, F. G. (1953–54). "Römische Bevölkerungsgeschichte und Inschriftenstatistik." *Historia* 2: 318–51.

Malthus, T. R. (1798). *An Essay on the Principle of Population.* Ed. A. Flew. 1970 edition. London.

Marchi, A. de (1903). "Cifre di mortalità nelle iscrizioni romane." *Rendiconti dell'Istituto Lombardo di Scienze e Lettere* 36: 1025–34.

McLaren, D. (1978). "Fertility, infant mortality and breast-feeding in the seventeenth century." *Medical History* 22: 378–96.

McLaren, D. (1979). "Nature's contraceptive—wet-nursing and prolonged lactation: the case of Chesham, Buckinghamshire, 1578–1601." *Medical History* 23: 426–41.

McWhirr, A., Viner, L., and Wells, C. (1982). *Romano-British Cemeteries at Cirencester: Cirencester Excavations II.* Cirencester.

Merrill, E. T. (1900). "Note on a certain periodicity in vital statistics." *Proceedings of the American Philological Association* 31: xx.

Miller, B. D. (1981). *The Endangered Sex: Neglect of Female Children in Rural North India.* New York.

Millett, M. (1986). "An early Roman cemetery at Alton, Hampshire." *Proceedings of the Hampshire Field Club Archaeological Society* 42: 43–87.

Milne, J. (1837). *Treatises on the Law of Mortality, and on Annuities.* Edinburgh. Reprinted in *Mortality in Pre-Industrial Times: The Contemporary Verdict,* ed. J. H. Cassedy. Farnborough, 1973.

Minois, G. (1987). *Histoire de la Vieillesse: De l'Antiquité à la Renaissance.* Paris. Translated as *History of Old Age from Antiquity to the Renaissance,* by S. H. Tenison. Oxford, 1989.

Mitterauer, M., and Sieder, R. (1982). *The European Family.* Tr. K. Oosterveen and M. Hörzinger. Oxford.

Moir, K. M. (1983). "Pliny H.N. 7.57 and the marriage of Tiberius Gracchus." *Classical Quarterly* 33: 136–45.

Molleson, T. (1981). "The archaeology and anthropology of death: what the bones tells us." In Humphreys and King (1981) 15–32.

Moore, J. A., Swedlund, A. C., and Armelagos, G. J. (1975). "The use of life tables in paleodeography." In Swedlund (1975) 57–70.

Moretti, L. (1959). "Statistica demografica ed epigrafia: durata media della vita in Roma imperiale." *Epigrafica* 21: 60–78.

Morris, I. (1987). *Burial and Ancient Society.* Cambridge.

Motomura, R. (1988). "The practice of exposing infants and its effects on the development of slavery in the ancient world." In *Forms of Control and Subordination in Antiquity,* ed. T. Yuge and M. Doi, 410–15. Leiden.

Nardi, E. (1971). *Il procurato aboreto nel mondo greco-romano.* Milan.

Needleman, L., and Needleman, D. (1985). "Lead poisoning and the decline of the Roman aristocracy." *Echos du monde classique/Classical Views* 29: 63–94.

Néraudau, J.-P. (1984). *Etre enfant à Rome.* Paris.

Néraudau, J.-P. (1987). "La loi, la coutume et le chagrin: réflexions sur la mort des enfants." In Hinard (1987) 195–208.

Newell, C. (1988). *Methods and Models in Demography.* London.

Nörr, D. (1977). "Planung in der Antike: über die Ehegesetze des Augustus." In *Freiheit und Sachzwang, Festschrift E. H. Schelsky,* ed. H. Baier, 309–34. Opladen.

Nordberg, H. (1963). *Biometrical Notes: The Information of Ancient Christian Inscriptions from Rome concerning the Duration of Life and the Dates of Birth and Death. Acta Instituti Romani Finlandiae,* 2, no. 2. Helsinki.

Ohlin, G. (1974). "No safety in numbers: some pitfalls of historical statistics." In *Essays in Quantitative Economic History,* ed. R. Floud, 59–78. Oxford. First published in *Industrialisation in Two Systems: Essays in Honor of Alexander Gerschenkren,* ed. H. Rosovsky, 68–90. New York, 1966.

Oldenziel, R. (1987). "The historiography of infanticide in antiquity: a literature stillborn." In *Sexual Asymmetry: Studies in Ancient Society,* ed. J. Blok and P. Mason, 87–107. Amsterdam.

Parkes, P. A. (1986). *Current Scientific Techniques in Archaeology.* London.

Parkin, T. G. (1992). "Age and the Aged in Roman Society: Demographic, Social, and Legal Aspects." D. Phil. diss., University of Oxford.

Partridge, C. (1981). *Skeleton Green: A Late Iron Age and Romano-British Site.* London.

Patlagean, E. (1969). "Sur la limitation de la fécondité dans la haute époque byzantine." *Annales: Économies, Sociétés, Civilisations* 6: 1353–69.

Patlagean, E. (1977). *Pauvreté économique et pauvreté sociale à Byzance, 4e–7e siècles.* Paris.

Patterson, C. (1985). "'Not worth the rearing': the causes of infant exposure in ancient Greece." *Transactions of the American Philological Association* 115: 103–23.

Penta, M. (1980). "Le viduitas nella condizione della donna romana." *Atti della Accademia di Scienze morali e politiche della Società nazionale di Scienze, Lettere ed Arti di Napoli* 31: 341–51.

Petersen, W. (1975). "A demographer's view of prehistoric demography." *Current Anthropology* 16: 227–45.

Phillips III, C. R. (1984). "Old wine in old lead bottles: Nriagu on the fall of Rome." *Classical World* 78: 29–33.

Pollock, L. A. (1990). "Embarking on a rough passage: the experience of pregnancy in early-modern society." In *Women as Mothers in Preindustrial England*, ed. V. Fildes, 39–67. London.

Pomeroy, S. B. (1975). *Goddesses, Whores, Wives, and Slaves*. New York.

Pomeroy, S. B. (1983). "Infanticide in Hellenistic Greece." In *Images of Women in Antiquity*, ed. A. Cameron and A. Kuhrt, 207–22. London.

Pomeroy, S. B. (1986). "Coprynyms and the exposure of infants in Egypt." In *Studies in Roman Law in Memory of A. Arthur Schiller*, ed. R. S. Bagnall and W. V. Harris, 146–62. Leiden.

Raepsaet, G. (1973). "A propos de l'utilisation de statistiques en démographie grecque: le nombre d'enfants par famille." *Antiquité Classique* 42: 536–43.

Ramage, E. S. (1983). "Urban problems in ancient Rome." In *Aspects of Greek and Roman Urbanism: Essays on the Classical City*, ed. R. T. Marchese, 61–92. BAR International Series 188. Oxford.

Rawson, B. (1966). "Family life among the lower classes at Rome in the first two centuries of the empire." *Classical Philology* 61: 71–83.

Rawson, B. (1974). "Roman concubinage and other de facto marriages." *Transactions of the American Philological Association* 104: 279–305.

Rawson, B. (ed.). (1986). *The Family in Ancient Rome*. London.

Rawson, B. (1989). "*Spurii* and the Roman view of illegitimacy." *Antichthon* 23: 10–41.

Rawson, B. (ed.). (1991). *Marriage, Divorce and Children in Ancient Rome*. Canberra.

Reece, R. (1988). *My Roman Britain. Cotswold Studies* 3. Cirencester.

Roby, H. J. (1884). *An Introduction to Justinian's Digest*. Cambridge.

Rostovtzeff, M. (1957). *The Social and Economic History of the Roman Empire*², revised by P. M. Fraser. Oxford.

Rousselle, A. (1984). "Concubinat et adultère." *Opus* 3: 75–84.

Rowland, J. Jr. (1971–72). "Mortality in Roman Sardinia." *Studi Sardi* 22: 359–68.

Ruggiero, A. (1981). "Il matrimonio della impubere in Roma antica." *Atti della Accademia di Scienze morali e politiche della Società nazionale di Scienze, Lettere ed Arti di Napoli* 92: 63–71.

Russell, J. C. (1948). *British Medieval Population*. Albuquerque.

Russell, J. C. (1958). *Late Ancient and Medieval Population. Transactions of the American Philosophical Society* 48, no. 3. Philadelphia.

Russell, J. C. (1985). *The Control of Late Ancient and Medieval Population. Memoirs of the American Philosophical Society* 160. Philadelphia.

Russell, J. C. (1987). *Medieval Demography*. New York.

de Ste. Croix, G. E. M. (1981). *The Class Struggle in the Ancient Greek World*. London.

Saller, R. P. (1984a). "*Familia, domus,* and the Roman conception of the family." *Phoenix* 38: 336–55.

Saller, R. P. (1984b). "Roman dowry and the devolution of property in the principate." *Classical Quarterly* 34: 195–205.

Saller, R. P. (1986). "*Patria potestas* and the stereotype of the Roman family." *Continuity and Change* 1: 7–22.

Saller, R. P. (1987a). "Men's age at marriage and its consequences in the Roman family." *Classical Philology* 82: 20–35.

Saller, R. P. (1987b). "Slavery and the Roman family." In Finley (1987) 65–87.

Saller, R. P., and Shaw, B. D. (1984). "Tombstones and Roman family relations in the principate: civilians, soldiers and slaves." *Journal of Roman Studies* 74: 124–56.

Salmon, P. (1974). *Population et dépopulation dans l'empire romain*. Brussels.

Salmon, P. (1987). "Les insuffisances du matériel épigraphique sur la mortalité dans l'antiquité romaine." In Hinard (1987) 99–112.

Samuel, A. E., Hastings, W. K., Bowman, A. K., and Bagnall, R. S. (1971). *Death and Taxes: Ostraka in the Royal Ontario Museum, I*. *American Studies in Papyrology*, 10. Toronto.

Schmidt, M. (1983–84). "Hephaistos lebt—Untersuchungen zur Frage der Behandlung behinderter Kinder in der Antike." *Hephaistos* 5–6: 133–61.

Schofield, R. S. (1986). "Did the mothers really die? Three centuries of maternal mortality, in *The World We Have Lost*." In *The World We Have Gained: Histories of Population and Social Structure*, ed. L. Bonfield, R. Smith, and K. Wrightson, 231–60. Oxford.

Schofield, R. S., and Wrigley, E. A. (1979). "Infant and child mortality in England in the late Tudor and early Stuart period." In *Health, Medicine and Mortality in the Sixteenth Century*, ed. C. Webster, 61–95. Cambridge.

Schulz, F. (1942–43). "Roman registers of birth and birth certificates." *Journal of Roman Studies* 32: 78–91; 33: 55–64.

Schulz, F. (1951). *Classical Roman Law*. Oxford.

Scobie, A. (1986). "Slums, sanitation, and mortality in the Roman world." *Klio* 68: 399–433.

Shaw, B. D. (1982). "Social science and ancient history: Keith Hopkins *in partibus infidelium*." *Helios* 9: 17–57.

Shaw, B. D. (1984a). "Latin funerary epigraphy and family life in the later Roman empire." *Historia* 33: 457–97.

Shaw, B. D. (1984b). Critique of *Death and Renewal* by M. K. Hopkins. *Echos du monde classique/Classical Views* 28: 453–79.

Shaw, B. D. (1987a). "The family in late antiquity: the experience of Augustine." *Past and Present* 115: 3–51.

Shaw, B. D. (1987b). "The age of Roman girls at marriage: some reconsiderations." *Journal of Roman Studies* 77: 30–46.

Shostak, M. (1981). *Nisa, The Life and Words of a !Kung Woman.* Cambridge, Mass.

Shryock, H. S., and Siegel, J. S. (1976). *The Methods and Materials of Demography,* condensed edition by E. G. Stockwell. London.

Siegel, J. S. (1980). "On the demography of aging." *Demography* 17: 345–64.

Sippel, D. V. (1987). "Dietary deficiency among the lower classes of late republican and early imperial Rome." *Ancient World* 16: 47–54.

Slim, L. (1983). "A propos d'un cimetière d'enfants à Thysdrus." In *L'Africa romana: Atti del I convegno di studio Sassari,* ed. A. Mastino, 167–77. Sassari.

Spengler, J. J. (1950). "Généralités." In *IXe congrès international des sciences historiques, I. Rapports, section 1, Anthropologie et démographie,* 9–37. Paris.

Stein, P. (1962). "Generations, life-spans and usufructs." *Revue Internationale des Droits de l'Antiquité* 9: 335–55.

Suder, W. (1975). "L'utilizzazione delle iscrizioni sepolcrali romane nelle ricerche demografiche." *Rivista storica dell'antichità* 5: 217–28.

Suder, W. (1981). "Le citta dell'Africa romana: mortalità." *Bulletin archéologique du comité des travaux historiques et scientifiques* 17B (Paris, 1984): 225–35.

Suder, W. (1983a). "La demografia dell'Africa romana: rassegna delle ricerche e della bibliografia." *Bulletin archéologique du comité des travaux historiques et scientifiques* 19B (Paris, 1985): 505–10.

Suder, W. (1983b). "Notes on mortality among the slaves in the Roman empire. An [sic] inscriptional evidence." *Antiquities* (Warsaw) 10: 119–22.

Suder, W. (1985). "Art et démographie: quelques remarques sur la chronologie des portraits du tombeau de Bôlbarak à Palmyre." *Damaszener Mitteilungen* 2: 291–95.

Suder, W. (1988a). *Census Populi: Bibliographie de la démographie de l'antiquité romaine.* Bonn.

Suder, W. (1988b). "A partu, utraque filiam enixa decessit. Mortalité maternelle dans l'empire romain." In *Centre Jean-Palerne, Mémoires VIII: Études de médecine romaine,* ed. G. Sabbah, 161–66. Saint-Éienne.

Swedlund, A. C. (ed.) (1975). *Population Studies in Archaeology and*

Biological Anthropology: A Symposium. American Antiquity 40.2.2, *Memoirs* no. 30.

Syme, R. (1960). "Bastards in the Roman aristocracy." *Proceedings of the American Philosophical Society* 104: 323–27.

Syme, R. (1980). *Some Arval Brethren.* Oxford.

Syme, R. (1986). *The Augustan Aristocracy.* Oxford.

Syme, R. (1987). "Marriage age for Roman senators." *Historia* 36: 318–32.

Szilágyi, J. (1959). "Contribution à la question de la durée de la vie moyenne dans l'Aquinium et d'autres régions de la Pannonie." *Antik Tanulmányok* (Budapest) 6: 31–81, 221–43.

Szilágyi, J. (1961). "Beiträge zur Statistik der Sterblichkeit in den westeuropäischen Provinzen des römischen Imperiums." *Acta Archaeologica Academiae Scientarum, Hungaricae.* 13: 125–55.

Szilágyi, J. (1962). "Beiträge zur Statistik der Sterblichkeit in der illyrischen Provinzgruppe und in Norditalien (Gallia Padana)." *Acta Archaeologica Academiae Scientiarum Hungaricae* 14: 297–316.

Szilágyi, J. (1963). "Die Sterblichkeit in den Städten Mittel- und Süd-Italiens sowie in Hispanien (in der römischen Kaizerzeit)." *Acta Archaeologica Academiae Scientiarum Hungaricae* 15: 129–224.

Szilágyi, J. (1965–67). "Die Sterblichkeit in den nordafrikanischen Provinzen." *Acta Archaeologica Academiae Scientarum Hungaricae* 17: 309–34; 18: 235–77; 19: 25–59.

Taubenschlag, R. (1955). *The Law of Greco-Roman Egypt in the Light of the Papyri, 332 BC–640 AD²*. Warsaw.

Treggiari, S. (1969). *Roman Freedmen during the Late Republic.* Oxford.

Treggiari, S. (1976). "Jobs for women." *American Journal of Ancient History* 1: 76–104.

Treggiari, S. (1979). "Questions on women domestics in the Roman world." In *Schiavitù, Manomissione e Classi dipendenti nel mondo antico,* ed. M. Capozza. Università degli studi di Padova, pubblicazioni dell'istituto di storia antica, 13: 185–201. Rome.

Treggiari, S. (1981). "Concubinae." *Papers of the British School at Rome* 49: 59–81.

Trennery, C. F. (1926). *The Origin and Early History of Insurance.* London.

Ubelaker, D. H. (1978). *Human Skeletal Remains: Excavation, Analysis, Interpretation.* Washington.

United Nations (1955). *Age and Sex Patterns of Mortality: Model Life Tables for Underdeveloped Countries. Population Studies* 22. New York.

United Nations (1956). *Methods for Population Projection by Sex and Age. Population Studies* 25. New York.

Vallois, H. V. (1960). "Vital statistics in prehistoric population as determined from archaeological data." In *The Application of Quantitative Methods in Archaeology,* ed. R. F. Heizer and S. F. Cook, 186–222. Chicago.

Vatin, C. (1970). *Recherches sur le mariage et la condition de la femme mariée à l'époque hellénistique.* Paris.

Victor, C. R. (1987). *Old Age in Modern Society: A Textbook of Social Gerontology.* London.

Vielrose, E. (1976). "Fertility of families in Egypt in the Greco-Roman epoch." In Polish with English abstract. *Studia Demograficzne* 43: 51–57.

Vrugt-Lentz, J. T. (1960). *Mors Immatura.* Groningen.

Waldron, H. A. (1973). "Lead-poisoning in the ancient world." *Medical History* 17: 392–99.

Waldron, T. (1982). Report on lead content of bones. In *Romano-British Cemeteries at Cirencester: Cirencester Excavations II,* ed. A. McWhirr, L. Viner, and C. Wells, 203–4. Cirencester.

Waldron, T. (1983). "Lead in ancient bones." In *Disease in Ancient Man: An International Symposium,* ed. G. D. Hart, 172–82. Toronto.

Waldron, T. (1989). "The effects of urbanisation on human health: the evidence from skeletal remains." In *Diet and Craft in Towns: The Evidence of Animal Remains from the Roman to the Post-Medieval Periods,* ed. D. Serjeantson and T. Waldron. BAR British Series 199: 55–73. Oxford.

Walek-Czernecki, T. (1938). "La population de l'Egypte ancienne." In *Actes du congrès international de la population, II,* 7–13. Paris.

Wall, R., Robin, J., and Laslett, P. (1983). *Family Forms in Historic Europe.* Cambridge.

Wallace-Hadrill, A. (1981). "Family and inheritance in the Augustan marriage laws." *Proceedings of the Cambridge Philological Society* 27: 58–80.

Ward, L. H. (1990). "Roman population, territory, tribe, city, and army size from the republic's founding to the Veientane war, 509 B.C.–400 B.C." *American Journal of Philology* 111: 5–39.

Ward, R. H., and Weiss, K. M. (eds.) (1976). *The Demographic Evolution of Human Populations.* London. Reissued as *Journal of Human Evolution* 5.

Weaver, P. R. C. (1986). "The status of children in mixed marriages." In Rawson (1986) 145–69.

Weiss, K. M. (1972). "On the systematic bias in skeletal sexing." *American Journal of Physical Anthropology* 37: 239–50.

Weiss, K. M. (1973). *Demographic Models for Anthropology. American Antiquity* 38.2.2, *Memoirs* no. 27.

Weiss, K. M. (1975). "Demographic disturbance and the use of life tables in anthropology." In Swedlund (1975) 46–56.

Wells, C. (1964). *Bones, Bodies and Disease.* London.

Wells, C. (1975). "Ancient obstetric hazards and female mortality." *Bulletin of the New York Academy of Medicine,* 2d ser., 51: 1235–49.

Wenham, L. P. (1968). *The Romano-British Cemetery at Trentholme Drive, York.* London.

Whittaker, C. R. (1976). Review of *Population et dépopulation dans l'empire romain,* by P. Salmon. *Journal of Roman Studies* 66: 234–35.

Wiedemann, T. (1989). *Adults and Children in the Roman Empire.* London.

Willcox, W. F. (1938). "The length of life in the early Roman empire: a methodological note." In *Actes du congrès international de la population, II,* 14–22. Paris.

Willigan, J. D., and Lynch, K. A. (1982). *Sources and Methods of Historical Demography.* New York.

Wilson, C. (1986). "The proximate determinants of marital fertility in England, 1600–1799." In *The World We Have Gained: Histories of Population and Social Structure,* ed. L. Bonfield, R. Smith, and K. Wrightson, 203–30. Oxford.

Wrigley, E. A. (1969). *Population and History.* London.

Wrigley, E. A. (1987). "No death without birth: the implications of English mortality in the early modern period." In *Problems and Methods in the History of Medicine,* ed. R. Porter and A. Wear, 133–50. London.

Wrigley, E. A., and Schofield, R. S. (1981). *The Population History of England, 1541–1871: A Reconstruction.* London.

Yavetz, Z. (1958). "The living conditions of the urban plebs in republican Rome." *Latomus* 17: 500–17.

Zubrow, E. B. W. (1976). *Demographic Anthropology: Quantitative Approaches.* Albuquerque.

Index

Abortion, 104, 126, 127–28
Adrogatio, 31, 114
Adultery, 115, 128
Africa, 7, 8, 9, 14–15, 60, 106, 113. *See also names of towns and provinces*
Age, exaggeration of: in census documents, 20, 165n.42; of pseudohistorical figures, 106–7; on tombstone inscriptions, 7, 14–15. *See also* Centenarians; Longevity; Maximum life-span
Age, underestimation of: of skeletons, 48; from tax data, 23–27
Age composition/structure, 73–75, 77, 84, 88–89, 92; Egyptian census data, 20, 21; epigraphic evidence, 6–8
Age-rounding, 9, 14, 19, 20
Age-specific fertility rates, 125–26, 127
Agrippina Maior (wife of Germanicus), 94
Album of Canusium, 137–38
Alexandria, 55–56, 63–64, 65
Alexis of Thurii (comic poet), 108
Alimentary schemes, 98, 99
Alton, Hampshire, 56
Amenorrhea, 130
Ancient demography. *See* Demography

Appian, 65–66
Appleton, C., 103–4, 122
Arganthonius (king of Tartesii), 106
Aristotle, 60, 61, 98, 130
Athens, population size, 4
Augustus, marriage legislation of, 31, 88, 89, 100, 111, 114, 115–20, 124, 132
Average life expectancy: calculation from census data, 19–21; calculation from epigraphic evidence, 5–19; calculation from skeletal evidence, 42; calculation from tax data, 25–27; calculation from Ulpianic life table, 31–35. *See also* Life expectancy

Bagnall, R. S. *See* Theban tax receipts
Baths, 119
Beloch, K. J., 5, 6, 8, 66
Benign neglect, 98, 99
Bergomum, N. Italy, 38
Birth cohorts, 72, 75–76, 78, 86, 92
Birth intervals, 126, 127
Birth rate (BR), 73, 78, 84–89, 92, 126, 177n.21. *See also* Fertility
Births, notices of, 19, 37, 59
Blumenkranz, B., 9
Boak, A.E.R., 67
Bononia, Cisalpine Gaul, 109

Index

Fronto, M. Cornelius, 94
Funeral clubs, 35, 37

Galen, 107
Gaul, 65–66
Gellius, Aulus, 113
Generational length, 33, 187n.85
Germanicus, Iulius Caesar, 94
Gorgias of Leontini (sophist), 107–8, 110–11
Gracchus, C. Sempronius, 94, 114
Gracchus, Ti. Sempronius, 94, 114
Gracchus, Ti. Sempronius, senior, 94
Greece, demographic regime in, 179n.1
Greeks: in Miletus, 99; in Rome, 11
Greenwood, M., 32
Gross reproduction rate (GRR), 84, 86–89, 92, 111–13, 119, 149, 160
Growth rate (r), 85–90, 150, 160

Hadrian, 109
Harkness, A. G., 6
Harris, W. V., 121
Hastings, W. K. See Theban tax receipts
Hendriks, F., 35–36
Herculaneum, 173n.163
Herod Agrippa, 65
Hesiod, 110
Hieron II (tyrant of Syracuse), 108
Hieronymus of Cardia (historian), 108
"High pressure" regime, 92
Hodge, W. B., 36
Hollingsworth, T. H., 42, 81
Hombert, M., 9–10, 16, 20, 27, 37
Homosexuality, 128
Hooper, F. A., 10
Hopkins, Keith, 7, 16, 21, 69, 104, 116, 123–24, 126, 129
Households, size of, 113
Housework, 119
Howell, N., 70
Humbert, M., 132
Hume, David, 65–66, 162n.2, 174n.167
Hutterites, 112
Hygiene, 11, 93, 104, 128

Illegitimacy, 96, 129
Infant and early childhood mortality, 92, 93–98; and average life expectancy, 71–72; and epigraphic evidence, 6; and Frier's life table, 76, 82–84; and population density, 11; relationship to adult mortality, 83; and skeletal evidence, 43; and Ulpianic life table, 31–32. See also Mortality
Infanticide, 68, 95–98, 127, 128
Infants, burial of. See Burial, of infants
Infertility, 114–15, 124, 128
Inheritance, between marriage partners, 31, 116–17
Inheritance tax, 29, 31, 39
Inscriptions. See Evidence, epigraphic
Isaeus, 108
Isocrates (orator), 108
Italy: alimentary schemes, 98, 99; census data, 20, 109, 110; population size, 4–5; as underdeveloped country, 70
Ius liberorum, 115–19
Iustae nuptiae, 128–29

Jerome, Saint, 36
Jews: in Egypt, 65; in Rome 9
Josephus, 65
Julius Caesar, 65

Kajanto, I., 8, 11
Keszthely-Dobogo, Hungary, 51
Kingsworthy, Hampshire, 54–55
Kom Abou Billou, Egypt, 10

Lactation. See Breast-feeding
Lead poisoning, 93, 119
Levison, W., 37
Lex Falcidia, 28, 29, 38
Lex Iulia de maritandis ordinibus. See Augustus, marriage legislation of
Lex Iulia de vicesima hereditatium, 27, 29
Lex Papia Poppaea. See Augustus, marriage legislation of

222

ANCIENT SOCIETY AND HISTORY

The series Ancient Society and History offers books, relatively brief in compass, on selected topics in the history of ancient Greece and Rome, broadly conceived, with a special emphasis on comparative and other nontraditional approaches and methods. The series, which includes both works of synthesis and works of original scholarship, is aimed at the widest possible range of specialist and nonspecialist readers.

Published in the Series:
Eva Cantarella, *Pandora's Daughters: The Role and Status of Women in Greek and Roman Antiquity*
Alan Watson, *Roman Slave Law*
John E. Stambaugh, *The Ancient Roman City*
Géza Alföldy, *The Social History of Rome*
Giovanni Comotti, *Music in Greek and Roman Culture*
Christian Habicht, *Cicero the Politician*
Mark Golden, *Children and Childhood in Classical Athens*
Thomas Cole, *The Origins of Rhetoric in Ancient Greece*
Maurizio Bettini, *Anthropology and Roman Culture: Kinship, Time, Images of the Soul*
Suzanne Dixon, *The Roman Family*
Stephen L. Dyson, *Community and Society in Roman Italy*
Tim G. Parkin, *Demography and Roman Society*
Alison Burford, *Land and Labor in the Greek World*